mNumbers=OldStyle1mNumbers=Lining1

$_s1^s1$

=2

THE PRESENCE

Alex Mistretta

THE PRESENCE

An Exploration into the Paranormal

Phenomenaresearch

TABLE OF CONTENTS

Section I:
GHOSTS

I

HAUNTED

PART I:

RESIDUAL

THE HORROR

It was blitzkrieg weather outside. The type of weather here in London that I presume still made the older generation a little nervous. I was nervous too, but not because of the weather and acts of war; just because of where I was going. I always enjoyed feeling a little nervous, the precursor to the release of epinephrine. I was putting my backpack on, and I filled it with the usual: a 35 mm camera, notebook, pen and a book on ghosts. You know the kind, a guide book of where to find ghosts in London, which incidentally is pretty much everywhere. So, yes it makes you wonder why do you need a guide book to begin with? So basically I just went around the corner, but around the corner was 50 Berkeley square and the "Horror of Berkeley Square".

It was 1982, the year of Margaret Thatcher and the Falklands war, the year of Blade Runner; and I had yet to see a real ghost. I arrived at Berkeley Square, and an unremarkable building in the rain stood in front of me. It was now a bookstore. There was no need to knock, it was open. I walked in and took out my camera and preceded to take pictures on the first floor. It looked like a library, and to a kid that only read books on ghosts, UFOs and Loch Ness, and a lot of comic books, it just looked like books only boring people read.

People were browsing and not paying much attention to what I was doing; well perhaps a look here and there annoyed by the flash of my camera. I knew from the literature that nothing of any paranormal value ever took place on the first two floors here. If you look through an assortment of books on the subject of ghosts, especially ones with pictures of apparitions in them, you'll notice that for some reason there's an unusual amount of photographs taken in staircases. I'm not entirely sure why to tell you the truth. The haunted likes to frequent and manifest on or near places of movement and transition; crossroads, bridges and in this case a stairway. Perhaps it is symbolic; going from one place to another, from one state of being to another. Be as it may, I started taking pictures of the stairway, leading up to the second floor where if I remember correctly more books were held.

There are four floors to the building, but the top two according to all accounts, were where the action was. These were the floor where, whatever presence there might have been, made itself known. Unfortunately, anything past the first two floor were of limit to the public; so that's where I went. I don't like to be told what to do and where to go. I managed to walk around briefly and took numerous pictures on the third floor. As I was about to get to the top floor, I heard someone up there, an employee of the store I assumed. As a result I never got to go to the top floor; annoyed and perhaps a little relieved.

These were the days prior to digital, so I had to wait a little while for the development of the roll. All the pictures came out perfect except the ones of the top two floors, it was as if they were veiled, and the best way I could describe it was like a solid mist in front of my camera. Years later in life the questions would come, did my expectation of a haunting caused me to psychically affect the development of the pictures? What environmental factors were present to affect the photographs? Did I just suck at taking pictures? But, not in 1982, not at age twelve. This place was haunted, just like the book said and it was very exciting.

The house itself gained a reputation for being haunted in the early 1800's. The story was that a young girl had died jumping out of the window of an upstairs bedroom. That room was the most intense area in the house. It was always very cold, groans were heard and furniture moved on its own volition. Then, people were attacked, supposedly by an entity either described as male with a huge black mouth or a shapeless monster.

In the 1840's Sir Robert Warboys whom ridiculed stories of a haunted room decided to spend the night there, with a pistol. By one o'clock in the morning, Warboys was dead with the pistol having been fired, and a bullet lodged in the wall of the room.

RESIDUAL HAUNTINGS

Since those rainy London days, I've developed a better understanding of the paradigm hauntings so uncomfortably fit into. I reflected upon my first question stated above. Did my expectations affect the result of the photographs? Taken further, this question puts the nature of hauntings in doubt. The world at large assumes that a haunting is caused by a person or persons who died and have failed to move on. Too attached to this life perhaps, or an inability to recognize death. It this model, the ghost walks around perhaps unaware that it died and tries to live it's life. Imagine how confusing it must be; not understanding the state that you are in and why the environment doesn't respond to you as it should. Is it no surprise then that in some cases the ghosts lashes out and hauntings than take a turn for the destructive.

I am not necessarily negating the veracity of that model in many cases; but it's pure simplicity concerns me. I think, and deduce, that the truth is much more complex. Some hauntings appear devoid of intelligence. In other words, they seem completely unaware of the present world around them. They do not ever interact with the living and appear to perform the same task over and over. These events, which can includes apparitions or/and the sound of footsteps, appear to function as a type of visual and auditory recording.

For example, an apparition will walk up or down a particular set of stairs and disappear near the bottom every time, unaware of being watched.

The same apparition may also walk across a particular part of the house; let's say the second floor. The unusual part is that the apparition is only visible from the knee up, as if it is walking across a floor that is a couple feet below the current one. Upon further research, it is discovered that the original second floor was indeed a couple feet lower some years before. The apparition has no awareness of the new set up. Nor does it appear to have any awareness of any current observers or physical obstructions. These apparitions will walk just as easily walk through walls as they will through a person.

How we perceive them lacks a certain consistency. They may be seen as white ladies, as looking like real people or as black shadows. The later I personally encountered some years ago in Chicago. A solid looking black mass, walked by three feet in front of me. It had a human form and seemed unaware of my presence.

There are several different ways one can look at residual hauntings. One is that cases with apparitions are bona fide ghosts that for some reason or another are unable to see outside their own time. Possibly unaware of death they continue to function in their environment unable to see changes around them. Another possibility is that there might not be a ghost or intelligence at all. What we may be seeing in simply an imprint of an event or a life that was recorded by the environment. Obviously certain environmental conditions need to be present in order for this to occur and for an observer to be able to view the ghostly events. What these are is not yet understood.

Furthermore, are dramatic events more likely to become residual hauntings. There does appear to be more haunted locations where a dramatic event such as a murder, or battle has occurred. Is there an interplay then, that we can tap into, between a dramatic tragic event and the environment? Are these event more likely to be recorded, and do these event make it easier for the observer to witness them?

THE WHALEY HOUSE

The Whaley House built in 1857 sits today in the old section of San Diego. Open for public viewing, the location isn't shy in proclaiming itself, the most haunted house in the United States. This brings in quite a few tourists a year; myself included. The lore associated with the house includes several entities, doors opening by themselves, objects moving of their own volition, footsteps and even invisible hands touching the occasional guest. Add strange mists inside the house, ghostly shapes and strange lights, this may be the real deal.

Numerous investigators have been successful in photographing one or more of these phenomena, myself included. I visited the house in 2001 and out of approximately thirty pictures that I took, four or five showed unusual blue orbs comparable to pictures taken by other investigators.

This is different from the plethora of orb pictures that have populated the paranormal community the last 10 to 20 years. The overwhelming majority of these are simply dust particles, or moisture in the air that reflects light. The orb phenomena came about around the same time as digital cameras became increasingly popular. This is no coincidence, the digital aspect enhances this effects. This is different from pictures and visuals of orbs that are a more solid in appearance that occasionally show up in haunted locations and in poltergeist cases. Some of these are visible to the naked eye while others fall outside our visual spectrum. Invisibility doesn't really exist. If we cannot see it, it only means that an objects wavelength cause that object to veer towards the infra red or ultra violet range of the spectrum. In fact, the great majority of paranormal and ghost phenomena exists in the infra red and ultra violet. Most digital cameras can extend into the infrared spectrum to a certain degree without the usage of specific infrared film. With a standard 35 mm camera you would need specific infrared film or a filter in order to capture anything at that end of the spectrum. This is also true of ultraviolet light.

I was on a case several years ago in Hollywood, with a team of researchers including Dr Barry Taff. This was a follow up to one of the more famous cases in the field, the Hollimont haunting. Both Barry and myself were very excited to be there. Barry because in the past this had been a very active location, and me because this was my first time at this location. Overall it was a letdown as not much happened, but at some point during the investigation the chandelier in one of the upstair bedroom starting to move on its own volition. This lasted for several minutes which gave us the opportunity to film the chandelier. Invisible to the naked eye was an orb of light near the chandelier; very solid moving in a straight line. It showed up on film. In fact you could see it through the camera while it was being filmed.

About a year prior to that I was on another case, also in Hollywood, where at some point while in the basement felt something hit my hear. I thought little of it at the time. However, someone took a picture of me from the back at that exact moment and a green ball of light was seen next to my hear. Fast forward and back to 2001 and at the Whaley house; I snapped a picture of an empty chair in the corner that when developed showed a black shape on the chair. Not quite as solid as the shape I saw walk in front of me in Chicago; this one was more translucent, and invisible to the naked eye. The house itself has a long and complicated history, including numerous deaths that occurred on the property. The ghosts of these dead are thought to be responsible for the manifestations on the property.

In this case, all this may indeed be true; but as is the case with the majority of haunted locations, the further back you go in time the harder it is to verify accepted facts. You'll find that at many locations, certain stories of suicide or death on the property are legends and actually never happened at all. Which, brings us to a crucial point about the nature of hauntings in general. If one experiences an visual apparition of let's say a man hanging in the courthouse, and stories are that a prior owner of the property hung himself a hundred years ago. However, upon further research, it is discovered that the event never took place; there was no hanging. In fact, the man multiple witnesses have claimed to have seen hanging in the courtroom through out the years never even existed. Is every eyewitness lying? Or, did the environment create a subjective state that made the eyewitnesses believe that they saw an apparition, when in reality there was nothing there? Actually no; and this is where hauntings get a little more complicated. Some of these apparitions of people that never existed have not only been seen by multiple witnesses, but even photographed.

On the subject of multiple witnesses skeptics cry mass hallucination; except that mass hallucinations do not exist. There is no psychological condition known as mass hallucination. Multiple hallucinations may occurs under the influence of psychedelics, such as in an ergot epidemic for example. Even in those cases of ergot contamination, hallucinations will differ from individual to individual. The model where everyone hallucinates the same visuals does not exist.

Mass hysteria does exist, and is often confused with mass hallucination; but is in fact a very different phenomenon. Mass hysteria refers to a set of irrational behavior, delusions which may include physical symptoms that spread though a population. For example in 2008 in Tanzania, female students at a school began fainting, crying, and running and yelling hysterically around school grounds. Twenty girls were affected. In 2008 girls in Mexico lost the ability to walk. No known physiological symptoms were detected, and the girls eventually recovered.

The most dramatic case of mass hysteria occurred in 1518 in Strasbourg France when hundreds of residents began dancing for days. In all these cases no cause for the symptoms were ever found. Nor were there any hallucinations reported. The majority of these cases involve young girls. You can make a case for societal expectation of roles and archaic perceptions of women. How that may lead to why more women than man have experienced mass hysteria, but I don't buy it. I am intrigued from a statistical standpoint on the number of young girls that also experience Marian apparitions and also Poltergeist outburst. It appears to be the majority. Is there a physiological link to all these events?

Before I venture to far of topic, the point is that while the ghostly scene that supposedly represented a past event is actually of an event that never existed, the ghostly scene is still real. The question becomes, how do we reconcile what appears to be an impossibility. Well, let me tell you about a ghost named Philip.

CONJURING PHILIP

During the 1970's a group of psychic researchers in Toronto decided on, what may be the most important parapsychological experiment that nobody knows about. They decided to hold a series of seances, but with a twist. The ghost that they were going to communicate with was made up. They called him Philip Aylesford. They also invented a full history for Philip. He was born in the early 1624, was a military man and engaged in an ill fated affair with a Gypsy. His Gypsy lover, was accused of witchcraft and burned at the stake. This resulted in Philip committing suicide at the age of thirty.

In the first few months nothing out of the ordinary happened. Some of the members of the group said that they felt a presence, but nothing that could be measured. At some point, the group decided to attempt table rapping. This is the classic depiction of a seance where questions are asked to a spirit. The spirit responds in yes or no answers by taping on the table. Usually once for yes and twice for no. I've personally attended several of these with positive results.

In any case, Philip began to respond to questions. But, not only that; all of his answers were consistent with the history the group provided for him. Then things took an unexpected turn, the table starting moving, even levitating about half an inch. The group started to invite witnesses and also begin to film the seances. Whispers were heard, strange mists started appearing and Philip could turn the lights on and off when asked. This is not hearsay, or a story of something that happened once upon a time; this was filmed. This was witnessed by as many as fifty people and more importantly it was reproducible. In fact, the experiment was reproduced by several other groups since the 1970's with positive outcome. One group in Toronto even "contacted" a man from the future called Axel.

PART II:

INTERACTION

DISCARNATE ENTITIES

Now we see the transition from replaying of past events, residual haunting, to the most common of hauntings. In these cases, on top of all the signs that we have just talked about in relation to residual hauntings, we add interaction with the environment and the observer. These include, but not limited too, cold spots, pushing or hitting people, communication (verbal and otherwise), unexplained noises, mists, and moving of objects. The interaction in theses locations can even include conversation to what was presumed a real person, that suddenly dematerialized or simply walks away. With the later, the individual only realizes later that in reality they were alone at the location. If there is such a thing as a discarnate intelligence functioning in our immediate environment; than this is it. These are the ghosts.

In these cases they may appear no different from a regular individual. One phenomenon that I mention in the Spectral chapter is the White Lady apparitions. These types of apparitions can appear unresponsive to the immediate environment, or be quite the opposite, and interact with the observer. White Lady are the name given to female ghosts that have a white misty appearance; some more corporeal than others. These have been observed all over the world.

DEATH TUNNEL

Abandon prisons, hospitals and sanatorium offer a very subjective environment. Often in decrepit conditions, it is no wonder then that these types of places have a reputation for being haunted. Be as it may, some, such as the Essex Mountain Sanatorium of New Jersey make a good case for the later. Much of the Essex Sanatorium has been torn down and is now mostly wilderness, but what is left is reportedly very active in terms of haunting type phenomena. Strange figures and lights with no apparent source, voices and people reporting been touched and pushed have all been experienced here.

Still, in terms of reputation, Essex falls short of the frequency of activity experienced at the Waverly Hills sanatorium. Now abandoned, sitting in Jefferson County Kentucky, Waverly was originally built in order to contain tuberculosis patients. In the early parts of the 1900's tuberculosis called the White Plague ran rampant in this area where the environment, which includes much swampland, was ideal for the propagation of the tuber- culosis bacteria. The death rate at Waverly was almost a daily at Waverly, before antibiotics were introduced. In order to spare the patients the sight of bodies constantly exiting the premises, the dead were rolled out in an underground tunnel nicknamed the Death Tunnel. The entire location has a reputa- tion for unusual lights, apparitions, people being pushed or hit by unseen forces and nondescript voices; ant he activity seems particularly intense in the tunnel.

These types of places are popular for television shows and researchers alike. Warranted or not, a decrepit empty and dark former sanatorium cry out I'm haunted. They are enticing, and create great visual for television. As such a great number of researchers, some more professional than others, have inves- tigated Waverly and have obtained unusual photographs and EVPs.

EVP stands for electronic voice phenomena. The idea is to record voices and sounds in a haunted environment that are inaudible to the human hear. The protocols involved are relatively simple; you turn on a recording device and wait and see. Some researchers directly ask questions and check later to see if answered. It works, I've done it.

Let's imagine an answer to a question such as "are you haunting this place" or "are you dead" provide a positive outcome. Upon review a little boy's voice answers yes in perfect English. So, everybody celebrates, you bring out the bubbly, put on Enrique Iglesias and you start dancing like a whirling Dervish. You've just proven the reality of ghosts. Three hours later, someone has a thought, "hum dude, how come the little dead boy speaks English, and we're in Cambodia?"

This is the problem with EVPs. While promising from a research standpoint, how do we determine where the voices are coming from? Now, there is no doubt that anomalous voice are recorded; but are they really from the deceased associated with the location been investigated? Why do we sometime hear English in non English speaking locations? Why are we obtain EVPs from locations with no history of paranormal activity?

We know there's a type of intelligence involved since direct questions have been answered. It's the provenance of that intelligence that concerns me. What is exciting is that I believe we can take this research much further. If we can record sounds from another plane of existence, perhaps we can also film?

1140 ROYAL STREET

In the 1830's this New Orleans address was home to Madam Delphine Macarty Lalaurie. A very popular lady, that perhaps only the south could produce. Known for her lavish parties and balls; and not so well known, she was into torture and death. She owned many slaves and seemed to substitute them quite often. In those days of the south, no one really questioned why there was such a high slave turnover, or where the old ones went. It wasn't until her personal maid committed suicide that suspicion arose; but you could hardly accuse a lady in good social standing of any wrongdoing without definite proof. Proof was found when a small fire erupted and the fire brigade found a torture chamber at the top of the stairs. Some of the slaves were dead, but many were kept alive tortured and mutilated beyond recognition. No legal actions were taken against Lalaurie, but many of New Orleans residents wanted her out. She fled to parts unknown, and rumors place her in Paris some years later.

The house has been renovated since then, with various owners and occupants it seems not staying long. In terms of activity related to hauntings, the house has it all. Apparitions, moving objects, screams and the sound of chains have all been reported inside the house. As you would surmise, the little room at the top of the stairs experiences the most intense activity.

AMITYVILLE

Amityville is probably the most well known tale of a haunted house; primarily because of a best selling book and the subsequent movie staring James Brolin. Numerous non fiction books followed, as well as a few movie sequels and a remake starring Ryan Reynolds a few years back. Almost everyone has heard of the Amityville horror, but few realize that the tale is a hoax, at least most of it.

The story surrounds the Lutz family. This is the family portrayed in both the book and movie as victims of diabolical demonic forces within the house. The real life story emerged when George Lutz contacted members of the Psychical Research Foundation and the American Society for Psychical Research. From the onset both organizations were quite skeptical of the claims as the case didn't seem to fit the established pattern of a haunting. To complicate matters further, a first hand investigation was impossible since the Lutz had moved out of the house. Skepticism increased when they found a contract signed with Ronald Defeo Jr. Defoe was the man whom had shot his family inside the Amityville house a few years earlier, and the contract dealt with whatever profits were to be made from the rights of the story. Furthermore, the Lutz family lawyer was suing them for trying to cut him out of the profits. As a result, the majority of Parapsychologists and paranormal researchers became convinced that George Lutz and Hollywood had made up the inverted crucifix, his possession, the passage to hell and pretty much everything else. But, everyone had forgotten about Ronald Defeo Jr.

On November 13, 1974 Ronald Defeo Jr. shot dead six members of his family while they were sleeping in their beds. Ronald had simply gotten up at 3 am and murdered his father, mother, two brothers and two sisters with no motive. Right from the start there was a strange feel to the story. For one thing, all six were killed in their beds with no sign of having attempted to flee. Logic would dictate that the first shot coming from a shotgun would have woken up the rest of the family and that they would have gotten up to respond. Yet, no one had moved from their bed. This fact did not escape the police either. They searched for answers but came up empty. The bodies had not been drugged and Ronald when questioned had no answers. If anything, he deepened the mystery. He claimed that he had no control and that something got inside him and coerced him into killing his family. He has never changed his story.

WHY IS THERE MORE GHOSTLY ACTIVITY AT NIGHT?

If you watch any of the paranormal shows that are currently on television, all investigations take place at night, and often with the unnecessary act of turning off the lights. Logic would dictate that if a location is haunted, it is equally haunted in the day time as it is in the night time. Yet, statistically there appears to be an increase in reported activity between midnight and 3 AM, given a standard deviation of up to a couple of hours.

Societal expectations aside, there may actually be a scientific explanation for this. It may have more to do with environmental factors and our ability to perceive the phenomenon than the actual source of the phenomenon itself.

At night, there is much less noise and interference from electrical devices, such as televisions and radio, including the electromagnetic waves these devices propagate. The ionosphere is also expanded, which is where electromagnetic waves bounce off. The later is why we can pick up radio stations that are further away at night. The ionosphere lies 46 to 620 miles above the earth and at night is ionized by cosmic rays which originate from quasars, neutron stars, supernovas and possibly black holes. Cosmic rays do not ionize the ionosphere as strongly as the sun and within this calmer environment, unusual electromagnetic disturbances, such as "ghosts" could stand out.

INFRASOUND

Infrasound is inaudible to humans because they are below 20 Hertz. Hertz refers to cycles per second and 20 Hertz is the lower limit of human perception. The ear is not always necessary in order to perceive infrasounds. The human body in some instances can feel infrasound vibrations however. Infrasound can be generated by nature in earthquake prone areas, by volcanoes, ocean waves, lighting, and severe weather in general. Wind turbine, and some home appliances such as fans and speakers may give off infrasound as well. Yes, there is a reason I'm bringing this up.

Studies indicate that infrasound can generate the perception of a presence in the room. It can induce a feeling of fear and uneasiness. It can also stimulate the flight or fight response in humans. This is displayed by chills or the "hair on the back of the neck standing up" which is a vestigial response in humans. It dates back to our more hirsute ancestors whose hair or fur would "stand up" in response to danger. This gives the illusion of greater size.

These reactions may further perpetuate the feeling of being in a haunted location. This may account for the correlation of storms and ghosts in many stories. Storms can create infrasound, which can induce the feelings of fear and an unseen presence. Experiment specifically with 17 Hz have produced feelings of fear, uneasiness, chills and even pressure on the chest. Pressure on the chest is also associated with the Old Hag phenomenon. This is where you wake up at night with the feeling that there is a presence siting on your chest. Visual hallucinations can occur during this event. In the old days, it was assumes that the presence was of a witch, demon or ghost. Today we know that this feeling is the result of being in a hypnagogic state when one falls asleep. Auditory and visual hallucination may occur during this time. It is due to stimulation of the temporal lobe.

As I alluded to earlier, infrasounds may be picked up by other parts of the body aside from the ear. One of these is the eye. The eye resonate at a frequency below 20 Hz. The eye can vibrate creating a visual hallucination corresponding to a gray moving mist, which can resemble an apparition. Obviously, infrasound cannot account for all the phenomena associated with haunted locations; but as researchers we need to be aware of non paranormal factors.

OUTDOOR HAUNTINGS

The mechanism for the creation of either a residual type of haunting or one involving interaction does not differ in an outdoor setting. All the environmental factors such as geomagnetic disturbances are equally engaged in an outdoor location. The reason for this section is that I have a particular interest in outdoor hauntings, and simply wanted to cover the subject separately.

Outdoor haunted locations often cover a much wider territory however. In these cases, where the phenomenon is not so localized, you seem to get a wider set of paranormal effect. This may include phantom creatures such as Black Dogs, ghost lights similar to UFOs, sightings of humanoids such as "fairies" and more disturbingly, disappearances. One more rare phenomenon is, for lack of a better term, is the time warp effect. The later is when you find yourself in a scene that appear to be from another time, such as the middle ages. Most cases that I'm aware off have occurred in Europe and especially in France and England. The event is usually of short duration and may even include interaction with individuals that appear to belong in that era. In a sense, this is a haunting in reverse. Instead of the past coming to you, you go to the past. I suspect that whatever physics are ultimately proven to be involved in hauntings, will equally be at play here as well. The idea that time is always linear is perhaps an archaic concept. It's called space time for a reason. In the Parapsychology chapter of this book, I discuss Remote Viewing and how military research indicate that time is irrelevant in retrieving information while using this process. The information is always there; the question is how to get to it.

HOIA-BACIU FOREST

These woods located in Transylvania have become known in the United States through the show Destination Truth. One of the members of the crew was lifted though the air by an invisible force, and thrown backwards by a few feet. All this was captured on camera and it picked by interest.

The forest has a long reputation of being haunted. Apparitions have been seen by locals; strange lights and black fogs are also reputed to be part of the manifestations there. There are stories of disappearances in these woods, but hard data on the later is lacking. Voices can at times be heard, and have been recorded.

People feel as if they are been watched, and certain physiological effects such as disorientation and nausea have been reported in the forest. Burns and cuts have also appeared on people with no apparent cause.

In the center of the forest is a large circle where vegetation never grows. Locals claim that this is the most intense area of disturbance, and where the disorientation and physical effect are most likely to take place. Soil samples taken at the site by the Destination Truth team, did not indicate anything unusual. To compound the strangeness, UFOs have also been seen in the area.

HIGHGATE CEMETERY.

Contrary to popular belief, cemeteries are rarely haunted. Highgate in North London is an exception. In the 1960's the cemetery was a popular spot for late night occult rituals and grave robbing. More than that, Highgate became infamous with the "Highgate vampire" case of 1970. In that year, the police arrested a man trying to climb the walls of the cemetery while carrying a wooden stake and a cross held together with shoe laces. Apparently not possessing Buffy's skill set; his name was David Farrant, self proclaimed vampire slayer. Farrant claimed that the cemetery housed a vampire. He was never charged, and upon release the judge told him to go see a doctor. I don't believe he ever did, but he eventually wrote a book on the subject and presumably continued his vampire slaying days.

As a result, Highgate increased its security, putting an end to the rituals, grave robbing and failed attempts at finding vampires; but not to strange events at the location. It only switched from strange living people to revenants. The later includes a white lady, reported from time to time floating along the tombs. The cemetery itself is very old with many little paths and grave stones which are almost in ruined. It is among these paths that figures are at times seen. These ghostly apparitions I have to assume, along with the grave robbing of 40 or so years ago probably originated the vampire stories. Today, the sightings of ethereal figures continue; as for the vampires, not so much.

THE BORLEY RECTORY

The Borley Rectory was build in 1863 over what once was the Borley Manor House which was itself built over an old abbey. Cold spots, apparitions, objects thrown about, ringing of bells, writing on the walls, footsteps, pushing or grabbing by unseen hands, have all occurred at the Rectory.

In 1939 the Borley Rectory burned down. The source of the fire is not known. Today, the Borley Rectory lies in ruins but the disturbances remain ongoing. The place has been investigated countless times with numerous sightings recorded and a few pictures showing ghostly figures that resemble monks. The Borley Rectory has often been called the most haunted place in England.

PART III:

POLTERGEIST

THE HUTCHISON EFFECT

Object levitating, holes forming in glass, metals and other objects melting together, metal and wood fusing without displacement, unexplained heating of metals, fracturing of metal, strange light effects, mists that appear to have no source and the disappearance of objects; are all effects described in more extreme poltergeist cases. These are also effects created artificially in a lab by a man named Jon Hutchinson. His self funded experiments begin in the late 1970's, and were both investigated and witnessed by the Stanford Research Institute and the CIA. Both of these institutions felt that the effects generated by Hutchinson in his apartment, which doubled as a lab, were real.

Yet, at the time, no one would link this to the Poltergeist phenomena. But they should have. Because this what it is; only recreated artificially and reproduced in laboratory conditions. If parameters could be met, which really is about manipulating the electromagnetic environment, then at least in part the phenomenon could in theory be created.

However, there is a problem. For one thing, Hutchinson wasn't able to replicate the effects at will. Sometimes it worked, and sometimes it didn't. More importantly as it relates to the Poltergeist phenomenon, the effects could not be replicated when Hutchinson wasn't in the room. They were unable to determine why that was. Perhaps the key to unlocking the energy responsible for poltergeist effect lies within this problem.

So, while the source of energy responsible remains elusive, this model clearly demonstrates that one cannot remove the individual from the equation. There is a synergetic effect between the environment and the individual. Remember, synergy indicates that when multiple parts of a system are joined, the effect generated is greater than the sum of all the individual parts.

POLTERGEIST EFFECT

In 1982, I saw a movie called the Entity. The movie based on a real case was about a woman who claimed to have suffered repeated poltergeist attacks in her home, and even rape by an entity. The case was investigated by a couple of Parapsychologists from UCLA. The premise of the movie was fairly accurate, but as the movie went on, it began to differentiate itself from the real life case. In real life the Parapsychologist from UCLA were Dr Barry Taff and Kerry Gaynor.

I met Dr Barry Taff about ten years ago now through a mutual friend in the UFO community. We hit it off right away and have since become good friends and now work together on cases. There was always something different about poltergeist outbreaks versus traditional hauntings. The model where it falls under the same umbrella is outdated, and Barry had 40 years of data to back it up. The many cases Barry and I have discussed over the years, and the investigations that I've personally been on further validates this split in the paradigm.

The poltergeist phenomenon differentiates itself from both residual hauntings and ghost hauntings in that it is transient. It does not appear to haunt a particular location, but rather an individual. It is usually of short duration, but can have several outbreaks years apart. It also travels with the individual that is "afflicted". It rarely involves apparitions. Typical poltergeist outbreaks involve loud bangs or crashing sound with no apparent source, objects been thrown about, furniture been rearranged, small fires, objects disappearing and appearing and unusual streaks of lights. The lights can also take solid form. They can be visible to the naked eye or invisible, only appearing when filmed or photographed. The opposite can also be true where multiple lights may be seen by a number of observer, but not on film. The former may indicate that some of the phenomena occurs outside the visual spectrum. This is true with traditional and ghost hauntings as well where events can be captured by camera in the ultraviolet or infrared spectrum. The later is more puzzling. How can lights in a darkened room be visible to the naked eye but not on film? Are these induced hallucinations caused by the poltergeist phenomenon? If this is true than it indicates the ability to directly effect the visual cortex of the brain. Now, if this is possible, are other parts of the brain also at risk of been manipulated?

More spectacular display include levitation and the merging of objects into one as described above with the Hutchinson effect. Writing on the wall by the supposed poltergeist is also a trait associated with several cases. Blood plasma streaking down walls or kitchen cabinets has also been observed, with no clear source. One more common aspect associated with poltergeists are small stones been thrown at individuals. Again there may not be a clear source for the stones. This may occur indoors where no stone are initially present. None of these are usually associated with traditional hauntings.

What is also unusual about objects been thrown about is that weight seems inconsequential. Objects from furniture to small rocks appear to fly about with the same ease and velocity. The trajectory is also odd, as the objects do not necessarily obey the laws of physics. Once an object is thrown it should fly in a straight path until gravity pulls it down. In physics an object flying in a straight line cannot alter it's trajectory unless it meet another force. However during poltergeist outbreaks, the objects thrown about can slow down or speed up, as well as take right angle turns. This signifies that whatever force is responsible for throwing the object in the first place continues to affect the object once it is in mid air.

It gets stranger. There are rare instances where objects are thrown at great velocity at an individual, but when the object makes contact with that individual it hits with very little force. This defies all laws of physics as we know them. This is a rare event, but it appears that there is little correlation between an object velocity and impact. Furthermore, some common objects that are thrown around are knives and scissors. Yet these, at least 99 % of the time, do not actually hit anyone. Also, again in 99 % of cases where objects are thrown, where objects disappear, combine at a molecular level; there are no heat detected at the source or on the objects itself.

Here is where it all gets really interesting; (although I hope it's been interesting up to this point or I really suck as a writer). As already noted, poltergeist events surround a particular individual. This is not random, there is a pattern in the type of individual selected. In a great majority of cases, the inflicted is a teenager, and in most cases a young girl at the onset of puberty.

That been said, adults have also been afflicted, again more women than men. Most adults in these cases have either undergone some type of trauma, have experienced dissociative episodes and/or are seizure prone. In fact seizure medication may inhibit the phenomenon according to Dr Barry Taff. We have also noted a direct correlation between the intensity of the phenomenon and the mental state of the individual afflicted by that phenomenon. The more agitated, distressed, nervous that person is, the more activity surrounds that person. Obviously, much more research is needed in this area, but the data points in this direction.

The poltergeist phenomenon also functions as a virus of sorts. As we have seen, it specifically surrounds a particular individual and very much responds to that persons mood and subconscious desires. It may also attach itself temporarily to other individuals that are in the vicinity. For example, researchers present during a poltergeist outbreak have noted that the phenomenon does "follow you home". Various poltergeist activity can at this point occur in your car (loud unexplained bang while your driving home); or at home where you may experience small fires, objects been thrown about and writing on the wall. This only occurs in the more intense cases, and the occurrences are to a lesser degree away from the primary source.

The effects are temporary and diminish in time. Just like the flue virus, It has an onset, followed by contamination and diminishing of symptoms as time goes by. This of course differs entirely from traditional hauntings where the phenomenon stays at one location, and does not diminish with time.

What all of this ultimately leads to is that the poltergeist phenomenon is generated by individuals. Similar to conjuring Philip where an entity is created. The difference is that in poltergeist cases we have not assign a specific paradigm to an entity, and thus the phenomenon is uncontrolled and seemingly chaotic. A poltergeist is the physical manifestation of the subconscious using a mechanism and energy we have yet to understand. The subconscious functions very differently than the conscious, and can appear once again, chaotic. It follows different rules and pattern than we are accustomed to in a conscious model.

All that said, a proper environment is still needed for an outbreak to occur. High electricity in the air, electromagnetic anomalies, and some other factors we have yet to consider are all potentially indispensable. In this model the environment feeds an individuals which in turns has the ability to create the forces that are needed for a poltergeist outbreak.

This is for now a working hypothesis, supported by the data that we have accumulated. We unfortunately have yet to identify the forces responsible. We know that they do not appear to be not any of the four fundamental forces, gravitation, electromagnetism and strong and weak nuclear forces. Those can be measured. Electromagnetism does play a part it seems; but the forces it interacts with to produce the effects that defy physics remains unknown.

This model incidentally, does not negate the presence of an intelligence in some cases. The problem is that if individuals have the ability to create the phenomenon or mimic a discarnate intelligence, determining provenance becomes problematic. And, what happens in cases where there is an intelligence and a poltergeist effect at a location where a residual haunting is also taking place? How do all of these forces interact?

2

PARAPSYCHOLOGY

REMOTE VIEWING

Parapsychology as a term, has fallen in disfavor in recent years; replaced by more accessible terms such as paranormal research and ghost hunting. Yet, neither terms really works, in terms of representing the field as a whole. Paranormal research is too broad, encompassing everything that is strange and ghost hunting speaks for itself. Both terms create in me a certain palpable uneasiness. This is probably an unconscious need to legitimize paranormal research in some form; but the reality is that research whether it be in the field or in a laboratory setting really falls under the Parapsychology paradigm.

While most people are familiar with the protocols of so called ghost hunting, due to the preponderance of such shows on television, few are aware that bona fide scientific research has been conducted in the lab by reputable institutions; both in the United States and abroad for decades. The former Soviet Union originated such research during the cold war which in turn created active interest from the part of the United States government. This resulted in the implementation of a Remote Viewing Program.

Laboratory Parapsychological research involves experiments where the goal is obtaining results that cannot be attributed to chance, and results that can be replicated. For simplicity sake, Parapsychological research in the lab is essentially divided into ESP and psychokinesis. Other avenues of study such as

Near Death Experiences certainly fit with the Parapsychological paradigm, and will be discussed in a separate chapter. Ghost hunting which if we follow this paradigm is thus parapsychological field work, which has been discussed in a the chapter ghost.

ESP, short for extrasensory perception includes telepathy and remote viewing. In essence the ability to acquire information about a person, an object or an event without the use of the five senses. One of the more profound aspect of ESP and more precisely remote viewing is that time and distance do not seem to be a factor in relation to the efficiency of acquiring information. It is as if time and space do not exist outside of the five senses.

Telepathy is the transference of information between two or more people, again without the use of the five known senses. Psychokinesis or PK is the ability of an individual to move objects, affect randomness, or/and have any kind of a physical effect on a person or object without the use of the physical body. As we will see in the ghost chapter, the Poltergeist phenomenon may have more in common with PK than actual traditional hauntings.

In the early days ESP experimentation was conducted through ESP card symbol tests. The symbols on the cards were either circles, squares, wavy lines, crosses and stars. Volunteers were asked to "guess" as to which symbol appears on a particular card. Twenty five cards or so were used and presented randomly. Upon completion, statistics were used to determine whether hits, "correct guesses", could be attributed to ESP or were due to chance.

From the 1990's on, testing for ESP entered the computer age. The former Princeton Engineering Anomalies Research Laboratory, PEAR for short, ran some experiments testing micro PK. A random events generator, REG for short, was used. The generator throws out numbers randomly, and volunteers were tested to see if they could affects the outcome. The results were proven to be statically significant, thus not due to chance.

PEAR also achieved statically significant results where volunteers influence whether balls would fall left or right on an apparatus named Murphy. The influence on actual objects with a physical weight show macro PK, and as we shall see in the Ghost chapter leads to poltergeist like effects. The point not to be missed here is that ESP acts upon entropy, creating order if you will, and trespassing upon the quantum physics world. The implications are staggering. Can we in this way effect and shape reality? Is this what happens when the observance in the quantum world of certain particles affects their behavior?

The hard sciences study what makes the rules. Parapsychology studies what breaks the rules, which sets it in direct conflict with most sciences. As a result, most mainstream scientist reject Parapsychology on a purely philosophical basis. But, not everybody rejects it. Certain theoretical physicists do not, because they too study what breaks the rules. Schroedinger himself stated that the quantum mechanical wave function serves as a field of consciousness. He furthered the idea by theorizing that the quantum wave function covers the planet; and may thus be accessible to our minds.

This could suggest that we are looking at the ESP phenomena backwards. We assume that ESP is the result of an individuals ability to sense and interact with the outside world by additional means not available to the majority of the population. What if instead, some people can tap into information that is already there, and thus in theory available to all. The trick is knowing how to tap into it. What is also of interest in Shroedingers comments is that the mechanical wave function displays the future of a particular system. The catch is that it does so as a probability. This model in essence prohibits the complete knowledge of future events, as you would only access one of several probable outcomes. This could explain why predictions are so unreliable.

What is fascinating with this model is that if all information is available, then there is a way to train individuals to access this information. This would be the reason for the United states development of Remote Viewing protocols. It may be fool's gold, but the idea that all information in space time is available was too good to pass up. If we take this idea even further, we can postulate that it may also be possible to build machines that can retrieve such information.

Theoretical physicists aside, the just mentioned government and military would be the second group that do not reject the practical applications of Parapsychology. Their interest is obvious.; it's about gaining an advantage. During the Vietnam war the CIA noticed that certain soldiers were able to sense the presence of the enemy or booby traps before there were any physical signs. If this ability could be harnessed; well it could change everything.

As a result, a large amount of research has been conducted for various psychic phenomena by the United States government, China, and of course, the former Soviet Union. What was discovered by all these nations is that ESP is not negatively affected by distance, or by time. The protocols and percentage of accuracy on observing an event does not deviate for observing a future event. In essence, ESP and thus remote viewing violates causality as it observes the effect before the cause. It has also been noted that ESP works better in the vacuum of space. In other words, electro magnetic fields affect psychic ability, but again, not time or distance. This is a clue.

What was also discovered is that the analytical part of the brain interferes with psychic abilities. This indicates to me that the subconscious mind is at least partly responsible for ESP. The idea would then be to inhibit the analytical part of the brain, in order to facilitate the connection between the conscious mind and ESP. This was one of the major discoveries of the remote viewing program. Once information is received by the subconscious mind, it only takes a few seconds for the conscious mind to seize that information and to begin analysis. As a response, remote viewers developed a set of protocols to keep the analytical part of the brain distracted and busy while they retrieved that information.

PHOENIX

Nina Kulagina is not famous, a name that for most people interested in the paranormal sounds vaguely familiar. A name overshadowed by a plethora of self pronounced phychics, healers, mediums and prophecy makers that have written books and made countless of television appearances. Yet Nina Kuligina is the real deal, and the most studied of the former Soviet Union's psychics.

The original X men had a character named Marvel Girl who could move objects with her mind. In the comics she uses what was then called telekinesis. In time, she would develop a wide range of psychic powers, and take the name Phoenix; but in those early days of the 1960's, moving tables and knocking people down with her mind was a formidable power. Today, the proper term for affecting objects at a distance is psychokinesis, and Kulagina was the Soviet's Marvel Girl. This is not a case of hearsay by the way, she demonstrated her ability in front of the Soviet Military and scientists. There are films of her moving objects, I've seen them. Not cause I'm special, or anything, they're on the internet.

Kulagina was discovered quite by accident at a hospital where she was under observation for exhaustion. A condition that would later be linked to her abilities; it seemed that whatever mechanism was involved in her abilities, left her drained after demonstrations. We have observed the same effect in certain poltergeist cases, where the individual at the center of the events becomes exceptionally fatigued after an outbreak. As we shall see when addressing the Poltergeist phenomenon in the ghost chapter, the idea is that certain individual are able to generate these forces unconsciously. Nina Kulagina could do so consciously, but on a smaller scale. Her abilities never demonstrated the force and variety of phenomena associated with Poltergeists. This may be because the conscious mind inhibits the phenomenon; perhaps an evolutionary safeguard against forces that we cannot fully control as a specie. So, why do have this ability in the first place; and how and when was it introduced to our lineage?

While in the hospital, it was discovered that she could determine the color of any object by touch alone. This is called paroptic vision. She was also able to speed up healing in others and expose photographic film just by focusing on it. In retrospect, her ability to speed up healing really should have been the focus of research, as it held practical applications. The effect on the body been healed could be observed in a control environment. By observing those effects, you should be able to determine exactly what physiological changes are occurring within the body, thus bringing insight to how Kulagina was able to accomplish this. However, it wasn't as immediately spectacular as PK.

As a result, the Soviets were never able to fully discover what mechanism was involved in her abilities, but some important observations were made nonetheless. It was determined that she could only affect objects up to a few feet, and that within that range she could move objects away from her, or towards her. More importantly, a high electric field was detected not only surrounding the object that Kulagina was moving, but also surrounding her person. Interestingly, no electric field was detected in the space between herself and the object. It was also discovered that she was unable to move objects in a vacuum and that thunderstorms inhibited her abilities. The later as we shall see in a later chapter appears to also inhibit the Out of Body Experience phenomcnon.

What may also turn out to be a form of PK is levitation. In theory, if your able to push an object away from you, using PK; you should be able to push yourself off the floor. In truth though, I suspect that PK and levitation both work in a more complex fashion then just using a psychic pushing. Still, PK and levitation probably remain connected in the type of force or energy used. There has been no bona fide studies of levitation in controlled conditions. The phenomenon however, has been observed by many, in very different locals through out history. Yogis, Tibetan monks, Catholic saints and seemingly ordinary individuals have been seen levitating. Some, even photographed and filmed. It is also an easy thing to hoax.

Levitation has been scientifically proven, albeit in different forms that may or may not be related to psychic levitation. The most common is magnetic levitation. The maglev train is an example of magnetic levitation, used in the commercial world. Biological organism can also be levitated this way. A famous experiments levitated a frog successfully a few years back, with no apparent ill affect to the animal.

Electrostatic levitation is of particular interest here as it uses electrical fields to counteract gravity. As we have seen, during PK experiments, especially in regards to Nina Kulagina, strong electrical fields were generated. The problem with equating those with electrostatic levitation is that you wouldn't have that space in between where there is no electricity.

3

SPECTRAL

SPECTRAL DOGS

I had just finished with a short report based on some of my investigations, most of it rather mundane I must admit. I had briefly mentioned Skinwalker ranch; a place in Utah known for cattle mutilations, UFOs, poltergeist activities and a huge white wolf like beast the size of a pony. This beast, seemingly impervious to bullets, has been known to attack livestock but also to disappear like a ghost, blurring the line between a flesh and blood creature and the paranormal. I can't quite recall why I brought this up at the time, aside from perhaps bringing a little excitement into the uninterested eyes staring at me.

I mentioned the beast, but purposely did not elaborate due to the fact that the name on the wall behind me said MUFON; in other words, this was a UFO event. I felt that this was perhaps not the proper forum to discuss the white beast. I was about to step down from the podium when a man stood up and said, I've seen the animal you speak off, or at least one very similar. Not in Utah he continued, but right here in California, in Topanga Canyon. Topanga Canyon is famous to UFO aficionados for a wave of UFO sightings in the 1970's, with occasional, if not consistent sightings to this day. Some that I've investigated myself. There are also tales of ghosts and strange creatures in the canyon, none that I've seen personally; at least not from a handful of late night drives through the canyon.

Back to the MUFON night, the man went on to describe the

beast he saw; large and white, wolf like but with no tail; at least as far as he could determine. The reason I bring this up is that it started me thinking of a similar fortean mystery that also straddles the paranormal zoological border, Black Dogs. Black Dogs are for most part known as a British phenomena; but cases within the United States and elsewhere do exist. This phenomenon refers to the anomalous appearance of black canids usually at night and outdoors. The animal is generally very large, quiet, with red glowing eyes. Other eye colors, such as green, yellow and silver have also been reported. Variation on color has been reported, but the great majority are black. The fur may differ however, as some are shaggy while others resemble Great Danes. It has been known to be aggressive in certain locations, but in most cases it just wanders, at times following the witness while keeping a certain distance. At some point, it just disappears; and I don't mean runs away, but dematerializes.

The jet Black coloration, perhaps somewhat exaggerated due to the surrounding darkness, and the glowing red eyes are also common attributes of what the British call the Man Monkey. The Man Monkey is the British equivalent of Bigfoot, in a sense. While Bigfoot is strictly a biological phenomena with no paranormal ties, this is Britain, the land of ghosts and these creatures behave as such. In fact, the Man Monkey behaves in the same manner as phantom Black Dogs. So what does a wolf like beast, Black Dogs, apemen ghosts and perhaps werewolves have to do with one another? Everything.

THE BLACK DOG OF BUNGAY

Bungay was and is a quiet town just twenty miles from the sea. Located in Suffolk county in Eastern England; it has a relatively small population of less than 5000. A 5000 that all know the story of the Black Shuck, and some that have even seen it.

August 4 1577 was a strange day in Bungay. A violent thunderstorm was raging, with rain, hail and a heavy darkness.

It was a sunday and people were attending the church of St. Mary's, with some trepidation I suppose, in light of the weather. The Bungay church was full as many were seeking refuge from the storm. Houses of the time weren't particularly sturdy in a storm. At some point thunder struck, the doors blew open and a large black dog came rushing in and proceeded to attack the congregation. Two people were killed before the beast ran away. Some report indicate that the dog materialized inside the church instead of coming in from the outside. In light of the doors blowing open before the animal, that is debatable, but that is how the story goes.

The dog wasn't done, as it next made an appearance 10 miles away at the church of Blyhburgh. There also, it attacked the congregation, but this time left "proof" of its appearance. It clawed the outside door of the church, claw marks that are still visible today.

Suffolk above and Norfolk county next door have a long tradition of spectral Black Dogs called Black Shuck. A modern phenomenon as well; these dogs usually appear outdoors on a path or road and will follow an individual but remain just out of reach, very rarely aggressive. In some ways the Black Dog phenomenon reminds me of the White Ladies. The White Lady phenomenon, which I have investigated on a handful of occasions is, for lack of a better understanding, a ghost that presents itself in the form of a floating whitish woman. They can be seen both outdoors and indoors, often linked to a historical place, which incidentally holds true for some Black Dogs as well. They are described as all white, hence the name. A fact I suspect has more to do with our visual system and perceptions then an actual state for the White Lady.

A few lucky witnesses have been close enough to touch a White Lady and have reported going through it as if there were nothing there. They do not appear capable of interacting with the environment. A few Black Dogs witnesses have been close enough to attempt to touch the animal, and their hands have gone right through as well.

The Black Shuck in Suffolk and Norfolk is very large, very black and has red eyes; the later which is not found in nature. There are no such thing as red eye dogs. It can be aggressive and many witnesses claim a sense of malevolence about, when a Black Shuck appears. I have always found the idea of malevolence intriguing but perhaps misplaced when it comes to these sightings. In truth what we are talking about is not a tangible malevolence, but the perception of malevolence, no doubt influenced by cultural expectations. Black Dogs are also called Hellhounds and are historically associated with the Black Man of the forest, the Devil.

Perceptions do not measure what is really there, but how our bodies interpret information. In these cases, malevolence does not lead to the devil, but to hopefully to reason. This is not to say, that the phenomena cannot be dangerous, as the following story may demonstrate.

In the nascent days of world war II, an American airman and his wife were staying at a small cottage in Walberswick Marsh in Suffolk. I suppose a nice refuge from the world at war and a severe storm, they initially thought. The storm outside had started when they both heard a loud noise coming from the front door, a very loud pounding in fact. Somewhat cautious, the airman looked out the window to see what the commotion was all about. What he saw was a large black animal, resembling a dog throwing itself repeatedly against the door. Afraid that the door would break and the dog would burst through, they preceded to barricade the door with all the furniture they could find. But, the dog kept pounding at the door, then on the walls all around the cabin. Unable to break through it seemed, the animal jumped on the roof where the airman and his wife could hear its footsteps for half the night. Then the noises went away. Remaining in the cabin until dawn, they finally dared to venture out and inspect the premises. The large dog was gone and they found no prints anywhere (Jon Downes).

A brief but important sighting took place in April of 1972 in Gorleston, Norfolk. At 4:45 in the morning, coast guard Graham

Grant watched a large Black Dog running along the beach. Nothing an unusual here, except maybe the size of the animal, until the dog disappeared suddenly.

This sightings is important on several level, one, we have a quality witness not in a suggestive state by any means. He was in a familiar place, at work, not in a reputed haunted location. Furthermore, there is very little place to hide or run to on a beach. Some cases where the animal is said to disappear suddenly can be the result of taking your eye off the animal briefly and the animal runs back into the forest. This holds especially true for sightings from a moving vehicle where it is difficult to keep an animal on the side of the road in view once you pass the animal. By the time you slow down or stop to obtain a better view, the animal can be long gone. In this case however the animal disappeared in full view with a witness from a stationary position. More importantly in my opinion is that the dog was seemingly unaware of been watched from a distance. This would suggest that Black Dogs have some type of existence on their own, an independent reality; which really was never a given since we do not know anything about Black Dogs when we are not observing them.

Located in Staffordshire, England, and reputed for its beauty, Cannock Chase is 26 sq. miles of woodland and heathland. A bright and popular place for picnics and mountain biking during the day. At night, it's a much different place.

It was huge with glowing red eyes, the witnessed described it. "I felt a sense of malevolence". Words spoken in regard to the Ghost Dog of Brereton, the local name for Phantom Black Dogs. The area also includes sightings of a ghostly Sasquatch like creature with dark brown or black hair and with glowing red eyes, known as the Man Monkey.

Phantom Black Dogs within and around Cannock Chase fit the pattern of reports elsewhere in Britain. There are several sightings on record of late drivers seeing the animal on the side of the road. Those who have been fortunate enough to get a good long look at the animal up close; usually people out and about on foot; haven't encountered any aggressive behavior. To further illustrate the Paranormal aspect of the phenomena, the dog disappears suddenly, sometimes accompanied by a flash of light. All that has been ascribed to phantom Black Dogs apply to the Man Monkey just as well in Cannock Chase, from behavior to their semi-objective state. The obvious glaring difference is the physical form the manifestation is based on.

MAN MONKEY

Bridge 39 overlooks the Shropshire Union Canal, just like it did 133 years ago. January 21, 1879 to be exact, a man and his horse were attacked by something resembling a gorilla, even though the Gorilla wouldn't be officially discovered for another 23 years. The man in question was walking alongside his cart and horse on the bridge at around 10 PM, when a creature came running out of the woods jumped on the cart and then on the back of the man's horse. The horse startled, took off with cart in tow and the creature still clinging to its back. The man was able to catch up and both out of panic and necessity took out his whip and attempted to strike the interloper off. He later claimed that it had no effect; the whip went right through the creature. This strange effect is also present in certain modern Black Dogs accounts, where the animal is solid as to interact with the environment, but not so to the touch. There are several cases on record where a late night driver unable to avoid a large Black Dog on the road, would go right through the animal, with no damage to the car and no animal in sight. Interestingly, there are also several late night drivers whom have encountered the Man Monkey on these same roads. However, to my knowledge, none have reported running it over and/or going through it. In any case, back in 1879, the creature jumped off the horse and ran off into the woods.

In time the creature would make occasional appearances, some quite recently, in the area near bridge 39. it was dubbed the Man Monkey, because of its apelike appearance. It is described at 5 feet to 7 feet in height, covered in hair, with glowing eyes, sometimes red, and walking upright. Now called the Man Monkey, is still a rather obscure phenomena, even by our standards. I knew of it peripherally through the work of the Center for Fortean Zoology and more recently Nick Redfern's book on the subject. The later, a good source for more recent sighting, especially in the Cannock Chase area which appears to be ground zero for this phenomena.

As an illustration of a point I made earlier, in the mid 1990's a waitress almost ran over the Man Monkey with her car at around 1 AM, given a consistent description of the creature. Some reports differ slightly where the creature is described as more lupine; or as a cross between a wolf and an ape. Perhaps, providing a link with the Wisconsin Werewolf and Dogman sightings in the American mid-west; a subject I've addressed in another chapter.

Something I would like to point here is that terms such as Man Monkey, werewolf and Dogman, beside sounding somewhat ridiculous, are loaded with built in expectations. These names more often than not originate in the press, where the more sensational sounding, the better, The Man Monkey is of course not a half man half monkey monster, nor are there bona fide werewolves running around in America. These are just terms people can identify with, not an objective reality. But there is something there; and once again, it stands to reason that there are no viable breeding population of these creatures; so we are left with a paranormal conundrum.

THE HANDS OF DARTMOOR

Dartmoor is a quiet place, with moors and fog that could remind one of England in the time of the Baskervilles. Fitting it seems, Dartmoor is one of these places that I seem to encounter repeatedly in my research. Dartmoor is famous for the Beast of Dartmoor which actually has little to do with Black Dogs, but rather a breeding biological population of large cats. But, Dartmoor is also famous for the Black Dog of Dartmoor which is exactly what it sounds like, phantom Black Dogs. Perhaps the strangest of all though, is the case of the hairy hands of Dartmoor.

Near Postbridge lies a rather desolate road named B3212. A fairly unusual number of accidents have occurred on that road within the last 100 years. In the early 1900's it was just a local source of interest, unknown to an outside world more concerned with war and the outbreak of the Spanish Influenza. At that time, Dr E. H Helby was the medical officer for Dartmoor prison and was rather fond of driving his motorcycle with a side-car around Dartmoor. In June of 1921 he was driving with two passengers, the two young daughters of the prison's governor, when at some point while on B3212 he lost control. He yelled for the girls to jump, which they did. They survived and he was killed.

Strange some thought, that he had time to tell the girls to jump, but could not correct his trajectory on a simple road. Officially an accident of course, but in the background the road's reputation raised questions. A reputation reinforced within two weeks with another accident and yet again two months later. The later an army captain on a motorcycle who claimed a pair of hairy hands forced him off the road. Accidents continued to occur from time to time with the stories of visible or invisible hairy hands as the cause. Survivors have claimed that these hands would take over their steering wheel overpowering them and forcing them off the road. In truth this would have remained in my mind as a ghost story, and might never have made the speculative connection of Hairy Hands with Black dogs if it wasn't for a certain mountain in the Scottish Cairngorm's and a peak called Ben Macdhui.

BEN MACDHUI

Mountaineers and hikers have reported an apprehensiveness on the mountain; a feeling of fear about the place. Some visitors have at times fled in uncontrollable panic, almost jumping off cliffs for no reason it seems. Others have felt a presence and heard footsteps behind them, but when they turn around there's nobody there. A ghostly entity called the Big Gray Man has been seen and is described as a huge gray mist shrouded figure or at times a ghostly Bigfoot type creature. This phenomenon has also been reported on neighboring peaks. Sometimes laughter and music are heard with no explanation of where it came from.

The great majority of visitors to the mountain encounter nothing, and visual sightings of the Big Grey Men is very rare. The majority of stories are about strange sounds and sudden fear. A presence is felt, angry, male, big, primitive and non human, are description mentioned. Physical sightings of the Big Grey Man aside, it is hard to formulate any kind of hypothesis based on people's feelings; but the descriptions given above seem to pop up consistently since the early 1900's.

Strange sounds can easily be explained, at least for individuals who aren't use to mountain noises. A feeling of apprehension can be attributed to the lonely misty environment, that can put one is a very suggestive state. We know that infrasounds and stimulation of the temporal lobe can lead to fear, the perception of a presence and even hallucinations. So, there could be a geophysical solution to the mysteries on Ben Macdhui.

A few report hearing footsteps, both heavy and slow; and on very few occasions, footprints. Tracks have been described as up to 20 inches in length with 7 feet between strides. One particular physical encounter occurred in 2004 to a man by the name of Tom Robertson. Robertson and Derek Blake had come to the mountain on a ghost hunt for the Big Grey Man. At around 1 AM they decided to retire for the evening. They were both inside the tent when they heard footsteps outside and a sort of mumbling. Then the tent caved in. A big hairy arm appeared followed by what they described as a Yeti like creature, and they started running.

This is the only story of it's kind on Ben MacDhui and when I first heard of it, I initially thought hoax. I'm still on the fence in regards to the veracity of the story, but the researcher who made this story public is Marc Frazer of Big Cats in Britain. Having done work with Big Cats in Britain; I wrote for their website; I'm familiar with Mark. He is an excellent researcher and one hundred percent honest, which is why I included this story here.

There are some obvious similarities to the Man Monkey phenomenon, but the Big Gray Man is somewhat less tangible, making this more in line with traditional hauntings. The paranormal link between the two is speculative, but not unfoundedly so; and there certainly are not a breeding population of primates in the UK living today.

THE SOURCE

I am certain that Black Dogs and the Man Monkey have a direct connection; less certain of the Hairy Hands and Ben MacDhui. Still, the later two contain aspects of the Man Monkey phenomena that cannot be ignored. What I can say with optimistic certainty is that they are all pieces of a puzzle; unfortunately with many pieces missing as to obscure the full picture. My working hypothesis at the moment is that what we are seeing is different aspects of the same phenomena, and at different stages in it's evolution.

Furthermore, you cannot fully separate the phenomena and the observer; the observer plays a part in how the phenomena presents itself. In physics this is called the Observer Effect, in psychology the observer expectancy effect, and in anthropology it is called Participant observation.

Expectations, cultural and otherwise, help shape the phenomena in some way; perhaps at a quantum level. Does that make it any less real? Not at all, Black Dogs and ghost apes are real with a physical presence capable of interaction with the environment., and with an awareness of being observed.

Once again there are of no breeding population of Bigfoots and ghostly Black Dogs in the UK and in other places, this is not a cryptozoological matter. Some researchers place the British Black Panther phenomena within the preceding paradigm. I couldn't disagree more. There are absolutely no supernatural overtones to the Black Panther phenomena. Britain is home to a biological, breeding, large cat, period.

Black Dogs and these Man Monkeys are of extreme importance in Paranormal studies, because they give valuable insight into how certain paranormal event present themselves. Much like the related Poltergeist and Ghost phenomena, all we can do is observe the outcome; but now we know that there is a link and we know of some of the factors involved. Gone are the days when Black Dogs were a representation of the devil, and gone are the days where we classify the preceding as just ghost stories. What it all points to, and where the phenomena lies when not manifested and observed remains a mystery, and thus accordingly the next step in research.

4

2.5 OUNCES

PART I

THE OUT OF BODY EXPERIENCE

OOBE

2.5 ounces is the physical weight loss experienced during an Out of Body Experience, or OOBE for short; as reported in several unrelated experiments (Mithchell, 1981). This figure was initially noted by Dutch scientists, and since, repeated in several other studies conducted at different locations worldwide. Further experimentation in both Remote Viewing and OOBEs have also detected anomalous lights, present at the location viewed or visited by either the remote viewer or the OOBE experiencer.

Experiments conducted in China and then replicated in the United States have measured a light source 100 to 1000 times greater than the background in remote viewing experiments (Swanson, 2003). The lights were detected at sites perlustrated by remote viewers. Similar results were obtained in OOBE experiments as well. The question is, is there a difference between the two?

Traditionally, remote viewing is described as the ability to retrieve information from a distance without the use of the five known senses. An Out of Body Experience is the ability, conscious or unconscious, to leave the physical body and travel to any location on the planet, and sometimes beyond. It has also been called Astral Projection; and the part of the self that has the ability to distance itself from the body is called the Astral body.

As we've just seen, there is a physicality to remote viewing in the form of detectable energy. Experimentation in the Out of Body Experience field indicate a similar phenomenon, albeit in less strictly controlled environments. So, the question is; what really differentiates the two aside from methodology?

The frustrating reality is that we don't yet know. Further experimentation is much needed in both these departments. What certainly is a clue to the greater understanding of psychic phenomena is that the type of light detected at remote viewing and OOBE sessions are similar to anomalous lights detected during Poltergeist outbreaks.

Where the two begin to differ is that during an OOBE the experiencers is able to view his own body and his immediate surroundings. During a remote viewing session, the experiencer does not report seeing his body, but rather finds himself viewing the target directly. Furthermore, OOBE experiments and experiences have reported further physicality to the phenomenon. Orbs of lights have been seen at the location of a reported OOBE, again, similar to ones witnessed at haunted locations. By orbs of light I mean a detectable solid energy source that may be in the form of a ball or streaks. This is not the dust particles or light reflection captured by digital cameras that is all too often photographed in ghost hunts.

There are also cases where the experiencers was seen physically at the location visited by the astral body. In these cases the astral appears solid and is able to interact with the environment. It can manipulate object as well as converse and behave as a normal individual. The astral has also been perceived as a shadow like entity, similar to shadows that have been reported and photographed in hauntings. Often in these cases, the astral is described as pale and white, reminiscent of the White Lady phenomenon. Clearly there is a range here from barely visible, to orbs of light, to entirely visible and tangible. What causes these differences is unknown? I suspect that environmental factors are involved, but we have yet to identify them.

THE BLUE NUN

Sister Marie de Jesus Agreda was born in Spain in April of 1602. Like many young girls in spain at that time she was very devout and took the blue habit of the Franciscan order early in life. But, sister Agreda was not like other nuns; she started having visions at the age of 18. The visions were very intense and could last all day, and eventually she started talking of spiritual travels to the New World. Her actual self never left the convent, but claimed to nonetheless bilocate to this far away land. There, she claimed to have met natives. She told them about God and Christ, and gave them rosaries (O'Brien).

Bilocation is the state of being in two places at once. Unlike the majority of out of body experiences, this involves a tangible second body indistinguishable from the first. Furthermore, this second body acts and functions no differently than the first. This phenomenon is said to have occurred to various saints, and to seemingly ordinary random individuals that were unaware of being in two places at once. Some Tibetan Lamas claim to have this ability as well.

Today, we might view bilocation as another aspect of the out of body experience, but in the 1600's in Spain it was viewed as potentially demonic; and the inquisition took those matters seriously. Remember, these were the geniuses that came up with the rock test for witches. A suspected witch was thrown into a body of water, usually a river, and saddled with heavy rocks. If the "witch" floated, which no one ever did, she was considered guilty of witchcraft and sentenced to death. If she drowned from the weight of the rocks, then she was deemed innocent.

The inquisition was not impressed with sister Agreda's piousness, and a trial, that divided many in Spain, began. Sister Marie de Jesus Agreda never deviated from her position that part of her did indeed traveled somehow to the New World. While the trial was in full swing, conquistadors and friars were returning to Spain from an unexplored area that we know today as the American South West. The natives they encountered there had no prior contact with Europeans; but were far from the "ignorant savages" the Spaniards were expecting. Many knew the story of Jesus and the cross, and some were in possession of rosaries that they showed to the Spaniards, with I would assume a tinge of pride. They explained to the Spaniards that a white lady dressed in Blue had visited them and spoken in their language, and shared with them the gospel. Back in Spain, these accounts saved sister Agreda from the inquisition.

The Blue Nun claimed that she visited the New World over 500 times, while her body never left the convent. When the Franciscans officially arrived in the New World and more specifically in the south west, they were greeted with tales of the Blue Lady, and 50,000 people that were ready to be baptized. All this, did not escape the attention of King Philip. Rumors have it that she bilocated to foreign courts while in the service of the king. Wether the later is historical fact is debatable, and not much is known about her life after this point. In 1988, her body was analyzed by Spanish doctor Andreas Medina. She was found to be incorruptible.

THE PHYSICALITY OF THE ASTRAL BODY

There are further clues as to the physicality of the astral body, albeit some of it anecdotal. There are reports that power lines can entangle the astral. Some experiencer also report that thunder storms can also inhibit OOBEs. This appears to point to the fact that the astral is negatively affected by electricity.

This effect was explored by Robert Monroe in an experiment with an electrified Faraday cage. A Faraday cage is an enclosure that keeps electromagnetic fields from entering; think a microwave, but in reverse. In Monroe's experiments, electricity was kept out and evenly distributed on the outside of the cage.

Robert Monroe in many ways popularized the term out of body experience through his research and series of books.

Monroe claimed and wrote about his ability to induce an Out of Body Experience at will using a set of protocols. Founder of the Monroe Institute, which still functions today and continues research in both the Out of Body Experience and in the understanding of human consciousness.

In this particular experiment, Monroe was placed inside the cage which was electrified with 50,000 volts. The idea was to determine if electricity interfered with the Out of Body Experience. Not only did Monroe become trapped within the cage during a OOBE, but he also became entangled by the electricity on the cage. He was also unable to cross the threshold of the cage. It was only when the electricity was turned off that he could travel beyond the cage. When the electricity was turned off, the Faraday cage in itself had no effect on the OOBE.

This could potentially be the most profound aspect of this phenomenon. For one thing, it gives us a clue as to the nature of the astral body. Whatever energy makes up the astral; it has a physicality, thus potentially mass, and it is affected by electricity. Wether the astral body turns out to be the seat of consciousness, the soul, or something that we haven't thought about yet remains to be seen; but it can potentially be trapped and has a physicality. As such it can be studied. Taking this idea to it's logical yet disturbing conclusion; what if the astral body is identical to the deceased, or to ghosts? This could indicate that we in theory could trap "ghosts" for study or communication. We could find out everything we wanted to know about the afterlife and the physiological make up of ghosts. At the very least, we could begin to identify the nature of the energy used during haunted events.

Now, what if we take this one step further, acknowledging that the astral has a physicality that can thus be manipulated. We can begin to think of a way of attaching recording equipment to the astral, including video. Furthermore, what if the astral body is involved in both OOBEs and in Near Death Experiences? Does this model point to the possibility that we may be able to bring back physical data, such as a recording, of the afterlife.

PART II

THE NEAR DEATH EXPERIENCE

The brain cannot survive more than a few minutes without oxygen. Lack of pulse, no recorded brain activity and a stoppage of breathing signals death. Yet, in some individuals, all of the above occur and they survive. But, unlike a coma situation, they come back with an experience.

As with the OOBE phenomenon, these people report floating over their body, seeing the self and seeing the doctors trying to save their lives. The scene is viewed from a certain sense of detachment, and a short while later they notice that a tunnel is starting to form and at the end a very bright light. The light keeps getting brighter and brighter, but the eyes aren't blinded. A disconcerting feeling to be sure; but inside the tunnel "guides" or deceased family members are there to greet them. They reassure; it's all part of the process, they say.

Sometimes, there is no one to meet inside the tunnel, so the experiencer heads into the light at the end of the tunnel. Past the tunnel into the light, they meet relatives or "guides". Another presence, more mysterious can also be encountered; a being of light that radiates love according to experiencers. Whatever preconceptions we may all have, there is no knowledge or exposition of who or what this being is. At this point a life review begins, all the good and the bad with no judgement attached. Often, the life review is from the point of view of all the people the experiencer has interacted with through their more recent life. Whatever happiness or wrong is felt from all these interactions, the experiencer feels it at this moment. There is no outside judgement, only self analysis. Yes, i said more recent life, as there are hints that there are more incarnations in the past and future, depending on the individuals need.

At this point they may be told that this is not yet their time and that they must go back. Some are given a choice, a choice to stay or a choice to go back; but most are told that they must go back as this is not their time. A few are allowed to stay a little longer and travel in this realm. They come back describing beautiful crystal cities of light.

Hallucinations brought about by electrical activity in the brain? Hallucinations brought about by the release of DMT in the pineal gland? These are some of the arguments against the reality of the Near Death Experience, or NDE for short. One argument for the reality of the phenomenon is that these experiences are relatively identical in all cultures. Shouldn't we expect hallucinations to be more individualized. Or once again, did nature in it's perfectness have a built in system easing the transition into death?

Some of the landscape encountered during NDEs is identical to ones experienced during OOBEs. The bright landscape with the beautiful cities of light have also been described by OOBE experiences. Furthermore, the tunnel described in NDEs can also be present during an OOBE. In other instances, entrance to this world during an OOBE can occur after flying through a complete darkness that seems never ending, or strangely through a pitch black hole in the wall.

In OOBE cases dead relatives may be encountered, but not nearly as often as with NDEs. In fact, this is very rare, and there are no guide either as the experiencer typically flies over the landscape on his or her own. On rare occasions, a dark dreary world is encountered. Not much is known about the later, but the former appears to be a fully functioning world filled with "people" that go about their business. The descriptions of this world is very consistent among all OOBE experiencers. Once you've access this world, you may return to it and it will appear exactly the way you left it. There are even cases of two individuals experiencing an OOBE and meeting on this world. Upon waking and meeting up; their description of their experience matches on all levels.

SECTION II: UFOS

1

QUETZALCOATL'S CHILDREN THE UFO PRESENCE IN LATIN AMERICA

PART I

CENTRAL AND SOUTH AMERICA

"Beings descended from the sky in flying vessels..." says the Mayan Chilam Balaam. The descending of gods is a myth shared by all ancient cultures. But these are not set in mythical places. From the Fertile Crescent to Marcahuasi, geographical specifics are given. Marcahuasi, referred to as "The place of the ancient giant gods" is a two mile long plateau high in the Andes of Peru. From Inca sites to the under water UFOs of Lake Titicaca, Peru is a major player in ufology. Marcuahuasi is famous for its enormous giant granite rocks that resemble human like faces. Ancient ruins nearby seem to indicate small people once lived here, with doorways three feet in height. In UFO circles this place has a reputation for sightings, including several clear photographs.

Latin America is unique in many ways in relation to this phenomenon. It has a history of beings from the sky in Mayan writing, and in oral tradition through several cultures on the continent. Mexico, Brazil and Peru have some of the most intense and well documented UFO sightings in the modern world. South America also has recent reports of the Chupacabra; providing a link to Puerto Rico which I'll address in part two.

George Adamski and many other contactees also claimed that beings were descending from the sky in those strange days in the California desert of the 1950's. Contact with tall blonde aliens who were willing to take a few lucky earthlings for a ride in their flying saucers represented Ufology in the 1950's through the 1960's. Labeled the Nordics, these beings claimed to have come from scientifically impossible places such as the planet Venus.

These tales, filled with scientific inaccuracies are largely discarded today. The idea that Venusians Scandinavians were coming to the California desert to offer rides in their flying saucers borders on the grotesque. As an interesting side note, the tall blond Alien type has also been reported in the Pyrenees region of France.

Is there an objective reality to tales of Nordic Venusians? Probably not. Is there a subjective reality to these tales? Yes, but in what manner remains to be seen. If we could answer that question, we would know the Ufo phenomenon modus openrandi. Because, like Mescalito, it is a trickster that weaves tales of UFOs and their occupants. They exist as objective reality but function at a subjective reality level.

Quetzalcoatl means "feathered serpent" in Nahuatl, the language of the Aztecs. The Mayan equivalent to Quetzalcoatl is Kukulkan. Similar to those Aliens in the California desert, Quetzalcoatl is described as tall, white with long white hair. He is also at times portrayed as having a beard. Native Mayans or Aztecs cannot grow facial hair. He is also associated with the planet Venus.

THE ZONE OF SILENCE

Much like it's fabled ocean counterpart, the Zone of Silence encompasses three geographical areas forming a sort of triangle with the states of Chihuahua, Coahuila and Durango. A world away from the mythic waters of the Bermuda triangle; in fact the Zone is mostly desert. Still, once upon a very long time ago these areas weren't so different. The zone was a thriving sea known as the Sea of Thetys. Today as it did then, the Zone sits north of the Tropic of Cancer and south of the 30 th parallel, a latitude it shares with the Bermuda Triangle and the Pyramids of Egypt.

UFO activity abound in the Zone, and both this place and the Bermuda Triangle share similar geomagnetic disturbances. Compasses go haywire, and deep in the Zone cars stall. Planes avoid flying over this area. Radio waves, short wave, microwaves and satellite signals will not penetrate certain areas; which is how the Zone received its name. In fact, all navigational instruments will malfunction, resulting in the only town within the Zone, Ceballos, having no television. Giant UFos, strange humanoids, mutated cacti, deformed animal life, and strange stone structures are all part of the lore associated with the Zone.

This area of Mexico lies close to the United States border which in 1970 resulted in a rather embarrassing situation for the United States. July 2nd to be precise is when panic set in at White Sands Missile Base. During a missile test, an Athena missile veered of course and headed straight for Mexico and crashed within the Zone, 400 miles away. The missile was carrying two small container of cobalt 57 which is radioactive. This fact added tension to a situation that White Sands was trying to keep quiet. No explanation was ever found or given for the malfunction.

Falling celestial objects, man made and otherwise are a common sight in the Zone, pointing perhaps to a geophysical anomaly beneath this area. Scientist have estimated that meteorites strike the Zone every three minutes The zone is also famous for its red and purple cacti and trees. These unusual colored plants grow next to regular green or brown cacti. If taken from the Zone, the cacti returns to a more normal green or brown.

Tortoises in the Zone display pyramid shape segments on their shells while tortoises in the rest of the world display hexagonal shapes. These tortoises also have no tail. Centipedes in the area are enormous at over a foot in length with purple heads and tails. Albino red eyed lizard and snakes are common, and insects grow to two to three times their normal size. All strange, but these are not the real mystery of the Zone; but they are markers to something much more mysterious.

In the mis 1970's a married couple, who were in the zone on a amateur rock and fossil collecting trip, found their vehicle stuck in the mud when a severe storm hit the area. Desert storms while rare can hit very quickly with a lot of force. The term Operation Desert Storm was no coincidence for the Gulf War of the early 1990's. In any case, back in 1975, Ernesto and Josefina Diaz were stranded with the fear of a flash flood in the back of their minds. Help was the last thing they expected in such a desolate place. So it was with some surprise when two very tall individuals in yellow raincoats came out of nowhere and offered to help. They told Ernesto and Josefina to get inside the car, and that they would help them get back on their way. Which is exactly what they did; their car was suddenly out of the mud and on firmer ground. Ernesto got out of the car to thank the two men, but they were gone. There was no sign of them, no sign of any vehicle and no tracks (Corrales).

Other ranchers and locals within the Zone occasionally report strangers that a very tall and blond. Sometime these strange individuals are seen on the side of the road deep in the desert with no vehicle in sight. Whether there is a correlation with the strange lights at nights can only be inferred.

Since the 1990's Mexico, and perhaps Puerto Rico and Kazakhstan, have been UFO central. Thousand of sightings, including mass sightings over Mexico city have been recorded and filmed. The reality of the phenomena should no longer be in question. Anyone can view the footage on the internet. They include apparent metallic spheres flying in formation, and on one filmed occasion flying around military jets at an air show.

These same objects have been seen in other parts of Mexico and Central America as well, from ancient Mayan and Aztec sites to the jungles of the Yucatan. Similar objects have also been seen in Argentina, Chile, Bolivia, and entering and exiting from Lake Titicaca. What differentiates the Zone of silence from other locations are the occasional giant sized UFOs flying at low altitude.

To further compound the mysterious aspect of the Zone; there are also ancient ruins in the desert. Archeologists think that these are thousands of years old. The architects are unknown, but like Stonehenge, the ruins are thought to have been built for astronomical purposes, So, like pyramids in the Egyptian desert and in the jungles of central and south America, like Stonehenge in Wiltshire; ruins in the Zone of Silence are about the skies. But, we were told this, perhaps even warned. The Mayan Popol Vuh tell us that, "Men came from the skies, knowing everything, and they examined the four corners of the sky and the Earth's round surface".

BRAZIL

The UFO field has a tendency to cover the same subjects repeatedly, with the same people telling the same stories. As a result, many areas where the UFO phenomenon presents itself in more aggressive ways are been ignored. Perhaps it is because they are in far away places with names we fail to recognize. Perhaps it is because some of the implications are uncomfortable, and fall outside the zeitgeist of accepted UFO theories. What we perceive this phenomenon to be is but a small part of the overall complexity of it. We have to go outside our comfort zone to these far away places, because there are answers to be found there. Places such as Brazil where the UFO phenomenon is raw, and more violent then anywhere else on the planet.

FIRST STOP: RIO GRANDE DO NORTE, NORTH EASTERN BRAZIL

The events in this region, and in Minas Gerais, are very unique to Brazil, but also very consistent within these two regions. More importantly for our purpose, they represent a microcosm of events taking place in the whole of Brazil. They usually take place at night in very rural isolated communities. The pattern of events involve a bright light that comes down just above the witness or witnesses, illuminating a large area. At this point panic sets in and the witness runs. The light chases and catches up to the individual. The light emanating from the object, or the object itself is very hot, causing burns to the individual. However, it's when the cold and the wind starts that things take a turn for the worst. The victim feels themselves lifted into the air towards the object, which by now is identified as some type of craft. The ones who are taken suffer memory loss, but the majority seem to be successful in escaping; very often by holding on to a tree. As a last resort, the UFO drops a hot oil like liquid on the victim. If still unsuccessful, the attack stops, sometimes dropping the victim as high as twenty feet to the ground. Benevolent space brothers, my ass.

The lucky ones escape with temporary symptoms, headaches, nausea, eye strain and diarrhea. The less fortunate ones suffer more serious and lasting symptoms. One man by the name of Moises became numb on the left side of the body for almost four months, and difficulties in seeing out of the left eye persisted for a year.

Januncio De Souza never saw the UFO approaching, it was just there above his head. Before he could react, a door opened on the underside of the object where he could see two figures sitting inside the object. He started to be pulled towards the inside of the craft, but held on to a small palm tree. The pull was strong enough for his feet to be levitated of the ground, but apparently not strong enough to make him let go. Perhaps in order to break that hold, a hot oil like liquid was poured on him. He held on nonetheless and the object left. He was sick for two days and had injuries resembling cigarette burns.

Another man, Luis Serra, went missing for three days after an attack, but suffered no side affects. Leonel Dos Santos was missing for a mere four hours, but became week, dizzy with a constant body pain for the rest of his life. Francisco Dos Santos went missing for a day, and had difficulty speaking for a week. There does not seem to be a correlation between length of abduction and severity of symptoms.

For reasons unknown Rio Grande Do Norte is the part of Brazil with the greatest number of recorded attacks. Whether this reflects the actual distribution of attack is unknown. These cases typically take place in rural villages communities which are still easily accessible, relatively speaking; and North eastern Brazil has also been the focus of study by researchers in the past. The frequency and pattern of events in more remote areas of Brazil is unknown.

SECOND STOP: MINAS GERAIS. THE FIRST MODERN ABDUCTION

As far as modern accounts of Alien Abductions, the phenomenon did not originate on lonely North American roads; rather, on a lonely Brazilian field in 1957, near Sao Francisco de Sales, Minas Gerais. It's very hot in this part of Brazil, which led farmer Antonio Villas Boas to work the fields at night. On one night like any other Boas notices a bright object, an object he initially labeled a red star. But stars do not change directions, and this object was certainly coming closer. In interviews given by Boas in subsequent years, he described the object as egg shaped with a red light in front. Boas did manage to obtain a good view of the object, since it landed a few feet in front of him.

Back on that night, he runs, at first to his tractor, but it dies. Now in a panic, he takes off on foot, but not very far. He is grabbed by humanoid creatures about five feet tall, with gray overalls, and small blue eyes. They do not seem able to speak, but rather emit these strange sounds, later described by Boas as yelps and barks. He is taken aboard.

Once inside the craft, Boas is stripped naked and covered by a gel like substance and left alone in a room. Some type of gas is released making him ill, but the feeling quickly dissipates. Shortly thereafter a female walks in, also naked. She is one of them, blue eyed with long white hair. Like the others, she doesn't speak, but makes the same high pitched barking like sounds. She doesn't have to speak, her meaning his clear, and Boas gets lucky on an Alien spaceship. Once finished, the female walks out of the room; but before she does so completely, she point at her stomach and then points upwards. Boas is released.

While the event was somewhat traumatic, the actual physical after effects were minimal and only lasted a few weeks. The familiar symptoms included nausea, headaches, and burning marks or lesions painful to the touch.

VALLEY OF THE OLD WOMEN

One of the more disturbing case in Ufology took place in this area in 1976 to Hermelindo Da Silva. Hermelindo was walking with only his dog as a companion around two in the morning when a bright light appears above his head. He starts to run, but four cables with hooks at the end descend from the object, apparently trying to get a hold of him. Along with the cables, a four foot tall humanoid in a silvery suit also descends and attempt to grab Hermilindo, who manages to fight him off. They struggle for some time, until the being relinquishes and retreats back into the object along with the cables. Aside from falling twenty feet, Hermelindo was unhurt. Three months later, the dog dies of unknown causes.

The Valley of the Old Women is unique for the preceding story; but also for the death of Cicilio Higinio Pereira. As with the preceding cases, Pereira was subjected to a bright light above his head and temporarily lifted up towards the light/object. He managed to get away; but became very sick, constantly vomiting and barely able to get out of bed. He never recovered, and died shortly thereafter. Unfortunately, a doctor was never consulted and thus an official cause of death was never given.

VARGINHA

On january 20 th, 1996, Liliane da Silva, her sister Valquiria and friend Katia Xavier were walking through a vacant lot in Jardim Andere, a section of Varginha. Liliane was the first one to notice the creature among the tall grass and weed to the left, twenty feet away and squatting in front of an abandoned building. The creature had "oily" brown skin, large red eyes and three projections on the top of the head. The girls screamed, which caught the creature's attention. It turned it's head to look at them.

Perhaps as a result of the screaming the creature crouched even further, and the girls fled. They ran to Liliane's and Valquiria's home, roughly twenty blocks away. Later that evening, the three girls, the sister's mother and a neighbor drove back to the lot, but the creature was gone; only the smell of sulfur remained. However the story doesn't end there and apparently this was not the only creature seen that day.

In fact, this was a busy night in Varginha, as a number of Army vehicles and personnel were seen parked outside Regional Hospital; where a section of the hospital was closed off to both patients and employees. Only the military and several unnamed physicians from outside the hospital were allowed access. Eventually the scene shifted to another hospital called Humanitas, in a more secluded area. At the time no reason was given for the commotion.

The chaos made it difficult to contain the story and numerous eyewitnesses came forward, saying that a creature matching the description given by the three girls was seen at both locations. It was hurt, perhaps even dead. Two nurses came forward and claimed to have seen the creature at one of the hospitals. Several military personnel also claimed to have participated in the recovery of another creature, separate from the one seen by the three girls, earlier in the day. Stories of a UFO crash somewhere in the area also surfaced, but with no confirmation. What eventually happened to these creatures is unknown, but the presence of American military forces were noted. Around the same time, in Puerto Rico, similar creatures were being seen; the Chupacabras.

PART II

CHUPACABRA

In the UFO and Paranormal world, the Chupacabra has become the poster child for paranoia and wild speculations. It has been called a vampire, a demon from hell, an alien pet, a government genetic experiment, and a blood thirsty kangaroo. While its identity remains clouded, I'm going to go out on a limb here and eliminate the blood thirsty kangaroo hypothesis, despite the 1950's.

In the middle of that decade, Tucson Arizona was in the middle of a series of sightings of creatures called by locals, killer kangaroos. Stories have it, that the kangaroos were responsible for cattle mutilations. Similar stories emerged out of Tennessee in the 1930's as well.

A link has been suggested between these reports and the Chupacabra of today. To be fair, there are some similarities between the Chupacabra and other bizarre creatures grazing the annals of ufology, cryptozoology and general paranormal research; but the Chupacabra in the form that it is reported today, seems to be a fairly recent phenomenon. One exception may belong to the Taino people of Puerto Rico who have stories about a vampire like reptile resembling and preceding the Chupacabra. As for killer kangaroos, they probably are a combination of the cattle mutilations that have plagued ranchers for decades in the United States and sightings of real life kangaroos.

Sightings of kangaroos aren't that uncommon in the United States. How they got there is a small mystery; but I'm fairly certain that kangaroos, if that's what they were, were not attacking cattle. I've been to Australia and have observed kangaroos and Wallabies up close. While kangaroos are bigger than most people realize, and can be aggressive; they are by no means dangerous predators capable of taking down an animal as large as a bull or cow. Kangaroos have been consistently reported for generations. The 1930's and the 1950's were without cable and the Discovery Channel and sightings of non native wildlife would probably have an element of apprehension and speculation that would not be present today. Little was known about kangaroos and the possibility of them being killers of cattle might have seemed like a reasonable deduction. As for the cattle mutilation cases, while not yet as rampant in the 1930's and 1950's as post 1970, was very much surrounded by an air of mystery. Perhaps because both phenomena had this air of mystery about them, they were united. Of course today, Chupacabras are also linked with animal mutilations.

The modern Chupacabra era began in the early 1990's on the island of Puerto Rico when numerous animals, mostly goats at first, were found mutilated and exsanguinated. Then, reports started coming in of a strange animal and strange tracks at the sites of the killings. There was a prior outbreak of mutilations in the 1970's on the island. The unknown culprit was called the Moca vampire. It's relationship with prior Taino "vampire" and modern Chupacabra remains to be seen. This area of research certainly deserves a better look; beyond just an assumed correlation.

At the time of this writing, Chupacabra sightings have extended beyond the Latin world into places such as Russia and the United States. This fact brings up a peculiar point. Whatever this specie turns out to be, it has no clear set geographical boundaries which is somewhat unusual if we were dealing with a regular member of the animal kingdom. This bothers me. Like the separation of church and state I like keeping my Cryptozoology and UFOs independent of one another. I believe and make no apology that Cryptozoology studies biological organisms related to present or extinct specie in the fossil record. There is nothing supernatural or UFO related to be seen. Then came the Chupacabras.

Chupacabras as described by witnesses cannot be placed within a zoological taxonomy that we are aware off, either from a current specie or one known from the fossil record. Furthermore, the link with the UFO phenomena is inescapable, which you may have guessed since, you know, this chapter is in the UFO part of this book. Chupacabras attacks have a tendency to occur on nights where UFOs are also reported in the same area. Sightings have actually been reported directly over the site of a Chupacabra sighting or kill, on several occasions.

To further complicate matters, genetics modification, or splicing, makes creating an animal resembling the Chupacabras near possible today. The temptation to create new life forms is nothing new, Chimeras were talked about in the ancient past; and a relatively unknown incident at a place called Poole island in the 1970's perhaps paved the way for the modern Chupacabra.

POOLE ISLAND

Maryland isn't the kind of state that you would think could harbor any kind of mysterious creature, and the Washington Post wouldn't necessarily be a source for mysterious creature reports. But in 1976 the Post published an article about a crabber by the name of Tom Sobotka, and the strange creatures he claimed to have seen near a place called Poole island.

The mid 1970's was a strange time. As we have seen, Puerto Rico experienced it's first major wave of animal killings and mutilations by the Moca vampire. Colorado and neighboring states was in the midst of the biggest wave of cattle mutilation in history, and disco was about to hit it big. 9;Whitemarsh, Maryland, was where Tom Sobotka applied his trade; where from 1973 to 1976 the area around Poole island, near Whitemarsh, experienced a series of sightings of creatures resembling

Bigfoot. All this Culminated in a military presence, a dead orangutan, a police cover up and a large body bag carried out by a dozen soldiers.

With all this in the background Tom Sobotka had an even more amazing story to tell. Pool Island's Bird river in the swamps is where Sobotka use to spend the majority of his time. In the Post and a subsequent article written by Mark Chorvinsky and Mark Opsanick of the excellent Strange Magazine, Sobotka made the following statement: "There are things out on the island that nobody would believe. Nobody goes out there but me. If I told you everything I saw there they'd lock me up".

Sobotka's father claimed that he knew a guard working at a military installation nearby, the Abeerding Proving Ground. The guard told him about strange experiments that were being conducted there, involving humans and mutations. Sobotka and his father had no way to prove their claims. Claims that involved mutated fishes that Sobotka observed in the swamps of Poole island; fishes that seem to have body parts belonging to other animals. He hinted at more, but never divulged what that might have been. Splicing did not exist in 1976, and rumored breeding experimentation was just that, rumors. The creation of new species and hybrids is carefully regulated today. At least as far as the public ic concerned; but if its scientifically feasible, someone is probably doing it somewhere.

PUERTO RICO AND THE CHUPACABRA

Back in Puerto Rico, by the end of 1990's over a thousand dead animals, including sheep, dogs, turkeys, rabbits, chickens, cattle, cats, horses and of course goats were attributed to the Chupacabra. In the deep end of paranoia, rumors and exaggerations; the pattern for a Chupapacabra kill emerged.

Mutilated animals with puncture holes are typically found on the animals neck and abdomen. More often than not the animals are exsanguinated, drained of blood. Some animals have been further mutilated where internal organs have been ripped out. Rabbits especially seem to bring out the worse in the Chupacabra as it will go through the trouble of absolutely destroying the cages holding the rabbits in order to mutilate Thumper. Rabbit cages aren't the only structures destroyed by the Chupacabra. It has been known to tear through barb wire and iron gates to get to its intended prey. The strength of the creature is quite remarkable.

By 1996 reports began emanating from North America. Florida was the first to be victimized. In march of that year, in south Miami, 69 animals were killed and eyewitnesses report a creature fitting the Chupacabra's description. Less celebrated reports also came from Massachusetts, New York and New Jersey. By that summer, reports of mutilations and of Chupacabras became common place in the American South West and in Mexico; and the killings in Puerto Rico escalated. Eyewitness reports of the creature were on the increase.

As a result, we now have a fairly detail description of the Chupacabra. The creature is between three to five feet in height, has big black and reddish eyes. The top of the head is round, the mouth has fang like dentition, and an appendage (tongue?) that can project. The creature is also equipped with spinal fins and wings, even though they aren't always reported. Footprints found next to dead animals show three toes with three long claws. It is apparently covered with short hair that has been reported has anything from brown, gray, orange, yellow and blue. The majority of eyewitnesses usually describe it as either ape like or dog like. In November of 1995 a man in Canovanas, Puerto Rico saw a Chupacabra attack his dog and described it as "monkey like and as running like a monkey, but definitely not a monkey".

In the beginning only animals were victimized, but eventually people were attacked as well and the creature was being seen more frequently around human habitations. In a small village in Mexico a woman claimed that a Chupacabra clawed her, and a man from another village said that he also was attacked. He displayed two punctured marks on his right arm. But, before you think that the Chupacabra just doesn't like Mexicans, a Puerto Rican man in December of 1995 claimed that he was attacked from behind and showed cuts on his abdomen. He described the creature as gorilla like. These incidents are fairly uncommon, and for the most part the creature doesn't seem to have it in for man. Instances like these are very rare and no one has been seriously hurt, as far as I know.

Towards the end of 2012 I found myself in a car with Reuben Uriarte, a well known UFO investigator and one of the original Chupacabras investigators. I actually met Reuben way back in the day when we were both part of the original UFO hunter documentary, which was part of the UFO files series. Back to the present and our ride on the 101 freeway I asked him about the Chupacabra and mentioned my obsession with it; I like to rank things, and the Chupacabra ranks pretty high on my paranormal subject list. We started talking about some of the cases and the goat sucker in general; a weird conversation I suppose for most people, but a regular weeknight for me. Reuben mentioned how he examined some of the Chupacabra's victims. What he found was that the internal organs in many cases were liquified. We know that Chupacabra victims have been found with one or two puncture wound, usually around the neck area. This obviously lead to the theory that the Chupacabra injects the victim with some kind of liquifying agent. That would suggest that they ingest the liquified insides for nourishment.

Spiders feed this way as they inject digestive enzymes through their fangs in order to feed on the liquified remains. This is not to suggest that Chupacabras have any relationship to spiders, but to point out that this is possible in the animal kingdom. Carnivorous plants also utilize external digestive enzyme to break down their captures prey. Most animals, including humans use digestive enzymes internally.

As far as Chupacabras are concerned, this ability could be of prime importance in identifying these creatures. If we could get a sample of the liquified remain of a Chupacabra attack, it could be analyzed and compared to known digestive enzymes; giving us a clue as to the zoological nature of the beast. If these creatures turn out to be genetic experimentation and more specifically hybrids; in theory then, digestive enzymes from any specie on the planet, and perhaps off it, could have been introduced. This includes plant digestive enzymes.

So, we know the Chupacabra doesn't like goats and rabbits. In addition it isn't fond of teddy bears either. In a rather idiotic episode, a less than brilliant Chupacabra in Caguas city, Puerto Rico tore the window of a bedroom open and savagely attacked a teddy bear. Episode like the later have prompted the police in both Puerto Rico and Mexico to take action.

In fact, in December of 1995 a police officer in Puerto Rico managed to shoot at one of the creatures. He failed in killing it but blood samples were obtained. The blood was analyzed first by a veterinarian and then by a laboratory in the United States. The veterinarian's report stated that the blood contains high levels of protein and acids, with traces of chlorophyll. The laboratory analysis revealed that the blood was similar to human type A but not compatible with human blood or any other animal. We do have to allow the possibility of contamination for the sample.

DISAPPEARANCE AND ALIENS

Ramon Quinones along with several other college students and two overseeing professors were camping in El Yunque in the Spring of 1967. Seating around the campfire, they noticed a rather loud buzzing sound that lasted several minutes. Perplexed but not particularly alarmed they waited for it to stop and went back to talking around the campfire, while Quinones strummed his guitar.

They noticed that it became very quiet outside their circle in the surrounding jungle; which allowed them to hear footsteps that seemed to be coming closer. They, I assume, expected a regular person to come walking out of the jungle. What they saw was far from regular; a tall luminous figure walking briefly in their line of sight before disappearing into the jungle. The figure was very thin and with a glow that emanated from the silvery suit it wore. Several of them rushed into the jungle trying to get a better look at the figure. Quinones who took his guitar with him became separated from the main group.

The rest of the tale was later recounted by one of the professors, named Gonzales. They were able to catch up with the figure, who aware of their presence stared at them for several minutes. In a state similar to a tiger's prey, where the tiger uses low frequency to paralyze its prey; the group felt paralyzed and in a trance and were unable to flee. The figure made no aggressive gesture nor attempted to get any closer. After about fifteen minutes, the figure vanished into the jungle. The group now free of whatever state they were in, panicked and several students fled. However, Gonzales noticed that Quinones was not among them. His guitar was found next to a tree, but Quinones was never found.

It is possible that Quinones simply panicked and was lost in the jungle. Whatever the case may be, the disappearance of Quinones opened the flood gates for UFOs and strange creatures in the El Yunque rain forest. UFOs are a common sight over El Yunque. Eyewitnesses point to the possibility of a flight path over El Yunque and landing somewhere in the middle of the island. Most of the UFO activity happens at night; but a few hikers have returned from El Yunque claiming to have seen strange creatures in the day time. We'll return to El Yunque shortly, but first a detour to Texas where they shoot Chupacabras.

TEXAS CHUPACABRAS

Dogs and coyotes afflicted with an unspecified skin disorder have been alarmingly abundant in the United States, and especially in Texas within the last ten years. Labeled Chupacabras by the mainstream media, these animals have been seen, filmed and killed in recent years. All subsequent analysis, including DNA have shown that these animals are in all cases coyotes, wolves, dogs, hybrids; or at the very least Canids.

Mange is a skin disease caused by mites that burrow beneath the skin. The mites causes severe inflammation which result in a thickening of the skin, and the animal's fur falls out due to the lack of blood supply to the hair follicles. The afflicted animal typically bites and scratches itself due to the itching which aggravates the skin's condition. Furthermore, bacteria can thrive in these conditions resulting in more infections, and a rather monstrous look for the animal inflicted.

All that being said, some wildlife officials have been perplexed by some of the physical characteristics on some of these animals. These includes traits such as longer forelimbs, bluish skin, unusually dentition, and elongated muzzle. None of these traits are caused by mange or any other known skin disease. These animals are canids without a doubt and not related to the Chupacabra phenomena; but some questions still need to be asked. What is causing these mutations; and, are we seeing the evolution of a new specie of canids in the heart of Texas? Whatever the case may be, let's be clear; these animals have nothing to do with the real Chupacabra phenomenon.

RUSSIAN CHUPACABRA

In 2006 reports of the Chupacabra, and a string of dead animals, emerged out of Russia. The animals were reportedly drained of blood with puncture wound such as the one's found in Puerto Rican cases. Eyewitness testimony described sightings of a creature resembling the Chupacabra as previously described elsewhere. The attacks begin in 2005 with the death of thirty turkeys and thirty sheep, all drained of blood. Initially in the central portion of Russia in a town called Chelyabinsk, subsequent sightings of Chupacabras moved the action to Siberia. As you may have noticed throughout this book, Siberia comes up often in relation to paranormal events. As it relates to the Chupacabra, sightings in Siberia centered around a village by the name of Novosibirsk. Unfortunately when dealing with reports emanating from Russia, a cautious skeptical view is required. A great deal of sensational news comes out of that region that are rarely properly investigated; Chupacabras included. Still the region has a history of sightings of a creature called Letayuschiy Chelovek. Relatively unknown to ufologists and cryptozoologists alike, this creature whose sightings date back a few centuries does bring the more modern Chupacabra to mind.

LETAYUSCHIY CHELOVEK

Letayuschiy Chevolek means flying human. People of the Taiga, especially in the Primorsky Territory in the far east are well aware of this creature. The majority of sightings come from hunters and soldiers, as this area isn't very heavily populated. One notable exception was a close up sighting by the Ivanitzky family in Petropavlovsk, in the 1990's.

The Ivanitzkys had just recently moved in into their new house, and from the first night on they were hearing strange noises, like very loud crickets. This went on for almost two weeks until the day where they found some kind of animal under the bed in their bedroom.

At first they thought that it might be a dog, and they threw slippers at it, trying to get it away from under the bed. At this point the animal came out. They claim that it grew in size and attacked them with a long trunk that appear to originate from the nose area. They began hitting the animal with whatever they had, and spraying it with household chemicals; until they were sure that it was dead.

It looked somewhat dog like with short bluish hair. It had wings, three fingered «paws», a flat human looking face, small forehead, no lips, small mouth, large eyes and a triangular hole for a nose. They through it out into a ditch and it was never seen again.

GENETIC ENGINEERING?

Back on Poole island the Chemical Research Developing and Engineering Center was also dumping a large amount of toxic chemicals In the area. At the time, the army claimed that no such chemicals were being dumped, but subsequent investigations by the Inspector General proved otherwise. In 1986 the army closed the facility down.

While the dumping was believed by some to be responsible for the strange events around Poole island. In truth, that is more movie science than real science. Poisoning from toxic chemicals do not result in monsters.

Tom Sobotka is of the opinion that human animal breeding experiments were been conducted at Poole Island, but so far, no real evidence has turned up. Honestly I find that theory a little farfetched. Not to mention that there are more suitable places available if your going to run secret unlawful experiments. I have had several phone conversations with individuals that claim that such experiments have taken place in the United States. The idea is that by introducing certain animal traits in soldiers at a genetic level, you can in essence create a particular soldier for a particular environment. I currently have no way of determining the veracity of such claims. Furthermore, is that even necessary in today's wars? While soldiers are indispensable for certain tasks in my opinion; the future of warfare appears to be in drones, and long distance weapons. That said, guerilla warfare as yet to really lose a war; so maybe.

Human animal breeding experiments have been rumored to have been attempted before, most notably from the Nazis and China. In this case it is hard to say what was really going on. We do know that soldiers were spotted carrying a large animal in a body bag and we do know that a dead orangutan was found, and I don't think he knuckled walked his way over from Borneo. As far as the chemical dumping goes it sure provided a convenient distraction. If people in the area claim to have witnessed strange animal mutations, well in can be attributed to the dumping and not to any government experiments; at least in 1970 logic.

EL YUNQUE

All of this brings us to another military installation and not a dead orangutan but live monkeys; and not in Maryland, but back in Puerto Rico and El Yunque. Inside El Yunque lies an impressive cave system that is thought to be the home of the Chupacabra. As there always seems to be in these tales, there is an American military installation in El Yunque, that holds a top secret status much like area 51.As we have already seen many UFO's have been spotted around the installation. Speculation on an alien origin for the Chupacabra remains popular. It has also been suggested that the creature may be a genetic experiment with alien biology; but explaining a mystery with another isn't going to provide concrete answers.

The Maryland case, if Sobotka is to be believed, dealt with breeding experiments; 1976 being too early for bona fide genetic manipulation. Today's technology let's us do so much more. Scientists have conducted genetic experiments on mice that has resulted in some less than attractive critters. These mice were injected with human DNA. All this research is public, all you have to do is turn on the discovery channel and see the results of these experiments for yourself. I recommend checking out the mouse with the human hear; or more importantly in regard to our discussion, the green glowing monkey. The later is where jellyfish genes were intoduced to monkeys, and even cats. The results were monkeys that glowed green, and that could pass that ability to their offspring. Imagine the stuff they do in secret. Imagine the animals they can create through biogenetics.

DNA of unrelated species can now be spliced together. Scientists have discovered DNA segments that are common in man, frogs, chickens, earthworms and even flies. Notice the diversity of organisms involved here. Organism that cannot breed can theoretically have their embryos fused to create an animal that combine traits. We aren't so far away from the minotaurs and chimeras of ancient Greece.

Could genetic experiments have been carried out, and then in the midst of Hurricane Hugo came loose? Hurricane Hugo hit Puerto Rico in 1989 and caused extreme damages, most notably in El Yunque. Remember how Chupacabra descriptions vary, different fur color, more ape like, more dog like; some reports include wings while others do not. Some offspring inherit some traits, others inherit others. Is the Chupacabra the result of genetic manipulation?

One last avenue I do want to explore is some of the more unusual aspects of the Chupacabra. One man by the name of Jaime Torres, who came upon the creature as it was sitting upon a branch in a tree, said that it was changing colors rapidly much like a chameleon. The color changed from purple to brown and finally to yellow. Suddenly aware of Torres, the creature let out a hissing sound that made Torres feel faint, and it took off.

The same effect was noticed by a police officer who was in pursuit of a Chupacabra. His symptoms were even more acute as he developed a severe headache and intense nausea which forced him to abandon pursuit. These are not isolated events. Others have reported the chameleon effect and the physical ailments. This survival mechanism, causing nausea and headaches could be induced by infrasound; a more extreme version of the tiger and the prey if you will. Infrasounds below 20 Hz have been known to create a feeling of fear, nausea and even induce visual hallucinations. There is no doubt in my mind that if these reports are accurate, Chupacabras have the ability to emit infrasound. I go into further detail on infrasound in the ghost chapter.

The chlorophyll found in the blood samples, assuming once

again that this analysis is accurate, raises a number of questions as well. I am not suggesting that we have a pissed off alien pet here; but, is it possible that genetic engineering has incorporated both native and non native species?

2

SIGNAL IN THE NOISE
RUSSIA

AN OLDER THREAT

Former USSR colonel Boris Sokolov once told US television reporters that his job between 1980 and 1990 was to study UFOs for the Soviet Ministry of Defense. He was quoted as saying that "for ten years the entire Soviet Union became a gigantic UFO listening post". He went on further and stated that the United States was equally interested in UFOs and that stealth technology was developed from recovered UFOs. According to Sokolov, pilots at first were instructed to take aggressive measures and fire at UFOs. Following a number incidents, where the crafts retaliated and pilots were killed, the Soviet Union adopted a non fire policy. It was also claimed that the Soviet's "Star Wars" program was called on the inside "the weapon of the aliens".

NATO General Secretary Lord Roberston also remarked that the Strategic Defense Initiative (SDI), the actual official name for the Star Wars program in the United States, was for terrorist threats and an older threat from the Universe. Mikhail Gorbachev in a speech in 1990 made the following statement "The phenomenon of UFOs does exist, and it must be treated seriously".

Quotes by reputable high level individuals on the subjects of UFOs, both from the United States and from foreign sources, aren't hard data. I am well aware of this; and they shouldn't be treated as proof of the ultimate reality of the UFO phenomena, but rather as a beginning for inquiry. More importantly, they demonstrate the global importance of the UFO issue. The UFO phenomena does not exist in a vacuum. If we are been visited; it becomes the most important topic on the planet. The later has not gone unnoticed by world leaders. Whomever has access to that technology has power and military supremacy. Whomever has access to their propulsion system; well, that affects the oil companies and in turn world economics and political positioning. This is the new cold war.

There is a geographical aspect to the phenomena, relevant today, and which gives us the possibility to study it as field work. This is true as well of the Central and South American UFO scene, which I discuss in another chapter. Eighty to ninety percent of UFO research and television shows focuses on the United States and the United Kingdom. Which considering the size and diversity of our planet, we are missing out on not only a plethora of data, but completely different aspects of the phenomenon as well.

The UFO phenomenon in many ways functions as a cybernetic system. Its actions impacts the environment and illicit a response. That response is sent back to the source who changes it actions and behavior accordingly. The human response to UFOs is intrinsic to its geographical location. Cultural diversity, religious adherence, history, as well as how UFOs are portrayed in the media affects that response. This will of course be different in Russia as it will be in the United States; and can explain the differences in UFO behavior based on their geographical location, and place in time. This action acts as a shield, a protection for the UFO phenomena; but it isn't foolproof. Their are cracks in the shield; if you look closely enough you can see a little of what lies behind it. But, you have to look at it from all angles, from Russia to Peru.

Furthermore, there is one thing that the phenomena cannot manipulate, and that is pattern. Pattern is inherent to the universe, the golden mean sees to that. By looking at all the aspects of the UFO phenomenon we can start to discern patterns, order in the chaos if you will. So, with that in mind, let's head to Russia where just like Russians at the airport, UFOs are louder, more visible with very bright colors.

THE LAND

VALLEY OF DEATH

Yakutia lies in the Russian far east and covers 1 198 200 square miles with only 1 million inhabitants. Consisting of large mountain ranges with the rest of the land mostly taiga and tundra; it is a inhospitable place. In the northwest section lies an area called "The Valley of Death", an area of interest due to the frequency of UFO sightings. Many years ago, according to local oral tradition, the land was plunged into darkness when a huge storm hit the valley. After the storm a large tower like structure could be seen for many miles away, reflecting the sun. The story goes to say that the structure was very loud and seemed to make its way underground. The ground itself was burned and a crater was left where the structure had been. Nearby, domed structures called "Iron Houses" by the local tribes of Tungus people stayed on the ground for centuries. Eventually, the environment took its toll on the structures and could actually be entered. The problem was that anyone who spent any length of time inside the structure died of a "strange sickness". I've always appreciated the term, strange sickness. A common term worldwide in historical texts and mythological tales; often coinciding with visitations from deities, weapons form the Gods; the Ark of the Covenant, that sort of thing.

Sometime a story is just a story, and a myth is just a myth; but in the mid 1930's explorers came upon these spherical objects roughly 25 feet in diameter within the Valley of Death. They were described as metallic, and appear to affect the growth of plants and grass around the structures. The explores, group of six men led by Mikhail Petrovich Koretsky decided to sleep inside the structures they labeled cauldrons for a night. Warm and comfortable they slept, but upon waking Koretsky developed painful lesions on one side of his face and another man lost all his hair.

Due to the remoteness of the area, the Soviets decided the place was perfect for nuclear tests. As a result in the mid 1950's a 10 kiloton bomb was detonated in the area. It exploded with a force of 20 megatons. That's two thousand time more powerful than expected. The Soviets had no explanation.

MOUNTAIN OF THE DEAD, URALS

In 1970 a picture was taken of a round UFO near Kholat Syakhel mountain in the Urals. There was nothing remarkable about the picture from a Ufology standpoint, it was a clear "good" photograph, but we have so many of those. Still, it was taken in an area rich in UFO lore. More importantly, it was taken next to Kholat Syakhel where a most unusual event took place eleven years earlier. An event which resulted in multiple deaths the police said was due to the "invincible force of nature". Kholat Syakkhel means mountain of the dead. A name given by the Mansi people who considered the mountain sacred and a place where spirit gathered.

Whether mountaineer Igor Dyatlov knew about the mountain's reputation, Is unknown. What we do know is that he departed with nine others in early February of 1959 and soon they would all be dead, victim of that invincible force of nature. This case is well documented, because the police did an excellent job reconstructing the event.

When the group failed to return a search party was sent out and found the following scene. The description below are based on the official police report and the search party's testimony. The group and their camp was easily located. One man was found to have died of exposure, but the others showed signs of severe internal trauma and the police stated that at least some of the victims rushed out of their tents and tried to flee. A tent was found ripped from the inside and footprints leading away.

The closest body to the tent was of the one female in the group, lying face down in a pool of blood. Next was Dyatlov's body found with a crack skull, but no outside visible damage to the head. Further away were three men, found with broken skulls and ribs and severe internal bleeding, but minimal damage to their skin. The bodies all had an orange tint to them and their clothes contained levels of radiation. One of the officials on site also mentioned that some tree branches in the area were burnt.

The police interviewed some of the local people in the area. They told the police that numerous orange spheres were seen flying above the mountain on the night of the tragedy. The objects were silent, the police was told. The rescue party also witnessed a «fiery» object in the sky, a sighting that lasted for about 20 minutes; invincible force of nature.

IN SPACE

THE FIFTH EXPEDITION

Several former cosmonauts have also gone on record in recent years claiming that they have seen UFOs from space. One of the better detailed sightings in space comes from cosmonaut Victor Afanasyev. In April of 1979 Afanasyev had the task of docking with space station Soviet Salyut 6. On route Afanasyev reported a UFO who followed him into space. After the fall of the Soviet Union Afanasyev made the following statement" It followed us during half our orbit. We observed it on the light side, and we when we entered the shadow side, it disappeared completely. It was an engineering structure, made from some type of metal, approximately 40 meters long with inner hulls. The object was narrow here and wider here, and inside there were openings. Some places had projections like small wings. The object stayed very close to us. We photographed it, and our photos showed it to be 23 to 28 meters away" 9;

This was a precursor to the events of Salyut 6, where just two years later a strange craft was filmed in space. In March of 1981 Soviet space ship Soyus T -4 docked with space platform Salyut 6. Their tasks were to investigate claims made by former crews on Salyut 6 of strange silvery clouds around the space platform. Prior expeditions called the second, third and fourth expedition, each had reported these unusual clouds. This was the fifth expedition. The expedition's protocols had been designed by professor A. I. Lasarev who authored a book about these events. In the book he mentions the silvery clouds and other unusual phenomena. The book was very well documented with exact dates, except May 14 to May 18 which were omitted from the book.

A meeting was held once the fifth expedition was back on earth, a meeting led by Lt. General Georgy Timofeyevich Beregovoy, There is no way to validate the following as it was reported by private conversation to UFO researcher Paul Stonehill; a Russian who moved to the United States in 1973. According to Stonehill's sources the cosmonauts observed a UFO in the second week of may, only 30 feet from the space platform. It was close enough for them to see it clearly through the portholes, and they saw occupants; and more importantly it was all filmed. I've made some inquiry over the years about the location of this film and about whether the story was true. Nothing concrete on the location of the film, or any other for that matter; but the answer appears to be the same for all claims made out of Russia. Some of it is true and some of it is not; some of it is information and some of it is disinformation. But, the frequency of events did not stop with the fall of the Soviet Union, the something that Gorbachev referred to in 1996 hasn't gone anywhere.

THE WATERS

ISSIK KULE LAKE AND LAKE BAIKAL

As a long time MUFON UFO investigator I've heard some crazy stories and I've investigated numerous sightings in and around the Pacific Ocean of the Southern California coast. As a result I've developed a specific interest in underwater UFOs or USOs. That combination, crazy stories and underwater UFOs, is alive and well in Russia and in the region as a whole.

I cannot ascertain the veracity of the following accounts, and some would probably say the majority of this book. Be that as it may, what follows has been making the rounds for years in UFO circles and in the 1990's when I was attempting to gather evidence from sources within Russia I myself had heard the following stories.

In the 1930's a Russian Ufologist was a rare thing and Alexander Gorbovsky was such a man. Gorbovsky was a historian by trade, (later in life he worked at the USSR Academy of Science); and in the twilight of that decade Gorbovsky found himself investigating a case about a strange find in a cave at Issik Kul lake, Kyrgizstan.

The main witness, who has remained anonymous, claimed that along with a few friends had discovered humanoid skeletons within the cave that were more than 10 feet in length. The skeletons were decorated with silver decorations of what appeared to be bats. Frightened they fled, but managed to take the silver "bats" with them which they subsequently melted before showing to scientists years later. As you can imagine, the scientist couldn't do much with the melted items, and were unable to determine the age or origin of what remained of the "bats".

In 2007, archeologist announced that they found the remain of a city sitting at the bottom of the lake. They gave a possible date of 500 BC. Very little is known about the people that once inhabited the city; but they were fairly sophisticated as the city seems to encompasses a very large area with walls 1,600 feet in length. The relationship between this city and the skeletons found in the cave is unknown, and obviously highly speculative, but tantalizing. Legends speak of four other cities somewhere in the depths of the lake.

Issyk Kul lake sits among the northern Tian Shan mountain range in eastern Kyrgyzstan. It is a saline lake who never freezes despite the very cold temperatures there in the winter time. Also in terms of sheer water volume, Issyk Kul is the tenth largest lake on the planet with a surface area of over 2000 sq. miles and a maximum depth of near 2200 feet. It is 110 miles long and 37 miles wide at its widest. it's a big lake, similar to another mountain lake on another continent, Titicaca. Lake Titicaca is also a location with a reputation in regards to mysterious ruins and UFOs. As is the case at Issyk Kul Lake, sightings in Titicaca center around UFOs coming in and out of the lake.

On the UFO front, issik Kul Lake would remain quiet for a while, until the summer of 1982 when the Soviets along with various military reconnaissance divers, including from Turkestan, conducted training exercises at the lake. The officers in charge were Lt. Colonel Gennedy Zverev and the source of this story, Mark Shteynberg who today is a well known author.

Shteynberg claims that one day before the start of the exercises, a Soviet Major-General by the name of Demyenko arrived at the lake with a warning and a story. They were told not to attempt at capturing "Swimmers" in the lake, and in fact to stay away if they encountered the Swimmers underwater. There are no detailed transcription of that conversation on that day, but I would assume that Shteynberg and Zverez demanded some kind of explanation. Possibly regretting that request, they obtained the following story from the Major-General.

Similar training exercises were taking place in Siberia, in Lake Baikal. The Major-General claimed that the Soviet divers encountered the Swimmers at 164 feet deep beneath the lake. The Swimmers were 10 feet in height and clothed in silver with what appeared to be helmets. No breathing apparatus seemed to be present.

The Soviet commander decided to attempt a capture of one or more of the Swimmers and subsequently sent down seven divers with that goal in mind. Some of the divers attempted to apprehend one of the Swimmers and were expelled by a force upwards towards the surface of the lake. Three of the divers died from decompression sickness. As a result, the Major-General was sent to Lake Issik Kul to warn them about the Swimmers. Demyenko failed to divulge why they thought that similar Swimmers were present at this location as well.

At any case the Soviet took the incident quite seriously and ordered an inquiry into Lake Baikal and other lakes where similar creatures had been reported, as well as UFOs seen entering or leaving these lakes. Protocols were set in place in order to deal with the presence of the Swimmers at those locations.

If any of this is true in whole or in part, the details are classified somewhere. I'm quite honestly on the fence when it comes to some of the wilder tales here. There is a difference in wild tales coming from government authorities versus wild tales from civilian sources. The later is more often than not an indication of fabrication, both from a hoaxing or a delusional standpoint. When governments starts talking crazy, outside of Congress I mean, about UFOs; disinformation comes to mind. Here is the thing though, at the center of all effective disinformation campaign is some type of truth. If there weren't, there would be no point in a disinformation campaign. So, what I do know to be true, is that these locations in Siberia have a high level of UFO activity, which is paramount to any research, especially if we are looking for repeatability. Let's start there, but, I am willing to go diving in these lakes; just in case.

3

THE DEEP

In around 2002 I received a phone call from a man living in Santa Monica telling me that he's been seeing strange lights over the ocean late at night. Calls concerning strange lights are routine in my world, usually not amounting to very much. I try to be diplomatic especially when representing MUFON; which hasn't always been my forte. But, calls and sightings about a five second flashing light someone may or may not have seen in the sky bores me to no end; and this is coming from a guy that watches the Luge world cup. Its more exciting than you would think.

Still, this time it was different, it sounded promising. He had another witness that claimed to have seen multiple objects flying over the water, and he himself had filmed the strange lights. There was more; the day following one of his more spectacular sightings, two men knocked on his door claiming that they were here to inspect the building for the city. They wanted to see his apartment and specifically the bathroom; from which he had seen and filmed the lights. He acquiesced, they went in, and locked themselves in the bathroom for several minutes. What was discussed, or whatever, by the two men in this rather awkward situation, is unknown. They thanked him and walked out. A paranoid mind set leads to a Men In Black scenario, and yes they were wearing suits. Unfortunately they didn't say much and never returned. With nothing else to go on, I had to leave that as an odd occurrence; or maybe a Men In Black gay porn thing.

The great majority of witnesses or/and experiencers of unusual event rarely want to take it past the telephone interview process, so I asked the following with very little expectations. Can we meet at the location of the sighting? Can I see and get the filmed analyzed? Can I meet the other witness? Yes to all three he said, and we made an appointment for several days later.

On a typical sunny Santa Monica day, I drove over to the location. I rang the bell and went up to the apartment of the first witness, justin (not his real name). We spoke briefly as I inspected the apartment. By inspecting, I mean looking at the style of the apartment, the books and DVDs he owns; which helps me get a better idea of who I'm dealing with. This is essential in establishing the veracity of a sighting. Does the witness own a plethora of UFO and Paranormal books? Is his sighting too similar to ones portrayed in books he owns, for example? Does his personality veer towards fantasy? Profiling really does work, and here I saw nothing that made me suspicious. Along those lines, it is also extremely helpful to study eye and body movement in relation to deception. Not quite as foolproof and simplistic as you see on television, but helpful nonetheless in some investigations.

I was anxious to see the film which he had readied on his laptop. The film showed several lights above the water moving up and down and side to side. They were blue and a weak yellow and appear to get brighter and dimmer. With no frame of reference it could be that the witness is moving the camera back and forth creating the illusion of movement. Furthermore zooming can also give the impression that the objects are getting brighter. This wasn't the case. While these objects were moving about erratically, a single red object flew behind in a straight path indicating that the objects were moving and not the camera. Now we had something. I made a copy in order to get the film analyzed.

What about the two men that claimed to be inspecting the building I asked? Strange he replied, "while they were here I didn't think much of it although they did lock themselves in the bathroom for a few minutes, which was odd". Then they left. He called the landlord to see if he new of any inspection, but he didn't. As I alluded to earlier, I immediately thought of the famous Men in Black; not will Smith and Tommy Lee Jones. but undisclosed government agents that have a habit of showing up post major UFO sightings.

There's also a second category of Men In Black, the ones featured in John Keels book "the Mothman Prophecy" and many other historical Ufological cases. These guys, also dressed in Black tend to show up in a brand new automobile with no license plate. They act very strange, ask non sensical questions and look odd. By looking odd, I mean not completely human, almost robotic. They may have a strange accent and a rather threatening disposition.

Back in Santa Monica, the second witness came in. She lived next door and had also observed objects over the water several times in the last two years; always late at night around 2 or 3 am, and flying in formation. Unfortunately, this was all the information I was going to get; at the request of Justin, I had to abandoned the investigation. At least the part that he was involved with. He admitted to me that since he started seeing these lights he's been waking up in the middle of the night feeling like there is a presence in the room. He started inquiring about the abduction phenomena. I told him that perhaps it was better at this point in the investigation process not to read about the abduction phenomena, and not to jump to conclusions. For one, just the fact that he witnessed something unusual puts him in a subjective state. He was looking for answers to questions we don't really have yet. There's still too much noise in the data, and I suspect that we are seeing a very small percentage of the real picture. The brain tends to fill missing data with a best guess approach, and the problem is that we have a lot of missing data.

UFOs in and around Southern California waters have a long history, notably between the coast and Catalina island. UFO research has often been held back by the perceived geographical randomness of the phenomenon; well that and a lot of crazy people. From a scientific standpoint, replicating the UFO phenomena for proper study is an impossibility; and really if you think about it, doesn't make any sense. This isn't a replicable non intelligent act of physics, and logging report after report has become an exercise in futility. We have hundred of thousands of UFO reports on record, with very few verifiable answers.

What we really should be doing is treating to UFO studies as field research, similar to wildlife research. A apt analogy would be the study of Great White Sharks. The idea is to go where the sharks are reported, study their behavior in their natural environment, but also study their immediate environment. Their environment, such as available food sources, dictate to a degree the shark's behavior. Other factors, such as water temperature play a part in where great whites live.

There appears to be a great number of ocean and even lake areas worldwide where UFOs are consistently reported. Some of the areas with the most intense activity are the waters around Puerto Rico, the Bermuda Triangle area and Lake Titicaca in Peru. I myself have investigated many coastal and ocean sightings in the Southern California area; but before we get to all that, let's go back to a more paranoid time of 1958.

A CONTINUAL PRESENCE

The Russians were known to possess a rather extensive fleet of submarines, and there were rumors that some were near the Pacific coast. This made the U. S Navy very nervous in 1958. With that in mind, 11 destroyers were sent out 50 miles of shore from San Francisco where Navy pilots had spotted a mysterious object in the water. Nothing was found, but in this time of increased vigilance, mysterious underwater objects began to be tracked by the navy's of the world. The Americans were blaming the Soviets, and the Soviet were blaming the Americans. Other nations were blaming whom ever had a different ideology; but the truth was that everybody knew, that something else was responsible.

For two weeks in 1960 the Argentine Navy helped by the United States Navy tracked an underwater object in the Golfo Nuevo of the Patagonian coast. Two objects were eventually tracked with the first staying submerged and out running the surface ships. Explosive were dropped to no affect. Quickly becoming an international incident, the rest of the world denied having anything to do with the incident. Especially concerned were the soviets, whom had tracked mysterious underwater objects in their waters as well. As we shall see a little later, as well as in the Russian UFO chapter, the Soviets have a rich history of underwater UFOs both in the oceans and in Lakes.

Rumors once again of secret Nazi submarines and a surviving Nazi presence in South America to Antarctica began to surface. Yes, many Nazis had escaped to South America and especially Argentina, but at the end of the war the Nazis were broke. Like everything else, it all comes down to economics. Despite the amount of Nazi gold that made it's way to undisclosed banks worldwide, it was unlikely that they were responsible for these objects that were so advanced, so fast, and capable of flying in and out of the water. No, something else was, is, responsible.

ANTARCTICA

A few years later, well into that turbulent decade, yet another strange underwater object made an appearance in the southern hemisphere. Not on the south American continent this time, but at a more dramatic location; Admiralty Bay, Antarctica. Brazilian scientist, Dr Rubens J. Villela was standing on the deck of an icebreaker when a large object described as a silvery bullet brook through the ice and disappeared into the sky. The force was such that large blocks of ice were thrown up into the air. The object apparently went through 37 feet of ice (Sanderson, 1970).

Taking into account the small percentage of individuals that frequent Antarctica, we wouldn't expect a high concentration of UFO sightings emanating from this continent, but the sightings exist. in 1965 Argentine and British sailors witnessed a UFO on Deception island, and in 1971 the crew of an ice breaker reported a UFO once again in Admiralty Bay. In 1983 meteorologists filed a UFO report from Prydy Bay, and 10 years later Cape Hallett became the location of a sighting.

Antarctica became quiet for a few years, but there appears to be a resurgence in sightings within the last decade. For whatever reason the southern hemisphere and more precisely South America is known to be an intense UFO hot spot. Whether there is a link between UFOs on the South American continent and the frozen waters of Antarctica remains to be seen. Back on Antarctica sighting reports suggest that UFOs are heading or coming from the area of Inaccessibility, which is the most remote area of Antarctica as measured by the distance from the Southern ocean. There shouldn't be anybody there.

There is a great deal of nonsense associated with mysteries in Antarctica as well, especially about entrance to inner worlds at the poles and secret Nazi expedition to the area. These stories do very little in increasing Ufology's credibility, but I must admit have always held my attention. There's always a signal in the noise, no matter how faint. Finding a signal among disinformative noise, well that's the key.

Following that line of thought, the story of Admiral Byrd that is so linked to UFOs and Antarctica, is problematic. Yet, there are some aspect of the story that are intriguing. Admiral Byrd was a well known explorer in the early years of the 1900's, when explorers were still heroes. He had become famous for flying over both poles, and for his ground expeditions into Antarctica. in 1929, with a grant from Ford and Rockefeller, Byrd took off towards Antarctica. He set up camp and organized flights over the continent, and this is where it gets weird.

Author F. A Giannim wrote a book about Antarctica and Byrd's exploits. In it he mentions a newsreel shown in the

United States that was shot from Byrd's plane. It was labeled "Land Beyond the Poles", which showed mountains, rivers and wildlife. Quite a few people have mentioned through out the years that they remember the newsreel, which today cannot be located. Curiously, Byrd's log and diary are unobtainable and resides with the US Naval Intelligence.

Lake Vostok's waters are under layers of ice and snow. The lake wasn't even discovered until the late 1990's, and immediately became an interest to NASA because of its resemblance to the surface of Europa, one of Jupiter's moon. The idea was that whatever life was able to flourish in this environment, could in theory be similar to possible life of Europa. Vostok is 2000 feet deep, 300 miles long and 50 miles wide. This is not a small lake. The waters aren't as dark or cold as originally estimated. Some light does filter through, and there are geothermal sources which heat the water to 50 to 65 degrees Fahrenheit, depending on who you talk to.

The lake lies in the Russian portion of Antarctica where research has encountered difficulties from the beginning. A story initially broke, that Russian scientists vanished while working at the lake. A story that was later denied by the Russians, and which started much speculation, especially on the internet, about the lake and what was found there. About the later, it was then announced that a new type of bacteria was discovered while drilling; which was also eventually denied.

The northern end of the lake has displayed magnetic anomalies where measurement were twice as high as expected, and more surprisingly extending to 65 by 45 square miles. Unfortunately, not much else is known as early on NASA and JPL abandoned their research abruptly. NASA made a statement, which was later retracted, that they were pulling out of Vostok due to the NSA involvement and for "matters of national security", which led to rumors flying left and right. To remedy the situation JPL issued a statement saying that the wrong acronyms were used, and what was meant was NSF, the National Science Foundation. The reason for the pulling out, solely due to lack of funding. I assume as well that behind the scenes, the Russians may have wanted all other agencies out, for political reasons and the fact that they own Vostok.

Once something is labeled mysterious, everything associated with that very thing becomes, well viewed suspiciously. This holds true for the following events which occurred during the time the Russians were drilling into the lake. Certain individuals were evacuated from Antarctica, including two skiers who were attempting to cross the continent on skis; and personnel from the McMurdo polar bases. It was also reported that some left McMurdo base voluntarily after falling sick. Much has been made of the later, but to be fair, McMurdo is nowhere near Vostok and this is most likely a unrelated event. They were also reports that researchers at Norway's Amundsen base, 150 miles from Vostok, found the number of personnel and equipment that were suddenly arriving on the continent extremely unusual. While there may indeed be something unusual about Antarctica, the preceding events are most likely all unrelated and links were created between them that weren't there. All that said, I wouldn't have included the preceding here if the possibility of a story didn't keep gnawing at the caudal area of my brain.

THE TRIANGLE

Let's get one thing strait, the number of disappearances over the Bermuda Triangle isn't particularly alarming; especially for ships. On average, four planes and around 20 yachts disappear each year (Quazar, 2004). Whether that constitutes an unusual amount or not is debatable. Due to the Bermuda triangle's reputation, more focus is put upon that part of the world than any other when it comes to ocean disappearances and accidents. All the worlds oceans, seas, and in some instances lakes have a great number of accidents, many unexplained. Typhoons, freak waves, pirates, storms are a fact of life in the open water. The Triangle, meaning from Florida to Bermuda to Puerto Rico lives partly upon it's reputation. The waters within the Triangle are often rough, and the weather can change most rapidly. Even Charles Berlitz in his classic book took some liberties with some of the accounts; the weather in some of the classic disappearances was at times severe. The later is a fact often neglected by researchers.

All that been said, there is still something very unusual in the Bermuda triangle, if not malignant. But, It's not the number of disappearances that is unusual or alarming, but it is the way they occur. May 1999, an Aero Commander on it's way to Nassau disappeared from radar for thirty minutes, with the pilot seemingly unaware of anything peculiar. Shortly after the plane reappeared on radar, it vanished once again, and this time for good.

In September of 1971, a military Phantom II fighter called Sting 27 vanished. Immediately, another Phantom II fighter, Sting 29 was scrambled to the area where Sting 27 when off radar. The pilot of Sting 29 reported a disturbance in the water and an oblong object over 100 feet in length. No further detailed was given. The official report mentioned a "suspected point of impact"; that was all.

Planes have disappeared above land, between radarscope (which is less than a minute), on approach, and in shallow water less than 10 feet deep. Some of the most chilling data come from conversations with pilots before vanishing. Pilots mention a problem, that they are disorientated, cannot tale where the sky and the water meet, instrumentation malfunctions, and a strange fog. Some pilots have also mentioned strange objects or aircraft in the air, that fail to appear on radar. Pilots, fearful of a mid air collision would change course; but the objects always adjusted their course accordingly. More alarming they would position themselves in front of the planes, causing the less experienced pilots to panic. Then, radio silence.

There appears to be no discernible pattern as to what type of plane or ship are more likely to experience an anomalous event over the Triangle. From small cessnas to DC 3's, DC 4's,

52 bombers and large tankers have all vanished from the sea. Boats have been found, derelicts, in perfect working conditions, but with the entire crew missing.

A remarkable, but not isolated account occurred in 1966 to a large 160 foot tug captained by a very experienced Don Henry. The tug and its crew where on their way to Florida, three days from Puerto Rico. It was in the middle of the day, and the weather was good. No reason to be concern, until the compass started spinning wildly and the radio went silent. The crew 's uneasiness was compounded by the fact that suddenly there was no horizon. Everything was grayish white. Worried about the barge they were tugging, captain Henry looked back to make sure it was still been tugged. The line told Captain Henry that the barge was still there, but he couldn't see it. It was enveloped in a strange fog. Captain Henry made the decision to speed up and try to escape whatever was enveloping his tug, but something was pulling it back. A few minutes later the resistance all but vanished, the fog disappeared, the horizon reappeared, and the tug was back on it's way. There was no damage. The only remaining effect was that the barge was unusually warm to the touch.

Radar can also behave strangely out in the Triangle, showing large object or land masses in the middle of the ocean. Investigation by the coast guards never find anything, and the signal eventually fades away.

The number of UFO sightings over the water's of the Triangle as well as USOs (underwater swimming objects) below has been a constant since the time of Columbus. The early sailors and explorers called the underwater disturbances "wheels of light". UFO's have been seen from ships, from shore and from experienced pilots, with a specific concentration near and on Puerto Rico. As a note of interest, an area off the coast of Japan called the Dragon's Triangle has experienced similar phenomena to the Bermuda Triangle, UFOs and all.

LAGUNA CARTAGENA

The Chupacabras were what initially made me turn my attention towards Puerto Rico. Honestly, I love those guys. It didn't take long to realize that the Chupacabra is only a small part of a much bigger story, you name it and it's happening there. Amid the chaos are three areas of primary interest on the island; the El Yunque rain forest, the waters of Lajas and Cabo Rojo and Laguna Cartagena.

In the afternoon of May 31 1987, a loud explosion and apparent earthquake was heard and felt in Southwest Puerto Rico. Seismologists initially stated that the epicenter of the quake was situated under a lagoon called Laguna Cartagena. A day later, the epicenter was changed to the Mona Channel, out in the ocean. Nothing was said about the loud explosion, perhaps hoping that it would be forgotten; but Laguna Cartagena wasn't quite done yet.

That night around 10 PM, a large cylinder shape UFO with lights at each end was seen flying and hovering for 15 minutes over the lagoon by multiple witnesses. There's a small community near the Lagoon and several members of that community were interviewed about the incident. They stated that this was not unusual for this area. Prior to the incident and more recently as well, UFOs have been seen over the Laguna Cartagena; and flying in and out of the lagoon. In fact, the night before the quake several local residents were awaken by a very bright light outside. When they went out, they saw a bright red object enter the water. Other witnesses claimed that later that night a strange object was seen over the lagoon as well.

In the days following the event, military jets and helicopters were seen flying over Laguna Cartegena almost around the clock. The situation took an unexpected turn when a kind of unidentified blue smoke started emanating from crakes in the ground around Laguna Cartegena. As a result a new military presence was notice, now on the ground. They were Americans.

CABO ROJO

Cabo Rojo is a coastal town in the south west side of the island. Oral history, or legend according to many historians, say that Christopher Columbus himself give the town it's name. Cabo Rojo is very well known for it's fishing and large number of fishermen. Yes the fishing is good and if you ask the fishermen what kind of fish lie just off Cabo Rojo's water; they will tell you. But, you'll detect a hint of omission. So, you will keep asking what else is in these waters, making the fishermen nervous. Some won't talk about it, others have complained to the local authorities. But, what can they do about strange under water lights and strange under water crafts, that have the ability to fly in and out of the water? And what can they do, about the noise of the jet's that always seem fly over these waters?

If, you are able to obtain a description of the objects; they are described as circular, metallic and at night very bright, but silent always silent. When they are seen over the town is either because they are heading out to see, sometimes plunging in the water not far from shore, or coming from the water and flying towards the mountains, towards Laguna Cartegena. Military jets come next, following, chasing. But the jets can only move at great speed in the sky, the circular objects can also move at great speed under the ocean. They will not be caught.

Pilots from the air, and boats, are the primary source of sightings of these under water lights in the Caribbean. As I briefly mentioned earlier, they have been reported for centuries, called "Wheels of light". According to Ivan Sanderson, well known author and well respected researcher pointed out in his book, "Invisible residents", specific areas that these lights have been seen thought out the centuries. Other areas of interest are in and near the Indian ocean, the Persian Gulf, and the south China seas. Sanderson's analysis dates from several decades ago, and to be fair statistics from the worlds oceans and seas can be skewed. Sightings can only occur when there is someone there to see it and report it. Commercial ships follow very specific shipping lanes and obviously some areas are busier than others. One would expect a greater amount of sightings from these places.

LAKE TITICACA

If you want to spend half the night on the internet, google Lake Titicaca, UFOs; because it will take you at least that long to sort out all the web sites, photos and videos on the subject. Many of them, questionable data from individuals that may or may not get out much. Still, the point being that this area of the world gets an unusual amount of sightings as well. Of primary interest here are the underwater lights that are reported underneath Lake Titicaca; and once again the display of strange objects entering and exited the lake by flight. As is the case near Bermuda and in Puerto Rico, rumors and talk of underwater UFO bases run rampant on the internet and at UFO conferences. This of course, pure speculation as no one has ever found a UFO base.

What is not speculation are the objects that appear to show a particular interest in this area. Perhaps it is because Lake Titicaca fills out two important criteria when it comes to the probability of a location becoming a UFO hot spot; deep waters and ancient sites.

Lake Titicaca, bordering Peru and Bolivia sits at an altitude of 12,507 ft and is the largest lake in South America. More importantly in regard to our discussion, lake Titicaca also borders the ancient Inca sites of Tiahuanaco and Puma Punku. It is also where the Inca's deity Viracocha first made his appearance. Viracocha is the Inca version of Kukulkan or Quetzalcoatl, and was said to have brought civilization to the world. The path walked by Viracocha is called the Sacred Valley and starts at Lake Titicaca, goes through Cuzco, Ollantaytambo, and Macchu Pichu. It ends in the pacific Ocean where it is said Viracocha disappeared. One of the legends associated with Viracocha is that upon his travels near the province of Cocha, locals threw stones at him. Viracocha knelt and looked to the sky, and a great fire emerged from the sky and burned the landscape and stones.

4

MUTILATED

I like my music loud, and it was very loud in the car on that deserted Nevada road. It wasn't going to bother anybody. Even with the visibility only the desert can provide, there was no one else to be seen on Nevada state route 375. That particular stretch of road borders area 51, and leads straight to a little trailer town called Rachel. Route 375 was renamed extraterrestrial highway due to its proximity to Area 51, and all the UFO rumors at a base that didn't officially exist.

I was on my way to Rachel on 375 and looking forward to eating Rachel's semi famous Alien Burger, when I noticed a black mass up ahead in the middle of the highway. It was a dead cow, and not the burger I had in mind. Naturally I got out of the car and inspected the cow. Imagination takes over quickly in such desolate surroundings, thinking mutilation; but knowing that it was more likely hit by a truck and dead on impact as a result. Anyway, I wasn't going to be able to tell by lunchtime. I took some photographs; and went on to Rachel, not encountering another car or person until I entered the restaurant and excitedly ordered an Alien Burger. Not bad, but I still preferred that Bigfoot donut I had in Willow Creek a couple years earlier.

THE KILLING FIELDS

It all started in 1967 with a mare named Snippy; not her real name. Her real name was Lady, but the press had confused her with the owners other horse and the name stuck. Snippy was found one morning lying in her tracks, as if something had circled her before she died. It was strange, all the meat from her head to her neck was gone, but there wasn't a single trace of blood on the ground. A slight smell hung in the air, not unlike embalming fluid. It was muddy, yet there were no other prints or markings of any kind anywhere near Snippy.

Not far from the horse a green paste was found. Nellie Lewis, one of the owners, touched the paste with her fingers and felt a burn, that continued for half an hour. The next day she felt ill. Nellie and Berle Lewis who lived on the ranch had seen strange lights in the skies in the nights preceding Snippy's demise, and from that point on, for better or worse, UFOs and cattle mutilations would be forever linked.

Interviewed in 1993 Berle Lewis shed more light on the mutilation. He mentioned that the bones were completely white, almost bleached with absolutely no meat left on them. The cut was perfectly smooth and he didn't think that the smell was embalming fluid, but definitely medicine like. The strangest part of the story was the missing brain, because there were no visible openings anywhere on the skull. A pattern that would repeat itself, mostly on cattle, through out the following decades. Investigated by state police and the FBI; and not a single suspect was ever brought forward. The cattle mutilation phenomenon expanded worldwide, especially prevalent in Argentina. But the majority of what essentially became a kind of serial killings, was primarily focused in North American pastures. This is the biggest unsolved crime in America, and these fields have become our Whitechapel.

BLACK HELICOPTERS

Horse mutilations are rare, cattle is usually the main victim, and by the mid 1970's the mutilation wave was in full force. In the early reports only UFOs were reported in areas associated with cattle mutilations. In time however a new phenomenon would emerge, the black helicopters.

The San Luis valley which straddles Northern Colorado and Southern New Mexico was and is the epicenter for this phenomenon. The helicopters are always unmarked, jet black or dark green, with tinted windows, and local authorities have been unable to ascertain their origin. All that we truly know is that they often appear following a UFO sighting, or just before or after a mutilation. In some cases they appear directly involved.

In the 1970's two loggers witnessed a black helicopter in the middle of the highway next to a dead bull or cow. Around the same time period another eyewitness claimed to have seen a black helicopter with a cow attached and hanging underneath. Both of those reports together may suggest that these heli-copters are transporting cattle for some reason, but does not necessarily link the two with the mutilations. Furthermore, the weight versus lift capability of these helicopters is obviously a point to consider. Adult bulls can weight up to 3000 pounds.

With all that said, an interest by these helicopters and pilots with the mutilation phenomenon is undeniable. One New Mexico rancher by the name od Eli Hronich lost 15 head of cattle in 18 months to the mutilators. Hronich also had a Black Heli-copter hover right above his head as he was inspecting one of his mutilated cows. He didn't appreciate the intimidation tactic. Hronich also experienced burning that lasted for a week in his fingers after he inspected yet another animal, this time a steer.

Sheriff Ernest Sandoval was one of the principle investiga-tors at that time in the San Luis valley. Sandoval felt confident that the helicopters were coming from across the Rio Grande, from a supposed deserted area. He stated publicly on several occasion that some of the mutilations were perpetrated by the helicopters; and as a result he instructed his deputies to shoot at them if they could, which they did. Admittedly, he has no expla-nations for some of the earlier mutilations, before the appear-ance of the helicopters; and no explanation for the strange lights that certainly aren't helicopters.

In 1995 the subject of Black Helicopters reappeared in the press when Idaho Republican Representative Helen Chenoweth complained that unmarked black helicopters were landing on private property (Fox news, 2006). She explained in a press conference and to the New York times that many local ranchers were upset and wanted something done. Militias and conspiracy theorist latched on to this and black helicopters became a symbol for "fascist" America, Big Government, and the mythical New World Order.

On a slightly divergent note, around that same year of 1995 I was attending college in Chicago, where I was in the habit of riding my neon pink mountain bike in the middle of the night. Neon pink was macho in the mid 90's. I liked the deserted streets downtown and the high sidewalks that provided mini jumps. During the spring or summer I would got out after midnight and ride for an hour or two and habitually head to the all night McDonalds afterwards. On the way back to campus, there was a couple blocks by the river and train tracks that were mostly deserted. An odd little block in the middle of as very urban area.

One night at about three o'clock in the morning, tired and in a stupor only available post McDonalds, I came around the corner and came face to face with a large black helicopter hovering above the street. It looked military; with an external sensor pointed straight in my direction. What it was doing above the streets of Chicago, I have no idea? What does this have to do with cattle mutilation, you ask? Probably nothing, it's just a story about a helicopter.

UNEXPLAINED

A number of copycat mutilations have certainly occurred, fueling speculation that cults and devil worshippers were responsible; anything to stir the conversation away from UFOs. In America, belief in the devil is always more comfortable and socially accepted than the belief in anything UFO or alien related. But in these copycat cases, blood is everywhere; which I suppose is kind of the point. Furthermore, footprints are always left behind and a knife had obviously been used, essentially a sloppy crime scene.

In bona fide mutes (as they are called in the business) there are no footprints, no tire marks, no blood in the immediate surroundings, and the animals often exsanguinated. Exsanguinated does not mean that the animals are completely drained of blood. This is a misconception that is all too often propagated in the UFO community. Exsanguinated means sufficient blood loss in order to cause the death of an organism. In mutilation cases, the blood loss is considerable; and yes there are cases where the cattle is entirely devoid of blood. One has to keep in mind though that in dead carcasses the blood pools to the bottom of the animal, and subsequently can seep into the ground; ergo, given the impression that the blood has mysteriously vanished. What is harder to explain is the cooked hemogoblin found on the mutes. Hemogoblin is a protein found inside red blood cells, and in this case would require a considerable source of heat to "cook" it.

Further analysis have indicated that incisions have been made with a high source of heat, such as a surgical laser. This source apparently used to remove flesh, all reproductive organs, the rectum, ears, tongue and various internal organs. Furthermore, some of the cuts appeared to have been made post mortem, which could also explain the lack of blood on site.

There are also instances of broken bones, and broken tree branches; indicating that the animals have been dropped from considerable height. In some male specimens lying on their side; the bottom horn has been found embedded deeply into the ground. This further fuels the debate between the pro UFO camp and the pro Black Helicopter camp, but engaging in that argument is missing the point. The real revelation here is the indication that the mutilations are been conducted somewhere else. This explains the lack of evidence at the location where the mutes are found; including the absence of any prints even in snow or in mud. Even Watson would concur, I believe.

A mystery it is, certainly; but not one that cannot be solved. We know that certain chemicals are been used in an undisclosed manner. People can smell it, and slime and white residue have been found on and near the mutilated animals on several occasions. Some ranchers have even been physically affected by some agent near or on the mutes; burning fingers, feeling sick, and the development of abscess have all been noted. Once we can identify what chemicals are been used, we can at least deduce what those chemicals are usually used for; and where they may be procured.

Many investigators have used the fact that dogs and even scavengers tend to stay away from the carcasses to make a case for a paranormal paradigm. While there is evidence that animals do stay away from the mutes and that decomposition is delayed, the cause may be that mysterious chemical and residue. It is very possible that the smell alone, much more potent to species with a better developed olfactory sense, keeps animals away. Some radiation has also been detected in some cases.

There definitely is something affecting the environment in the immediate surroundings. In a case in Missouri, hundreds of flies were found dead on a mutilated carcass; and in Oregon in 2002, all ants within a 20 feet radius of a mute were also found dead (Granger, 2003). This could further explain the cases were animals, s cattle, dogs and even coyotes have been observed circling the mute at a certain distance. Again are they detecting a foreign agent?

THE LONGINUS EFFECT

Ironically the San Luis Valley was known as the Bloodless Valley by native Americans. It was considered sacred and tribes would avoid warfare in the valley. In some way, the act of cattle mutilation is a direct affront to that idea; and the spilling of blood is also in direct contradiction to what the San Luis Valley stood for. This concerns me, because a message is been sent. Whatever forces are ultimately responsible for the mutilation, certainly have the capabilities to dispose of the cattle elsewhere. But, cattle do not go missing for very long; and they are deliberately dropped for all to see. I may be reaching here slightly but it does portray a sort of arrogance and the willingness to violate a sacred place. This is not a hidden phenomenon, the bodies are there to see

Logan County, Nebraska, lost over 60 head of cattle to mutilations in a year and half time period in the mid 1970's. Sherif Harry Graves investigated the majority of these cases and was perplexed when he couldn't find signs of predation. None of the usual signs, such as bite marks and prints were present. Graves also found three circular indentations in the ground next to one of the mutes. They were 2.4 inches deep and 5.9 inches in circumference. This would not be the last time that these three circular indentations would be found next to a mutilation. So far, no one has been able to determine the object responsible. It has been speculated that these were the markings from a laser that was used in the field to cut open the animals. This is somewhat unlikely, especially in the 1970's. Portable lasers did not exist, and the ones in labs were enormous machines. If lasers were indeed used by an earthly source on these animals, it would have been much easier to bring the animal to the source.

Stranger still was a case that occurred in Colorado in the spring of 1975. A cow belonging to a Mrs. Caswell was found wandering aimlessly, and changing directions constantly; it also appeared groggy. Concerned, Mrs. Caswell quickly had the cow checked out. The first physical sign that something was very wrong was that the anus had been completely carved out in a circular pattern. Mrs. Caswell stated that you could see inside the animal. it was also discovered that the cow was blind, due to a straight cut down the middle of both globes of the eyes. Unless you were dealing with the world's smartest coyote, the precision involved clearly eliminates natural predators.

The strangest story however belongs to carpenter Larry Gardea. Mora county is fairly remote as far as New Mexico is concerned, and on September 13, 1993 Gardea was out hunting bear. While walking in a field he noticed two motionless cows next to a chain link fence. Both apparently dead, one on her knees, the other was laying on her side. Upon closer inspection, the cow on its side was missing its rectum, once again carved out in a circular manner. There were other cows in the field, and they suddenly began to panic and run for reasons he initially could not fathom. That is until he noticed a humming sound in the background, and speculated that it may have caused the cows to run. Then it got really weird.

One of the cows didn't get away, and it started to levitate slightly, before falling back down to the ground. Now in complete distress and bawling loudly, the cow appeared to be pulled by an invisible force towards the source of the sound. There was no object there to be seen, just that humming. Gardea took two shots in that direction which somehow freed the cow. Gardea flees to get the police. The police had no explanation, but told Gardea that two days prior a UFO was reported in the area. Additional sightings had occurred in the area in August and also after the Gardea incident in late September (Van Eyk, 2011). Again, no direct correlation between the mutilations and the strange lights in the sky; but there they are, always in the background.

Investigators in the 1970's and today are torn between suspecting the Black Helicopters and UFOs. The helicopters arrived later on the scene, leading to speculation that they were there in response to the UFOs. That debate still hasn't been resolved; nearly 30 years later and the UFO presence remain in areas of mutilations. The unmarked Black Helicopters have not gone away either; but by the 1990's yet another type of aircraft started making an appearance around mutilations, large silent triangular crafts.

The giant triangle phenomenon is a relatively new addition to the Ufo world, beginning it's run in western Europe. Belgium has given us Tintin, Van Damm, and the first giant triangle wave in Ufology. I guess from a cultural standpoint, two out of three isn't bad. In these early days of the 1990's hundreds of reports were emanating out of Belgium and France. These includes many official police reports that are quite detailed and descriptive in regards to the triangles. i've read them.

These aircraft are much larger than traditional UFOs and completely silent, with rows of lights on the outer edge of the triangle. Some were photographed clearly; and subsequently rumored to be the next generation of stealth technology, perhaps using anti gravity propulsion. These craft begin to be seen in the United States as well, especially near military installations, and yes over a little town called Rachel where I sat and had my Alien burger

I've investigated over a dozen of these large triangular craft sightings myself. Most were out in the desert areas of Southern California. Surprisingly, a couple were multiple witness cases over Los Angeles. In all cases, from my files to the cases in Belgium which I spent quite a bit of time on, these are identical aircraft; and I believe that these are ours. I base that assumption on the fact that they are often seen in places close to military installations such as Groom Lake; and the fact that in all case they are seen as flying in a straight path and not exhibiting any of the traditional movements and flight inconsistencies attributed to traditional UFOs.

Does this mean that the technology used in these aircraft were all developed here? I don't think so, I suspect we had a little help. Perhaps not in a straight forward manner, but through many years of reverse engineering "Alien" tech by our best scientists and engineer in places that do not officially exists. The fact that some of these aircraft as so large, one witness told me that you could land a 767 on top, and can glide at a very low speed and suddenly accelerate, indicate some type of anti gravity propulsion system. What that might be is beyond the scope of this chapter, but the advantage of negating gravity is that the size of an object in flight becomes irrelevant.

Ben Rich former head of Lockheed's Skunk Works gave a speech at UCLA in 1993, two years before his death. At that speech he stated that "we already have the means to travel among the stars, but these technologies are locked up in black projects, (...) we now have the technology to take ET home." This speech is not an urban legend as some would have you believe. I know people that were there, and who spoke to Ben Rich afterwards. Rich before becoming the head of Skunk Works was an engineer that worked on the U2 and SR 71 Blackbird. If anybody had the answer to the triangular craft mystery, it was this man. After his speech at UCLA, he hinted that the technology involved might not have originated with us, which brings us back to my point that the giant triangles are most likely ours with shall we say "special" technologies. As far as the link between giant triangular crafts and cattle mutilation, it lies solely on the observation of these crafts near mutilation cases in the early 1990's. But, the key to the mystery still lies with the more traditional UFOs spotted at the scene, and the Black Helicopters; and the answer will in all likelihood involve both factions.

BOVINE BIOLOGY

In 2002 the sequencing of the genome of the cow begin. It included hundreds of scientists, from 24 countries; all under the direction of the Bovine Sequencing and Analysis Consortium, and the Bovine HapMap Consortium. Fifty million dollars and six years later, the entire cow genome was sequenced and some surprises were in store.

For one thing it was discovered that cattle have more in common with humans than the usual test subjects of rats and mice. Cows share about 80 % of their genes with humans; and cow proteins are more similar to human protein than rats and mice (Tellam, 2009). It was also discovered that cows have a superior ability to resist diseases. In other words, on studies pertaining to diseases and environmental factors that lead to diseases, cows make much better tests subjects that mice and rats which are what all universities and research projects use.

I once visited the labs at a major university where neurophysiological experimentation was conducted. There was a room where all the test subjects, mice and rats, were kept. It was a slightly surreal experience to see this many cages and this many animals all in one room. If we were to hypothetically switch the rats with cows, it would take a football field to be able to contain this many subjects. More problematic than the physical logistics, would be the moral issues associated with experimenting with this many cows. From a practical standpoint, it is not feasible; but in secret?

Prior to these findings, it was always known that cows were an integral component in the food chain leading to humans. They eat the grass and in turn we eat the cows. Though a biological process called biomagnification, whatever environmental "impurities" exist in what cows eat gets transferred to humans and is actually amplifies as it goes up the food chain. So yeah, If I want to study the environment and how the food chain fits in in regards to the human population, I'm abducting cattle too.

One interesting aspect related to the cattle mutilation, at least in the United States, is that a great number of mutilated cattle are from areas that were once home to nuclear tests. This just might be a coincidence. Obviously, they needed open land with a lot of room to conduct nuclear tests, and ranchers need land with a lot of room for their cattle. So perhaps, that is where the relationship lies, but the correlation is intriguing.

Still, there appears to be in increase in UFO activity in the United States since the birth of the nuclear age., followed shortly by the cattle mutilation phenomenon. There is no doubt humans are involved with the mutilations in some capacity; hence the presence of unmarked Black Helicopters near mutilations sites. There is also no doubt that there is a UFO presence

around cattle mutilations, and some of the mutilations themselves point to a superior technology. Whichever the case, this
is clearly in my opinion an environmental study, and a study on
the effect on the human population.

5

ALIEN HISTORY

In 1952, Oppenheimer was innocently asked by the press if the nuclear tests at Los Alamos were the first to be conducted. "Well yes, at least in recent times", Oppenheimer replied without a hint of a wink. Whomever asked the question probably never gave the answer a second thought, too busy looking down at the pen and paper. In fact, no one did, but perhaps they should have.

In Pakistan, ancient skeletons found at Mohenjo-Daro and at Harappa showed possible traces of radiation. I say possible because while every book and documentary on the subject mentions this as fact, to be fair, I haven't been able to locate an original source for the claim of radiation. In the 1960's, China used areas of the Gobi desert for atomic testing, so it isn't surprising to find areas of fused silica in the Gobi: but what about certain areas of Iraq and Israel where the fused sand is ancient? Geologists have no explanation for this phenomenon that mimic the results of nuclear explosions.

Twenty years after Oppenheimer's cryptic comments, NASA sent out Pioneer 10, and a year later in 1973, Pioneer 11. Both contained a plaque with a drawing of a naked male and human female accompanied by various symbols and mathematical constructs explaining our planet. The idea was that if either Pioneer 10 or 11 were intercepted by extraterrestrials, they would be able to obtain basic information on the race that sent them. In what may have been ill advised, or at the very least naive, the plaques also contained information on the location of our planet. If that weren't enough, in 1974 the Arecibo message was sent out into space. It was a radio wave aimed at M13, a star cluster 25,000 light years away. if something out there in the cosmos, wanted to come here, now they had a map and a signal to follow. The reality is that from a first contact standpoint, it may all be a moot point. I suspect, no I'm certain, that a presence was already here. So, instead of looking out there, maybe we should look within. Within history and maybe even literally within ourselves.

A PRIMITIVE PRESENCE

During my Anthropological studies in school I became intimately familiar with cave painting traditions worldwide, and the importance of cave paintings in human cognitive development cannot be understated. Art shows a considerable evolution in abstract thinking, which is why we encourage children to draw. As such, it is somewhat difficult to assign an objective reality to the number of "alien" like figures portrayed worldwide in pictographs. What is remarkable however, is the similarities in morphology and apparent clothing, often including what appears to be headgear or helmets. These "alien" figures have all been observed in cultures, from Australia to Europe, that traditional thinking dictate never met at so early a time in history. Giant figures are also a common theme in early cave painting and outdoor rock painting.

Now, we must be very careful in assigning a extra terrestrial identity to these figures. As based on the observable existing human form, some artistic liberties may have been at work, and imagination was beginning to creep upon our specie. All that taken into account, certain cave paintings that represent everyday life, such as hunting and the depiction of local wildlife, include what appears to be flying saucers above the hunters heads. Also, of peculiar interest are the "alien" figures in cave or rock paintings accompanied by the same "flying saucers". It's the correlation that is interesting.

I am deliberately not using the term UFO here. UFO stands for Unidentified Flying Object and nothing more, and UFOs come in many shapes. The term flying saucer is a little more descriptive and most of these paintings take the shape of the classic flying saucer. One remarkable find was revealed in 2010 from India. It was discovered deep in the jungle, in the state of Madhya Pradesh, and shows a humanoid figure that appears to have a visor standing next to a flying saucer like object. India has a considerable history with UFOs, from depiction of flying objects called Vimanas in ancient texts to recent sightings on it's border with China.

Not a single culture has escaped the humanoid and the saucer motif. There can only be two reasons for this. One, that the humanoid saucer motif represents reality. The second possibility is that the humanoid saucer motif represents an archetype. Both hypotheses are the foundation for a mystery. The first mystery is, who is the humanoid, and what is the saucer in reality? The second mystery is, how does the same archetype develop in primitive cultures worldwide, that have no contact with one another? Why would the brain be predisposed to the development of the humanoid saucer motif?

EZEKIEL'S WHEEL

It has always struck me how God seems to change between the old testament and the new. In the old testament He is forceful and vengeful, even angry at times. Miracles abound, He creates, He destroys, He speaks, He kills. He order's man to worship only Him, to be obedient to only Him, and He sends angels to transmit messages from Heaven. In time though, He becomes silent, no more great miracles, and no more messages carried by angels.

The first gods of old, that we know off, were the Sumerian gods, and according to Sumerian writing, they came from the stars. They looked just like man because they created man in their image (Sitchin, 1990). At first they were very involved in the affairs of man. They created, they ruled, they gave man laws to follow, they performed miracles and they showed a great range of emotions. They had aircraft's that took them from and to the heavens. Then, they grew silent, they no longer took visible part in the affairs of man.

Sumerian civilization began at around 3800 BC with no known precedent. Prior to this date, the Tigris-Euphrates valley was home to the Ubaids, a village farming society. But in 3800 BC the Sumerian culture exploded on the scene with the first schools, first cities, first cosmology and teachers in all areas of mathematics, law, zoology and geography. The Sumerians followed by later Mesopotamian cultures, told in tablets of how the gods came from the heavens and created civilization. There were many of them with different functions, reminiscent of later Greek pantheon. The leader of the gods was called An, he was the chief and his symbol was a star. For generations the gods ruled, they had created man and thus had the right to oversee their creation, they were dominant.

One symbol in Mesopotamian mythology that is of particular interest to our discussion is the sun disk. The sun disk is a circle with wings on each side. In Egypt it was the symbol of Ra, the chief of the Gods. The sun disk, also called the winged globe, is an extremely prevalent symbol in the ancient world. It can be found all over Mesopotamia, Persia, Australia, South America, and in North America among the Hopis. The sun disk was a global symbol in a world of cultures that never met.

The circle or sun is a symbol for creation and the creator, because it is perfect, it is whole. The wings around the circle are symbolic for the gods coming down to earth, and also serves as a symbol of the messengers transmitting knowledge emanating from the gods. It is no wonder then, that the angels are depicted as wearing wings. If you couple symbolism with tangibility, the sun disk represents flying, and thus a flying round object belonging to the gods.

The wings of the sun disk also sit atop the Caduceus, above

intertwining snakes. In Greek mythology the Caduceus was carried by Hermes. The caduceus today is most often used as a symbol for medicine, especially in the United States. However, that's due to a confusion with the Rod of Asclepius, which has only one snake intertwine with a staff. Asclepius was the God of healing and medicine.

And here lies both the seduction and agnosticism of the ancient alien theory. It starts with a snake in the Garden of Eden, and a gift of forbidden knowledge. Knowledge becomes science, medicine, healing, now represented by intertwining snakes. Intertwining snakes become symbolic of the DNA double helix. Following the ancient alien astronaut theory, the deduction is then that ancient knowledge, represented by the symbol for DNA, was brought to man from the stars. Taken a step further, and perhaps to its logical conclusion, part of man's DNA originated with the gods. Ergo, we share a biological link with extraterrestrials. As I said seductive, lacking in definite proof perhaps, but permeated with a certain logic supported by ancient text.

There are no doubts that certain themes ubiquitously show up in all ancient traditions. Gods that came from the skies and interfered in some capacity with our development. They didn't hide in their saucers in those days. More disturbingly are the tales of hybrids, where the gods, or emissaries of the gods, found our women favorable. "The Nephilim were on earth in those days, and also afterward, when the sons of God came in to the daughters of man and they bore children to them. These were the mighty men who were of old, the men of renown" Genesis 6:4. The result, according to the Bible were giants that resided in Canaan. Interestingly enough, Israel, who has a rich history of UFO sightings, went through a particularly notable UFO wave in the 1990's. What differentiated these sightings from others in the past were the number of landing cases with occupants that were reported. The occupants, were all described as giants.

It seems, ancient tales never strays very far from the theme of genetics. The question is, are these tales a description of true events that we have labeled mythology, or are all these tales purely allegorical? Perhaps, a little bit of both? The line between reality and apophenia is a thin one, and once that ambiguous paradigm has you, you'll find clues in the strangest of places. Places such as Rosslyn Chapel, where the Prentice Pillar resembles the DNA double helix. A classic case of the aforementioned apophenia? Probably so, probably so, until I remembered one thing; just down the road is the Roslin Institute, where Doly the first cloned sheep was created.

The concept of hybridization between humans and "aliens" is tantalizing, but may appear faulty due to a genetic incompatibility between a specie evolved on Earth and a specie evolved elsewhere. Furthermore, logic would argue against an alien specie being a DNA based organism. However, there is a way around that, it's called panspermia. Panspermia is the theory that life originated outside of our planet and was brought here in the form of micro-organisms by meteors and meteorites. It is theorized that life on earth began between 3 billion to 4 billion years ago, a time of heavy bombardments by meteors on Earth and Mars.

Extremophiles are organisms, bacteria, microbes, that thrive in the most inhospitable of conditions. They can survive in non oxygenated environments, and even survive in the vacuum of space. Some are able to lay dormant for millions of years. They can survive in acid, in extreme radiation, and in several cases, have the ability to transfer their DNA to other extremophiles. More importantly, some can survive trips though space on meteors and comets.

Remember, ALH84001, the Martian meteorite that appeared to contain fossil bacteria? Still controversial, and yes, dismissed by some scientists, but contrary to popular belief, that particular meteorite wasn't the only one that may have contained fossilized bacteria. The point is that, the theory of panspermia is valid, and is quickly gaining ground in scientific circles. Panspermia may also explained sudden outbreaks of new diseases and previously unknown bacteria and viruses. What does all of this have to do with a shared genetic history between us and aliens, you say? Well, here is the most important point, in all this. if earth was seeded in this manner, and some viruses and microbes are in essence extraterrestrial in origin, then interplanetary life is DNA based! This is profound, because microbes which include bacteria, some algae, and amoebas, are the oldest inhabitants on Earth, dating to some 3.5 billion years ago. Microbes have a function in every processes on the planet, including providing oxygen.

The question still remains though, were we biologically inter-fered with a some point in our history, and can we prove it genetically? We can conduct all the DNA test we want, from mitochondrial DNA to nuclear DNA, but, if we don't have alien DNA in our database to compare it to, we are not going to get a clear answer. This doesn't mean that we shouldn't start looking, because I firmly believe that one of the next steps in looking for signs of extraterrestrial life is within. We need to also start looking at so called junk DNA, RNA. I suspect that we may have a few surprises in store. Ultimately, it may not be about proving that aliens visited our planet in the distance past, but more about determining how far back into pre-history do we have to look? If they were here before we were, then, whose planet is this really?

MALI

In 1946, the year before the Roswell crash, two french anthro-pologists arrived in Mali, west Africa. Their objective was to study a small tribe of cliff dwelling farmers called the Dogons. The Dogons have a very specific mythology surrounding the star Sirius and a small star they call Po. This star according to the Dogons is composed of a very heavy substance and orbits the dog star we know as Sirius every fifty years. They also explained to the anthropologists that Po follows an elliptical path around Sirius. Modern astronomers call this star Sirius B. Sirius B sits at about 8.6 light years from earth and is a white dwarf star, thus extremely dense. One cubic meter of matter from this star weighs about 20,000 tones. It is invisible to the naked eye and does follow an elliptical path.

Sirius was identified in ancient Egypt where it was called Sopdet. Sirius B on the other hand is a much more recent discovery. Its existence was suspected by astronomers in 1844, but not officially discovered until 1862 by Alvan Graham Clark. It was determined to be a white dwarf in the 1930's, and photographed for the first time in 1970.

The Dogons claim that their knowledge of this star system, including Sirius B dates back into antiquity. They further claim that a race called the Nommos came from this star system. They were described as amphibious, and preferred to reside in water. Tales of similar beings also existed in Sumeria, called the Oannes; and perhaps as we have seen in the Russian UFO chapter, in several modern accounts in Russian waters.

VIMANAS AND MISSILES

In India the International Academy of Sanskrit Research has translated ancient texts they call Aeronautics. Here are some inserts from these ancient Indian texts. «The Puspaka car that resembles the Sun and belongs to my brother was brought by the powerful Ravan; that aerial and excellent car going everywhere at will that car resembling a bright cloud in the sky and the King got in, and the excellent car at the command of the Raghira, rose up into the higher atmosphere.» The flying crafts were called vimanas. «The movements of the vimana are such that it can vertically ascend, vertically descend, move slanting forwards or backwards. With the help of the machines human beings can fly in the air and heavenly beings can come down to earth».

One text in particular, the Mahabharata speak of wars: «Gurkha flying in his swift and powerful vimana hurled against the three cities of the Vrishis and Andhakas a single projectile charged with all the power of the universe. An incandescent column of smoke and fire, as brilliant as ten thousand suns, rose in all it's splendor. It was the unknown weapon, the iron thunderbolt, a gigantic messenger of death which reduced to ashes the entire race of the Vrishnis and Andhakas.» Perhaps we were a little to quick to blame God for Sodom and Gomorra?

Ancient India covered a much greater territory than modern India, which included Afghanistan and Pakistan. From the Indo Pakistani war of 1965 to recent conflicts, Pakistan is no stranger to missiles and bombs. Was the first missile to hit the region launched between 2500BC and 3000BC? You may be tempted to through my book in the ocean at this point, but don't pollute and stay with me a little longer, because there was once a city called Mohenjo Daro.

Pakistan wasn't called Pakistan in those days, it was part of Mesopotamia, the birth place of civilization. Unfortunately, all the places that gave birth to society as we know it, and the places that keep records, are the places we destroy. Philosophical meandering aside, this becomes a serious issue when it comes to uncovering are hidden past. The Library of Alexandria which contained a book called "The True History of Mankind Over 100,000 years" destroyed, burnt (Sagan, 1988). During the 19 th century a French priest on Easter Island decided to burn all the Rongorongo tablets he could get his hands on. Library of Antioch, library of al-Hakam II, Imperial library of Constantinople, and the majority of the Mayan codices, all destroyed. Imagine how different our history books would be with all that knowledge. The truth, as is the case with the fossil record, we have reconstituted our history from a very limited and often bias data. The truth isn't out there, it's been burnt.

Mohenjo Daro was a thriving city with over 30,000 residents, until about 2000 BC when it was abandoned or destroyed. Archeologists have recovered pottery, statues, remains of large buildings, essentially all the things you would expect from a major ancient culture. What was unexpected was the radiation and and the fused pottery. Eerily, some of the inhabitants were found by archeologists in the streets lying there, unburied, as if they had died suddenly by some catastrophe. Many were holdings hands. I do want to point out here that this story is compiled from a plethora of sources, from books, to the internet, and to personal conversations I've had with other researchers. As I stated earlier, I don't have the original sources for this story.

In any case, the radiation at Mohenjo Daro may have been left as just an unusual archeological trivia, if only it had been the only place. Radioactivity at another ancient location was also found, this time in present day India itself, at Rajasthan (Oxford Journals, 2013). Radiation was detected for three square miles which led the Indian government to cordoned off the area. Further indication of radiation at Rajasthan are the unusual amount of birth defect and cancer in the area in modern times (Coppens, 2012). The Mahabharata also talks about columns of smoke in the shape of parasols, food contamination and peoples hair and nails falling out. Some of the effects discussed in these texts are also present in the Old testament when discussing some of the effect attributed to the Ark of Covenant.

DROPAS

In 1938, Archeologist Chi Pu Tei was sent by Beijing University on expedition into the Bayan Kara Ula mountains, near the China Tibetan border. His job was to survey a series of caves. A rather straightforward task for an experienced archeologist, but as his group entered one of the caves, they came upon a series of unmarked graves. They might, out of respect, have left the graves alone, if it weren't for the drawings on the wall. The drawings showed stick figures with elongated heads, among what appeared to be celestial bodies.

There must have been some discussion at this point about what to do with this discovery. These were archeologists, and they ultimately decided to do what archeologists do, they excavated. Even with the drawings on the wall serving as a kind of warning, what they found was still unexpected. The bodies were very thin, with very large skulls, and all under 4 feet in height.

Whether the archeologists knew at the time of the local legends, I cannot say. Local legends that tell of diminutive beings that once lived in the region. These beings looked so different as to inspire fear, and resulted in their extermination. They were described as having yellow skin, and it was said that they came from the clouds. Whether there is relationship between the bodies found at the cave and local legends is also unknown.

A great deal of books have been published on travel and mysteries in China and more specifically Tibet, some even by authors that have actually been there. Mysticism and UFO connections in Tibet is a subject I've been fascinated by since early childhood. I could go straight from watching the Super-friends on television to reading the Tibetan Book of the Dead. I was a peculiar child.

Stories of lost mystical cities, secret monasteries with strange bodies underground are regular occurrences in these books. The most popular series was of course from Lopsang Rampa who turned out to be a plumber from Plympton, England, named Cyril Hoskin. I have no idea how good Hoskin's was at unplugging your toilet, but he as a writer he was enthralling. The problem was and is, that as with most of the information in these types of books, the data is iffy at best. I'v personally heard stories of strange underground bodies in Tibet by several sources, but as with most of these books and tales, including the Bayan Kura Ula stories, definite proof is all to elusive.

In the 1970's, a new story emerges of a small statured tribe in China who claimed to have ancestors from a planet around Sirius. Many, even today, think the story pure fiction, perhaps inspired by the Dogon story of western Africa. The story did appear in some form in a fictional book, called Sungods in Exile, which lead many to declare the entire episode a hoax. However that story was based on earlier non fiction sources in China (Coppen, 2012). The tribe was called the Dropas. Unfortunately, as time went on, it became extremely difficult to separate fact from fiction. Especially post cultural revolution, where some of the artifacts associated with the Bayan Kara Ula site are unaccounted for.

In 1995 however, the Associated Press ran a story that a dwarfish tribe was found in Central China, at a location roughly three hundred miles from Bayan Kara Ula. These people were said to be under four feet in height. The Chinese never denied the story, but claimed that their diminutiveness was a result of generations of mercury poisoning. Unlikely, as mercury is a poison, and not known to affect DNA is such a way as to create such adaptive mutations.

EVE'S HIDDEN CHILDREN

Every once in a while a story breaks of unusual elongated skulls discovered that may or may not be non human. However, the majority of these are clearly human, and the elongated skulls the result of skull binding. Skull binding was practiced all over the world, and if conducted on a young enough child when the skull is very pliable, can give a very alien appearance. The question I suppose, is not wether these skulls are part alien, they are not, but why were elongated skulls so important to primitive society to begin with?

That said, there has been a few discovered skulls that are more intriguing than others, skulls that exhibit other unusual aspects that are not due to deformity. I very briefly examined such a skull a number of years ago. It had a very large cranium, but was extremely light. It also possessed exceptionally large eyes, and a lack of sinuses. The muscle attachments on the skull were also reduced in size, especially for the jaw muscle. The entire jaw was missing, but I assumed that it was quite thin. The skull was found in a cave in Mexico, and dates to about 900 years ago. Subsequent DNA analysis of the skull established it as partly human but with some differences on the maternal side. Its paternal lineage was a mystery.

Its most striking aspect to me was the location of the foramen magnum, which was advanced forward. The foramen magnum is an opening underneath the skull, on the occipital bone, for the spinal cord. The position of the foramen magnum is directly linked to locomotion. In modern humans it is further up the skull as compared to great apes and primitive humans, in order to accommodate our fully bipedal locomotion. In fact, through out human evolution, the foramen magnum has been slowly moving upwards as our walking upright has improved. One of the result of our form of bipedalism is that our heads are almost directly over our bodies, reducing the effect of gravity on the head. This means that in humans the neck muscles are smaller than in great apes, where the foramen magnum is further back in order to accommodate their form of locomotion witch includes quadrupedalism.

On the Mexican skull, the foramen magnum was placed even further up on the skull, as compared to modern humans, which would have resulted in a very straight posture while standing and walking. Furthermore, the reduced weight of the skull and the fact that the skull was very much on top of the spinal cord, could explain the lack of jaw muscle attachments. It wouldn't have needed heavy jaw musculature. The location of the fora-men magnum was the most striking feature on the skull. I don't know how to explain this. It looked like the next step in human evolution, if human evolution continues on the path that it is on. It looked like a skull from 2 million years in the future.

In 1999, bodies that were buried at least 500 years ago were found underneath the Vatican Library. For whatever reason, this is a story I completely missed when it first came out, it was only while watching a UFO documentary that I stumbled upon it. The bodies and skulls were found during the restoration of the library. A photograph was sent out of one of the skulls that stirred up the already agitated UFO community. The skull was very large with extremely large eyes, and in the context of the modern ufological paradigm, it resembled a Grey.

Several members of the Vatican expressed concerned over

the find, saying that there was a reason that, whatever the bodies were, the bodies were buried. Then, silence, the site was off limit and anyone associated with the Vatican refused to talk about it any further. As a result, much of the case hinges on the picture of one of the skulls that was sent out anonymously, most likely from one of the workers. The Vatican never actually denied the event or the provenance of the photograph. What happened to the bodies is unknown.

Out of all the major religions, Catholicism never seems to stray very far from the UFO phenomena. We've established a link with Marian apparitions in an earlier chapter, and we can safely assume that the Vatican has files deep inside their vaults. This is nothing new, religious art has been trying to give us clues for centuries, but no one looks at art anymore. A 15 th century painting inside the Palazzo Vecchio, in Florence, show a UFO above the Madonna. A medieval tapestry, depicting the life of Mary, shows a large classic flying saucer in the sky. A 14 th century fresco shows a flying object with a man inside. An 18 th century painting, by Aert De Gelder shows a UFO shining a light over the baptism of Jesus. The "annunciation" by Carlo Crivelli, 1486 shows a round object in the sky shinning a light unto Mary. If there are MIB's out there whose job is to keep the truth away for the general populace, well, I want that job. Its apparently the easiest job in the world, we're not even remotely paying attention to begin with. Too busy looking down at our phones I think.

ELVES AND FAIRIES

In 2010, Arni Johnsen, a former parliament member in Iceland was in a car accident when he flipped his car on a winter road. He claimed that Elves helped him and saved his life. Welcome to Iceland. The belief in Elves are apparently a controversial subject in Iceland. Surveys have indicated a belief in Elves from 10 % to over 50 % of the population.

This is obviously a large discrepancy in the results, which most likely reflect they way the surveys were both conducted and phrased. The higher number is in my opinion more indicative of the belief in the supernatural as a whole than the traditional elf motif.

The reason I brought up the Arni Johnsen accident is that it reminded me of the incident in the Zone of Silence where stranded motorists were helped by two strange individuals that quickly disappeared. See the Quetzalcoatl chapter for that incident in a little more detail. Sightings of Scandinavian type individuals have been encountered in the Zone of Silence on several occasions. Like the Elves in Iceland, they are at times seen on the side of the road in remote areas. In Iceland, they are usually associated with certain rock formations or large boulders which are said to be gateways to their realms. The beings from Mexico have no such connection, as they are usually associated with the unusual number of UFOs in the area.

To be fair, Arni Johnsen never mentioned that he actually saw any Elves, just that he thought that they protected him from harm. Contrary to popular belief, elves in Iceland aren't necessarily portrayed as very different physiologically from man. They can be quite tall, bringing us closer to the beings encountered in the Zone. I'm obviously not advocating the existence of bona fide Elves, but once again pointing to similarities in a phenomena that I believe has the same source, only viewed differently through cultural eyes.

They are several myths associated with the origin of Elves. One of them, is that they were the children of Eve that she decided to hide from God. Not thrilled with this development, God then stated, "What man hides from God, God hides from man" (Jon Arnason, 1864). If you want a more typical elf like creature that's a little more alien, even similar to the elongated skulls that we have been discussing, that you have to go to the land of the Fairies, England.

Just a few hundred years ago, reports of strange small beings people would encounter in the forest was not that unusual. We know them as fairies. Fairy encounters could result in a tempo-rary abduction where you could be taken into their world. As a result, you could be gone for hours, even days, with no memory of where you were. Today, we call these Alien Abductions and missing time, and as we have seen take a more destructive tone in Brazil.

Fairies, as well as elves, could sometime take your baby, or replace it with one of theirs. These type of tales have morphed into modern claims of human and alien hybrids. In some ways, this brings us back full circle to stories of the ancient gods and human hybrids.

The point is that whatever the modern UFO phenomena turns out to be, it has always been here. It is not static however, it's too smart for that, it changes with the times. What were once gods, became fairies, and elves when it became dangerous to believe in gods. Some, perhaps the elongated skull beings, became demons and jinn's, the later, often associated with modern UFOs in the desert.9;

If you look at UFO sightings and more particularly cases of close encounters, they seem to reflect the time the encounter takes place in. The ancients saw gods, Ezekiel saw angels, the middle ages saw fairies, in the 1950's contactees described the inside of UFOs resembling science fiction movies, and now the Greys. The outside appearance however for most part has remained the same since prehistoric man. From cave paintings to the most recent sightings, metallic flying saucers display the same behavior, flying pattern and appearance.

The discrepancy between the two is extremely important because it tells us that two very important things, that the actual UFOs represent an objective reality, but that close encounters are manipulated to reflect our expectations of what non human beings are suppose to look like and behave. This implies that close encounters, at least in part, take place in an alternate state of mind, perhaps what the catholics call ecstasy, or/and that our perceptions are manipulated. This means we can never trust the messages and descriptions from a close encounter, abduction or any other form of contact. The event is absolutely real, but the information given is problematic.

MARS

Some years ago I met a scientist that worked at NASA. His work included photo analysis of photographs brought back from Mars. He was given a lecture about the possibility of archeological remains on Mars, and after the lecture we had a chance to speak briefly. One of the first things that he told me was that the colors we associate with the Martian sky and landscape is false. In truth the sky and ground looks much like it does on earth, with a blue sky and various degrees of brown, beige, and red soil. We know today that this true. Recent photographs of the red planet show a surprising earth like landscape.

We know that Mars once had oceans and rivers, and that ice is still present at the poles. There are also recent photographs that show structures resembling vegetation. You can even detect some green in the photographs. These were the pictures that led Arthur C Clark, some years back, to declare that there was vegetation on Mars. His statements were also based on the fact that these tree or plant like "structures" diminish and increase depending on the Martian seasons. You can view these pictures on NASA'a website.

Back to my conversation with the NASA scientist and the second thing that he told me, there are artificial structures on Mars. He went to say that the famous Face on Mars wasn't the only face, and that there were pyramid like structures on the planet. That theory was nothing new, of course, he wasn't the first scientists that mentioned these artifacts. What was new was that he told me that there are very clear pictures of these artifacts, including pyramids, that he himself has seen; but before any Martian pictures are released to the public, they are passed through a filter. The reason for this process is to eliminate details, so that artificial artifacts appear natural.

The UFO community is an excitable bunch, prone to jump to conclusions. Case in point, recent pictures from Mars that appear to show artificial giant tubes, machinery, a skull, and even a figure walking behind a bolder have been used to argue for an extraterrestrial presence on Mars. No doubt, these photographs are intriguing, especially the giant tube like structures, but I think we need to exercise caution before we declare any of these proof of life. There's just aren't enough detail in the photographs.

Now, the pyramids are another story. For one thing, they are grouped in a specific area, in Cydonia. If this were due to an optical illusion, or if they were common natural structures, you would expect to see them randomly spread out across Mars. If you were to look at the photographs of the pyramids from above and not told their provenance, you would think that you are looking above the Giza plateau of Egypt. There is no way around this, they look like Egyptian pyramids, only larger.

To compound all this, near the pyramids are structures that appear artificial as well, including the Face. Once again, looking at this site from above, remember these are satellite pictures, is similar to looking at ancient ruins on Earth. There's a point where "coincidences" start to add up. There has been a lot of talk that the area of Cydonia may have been a city once upon a time. By talk, I don't mean by fringe mavericks like myself, but by reputable scientists, some from NASA itself. The questions is, if there was life on Mars where did it go?

History and the future aren't what they once were. They have mutated, alongside our whims of what is constitutes history and reality, and on the opposite side of what constitutes mythology or allegory. The problem is that the separation between history and mythology is very subjective. I have read passages written by ancient people translated by historical scholars where part of a paragraph is taken at face value and part of the same paragraph considered allegorical or myth. I have asked why, and the answer is always the same. It is because we know that this part is true, the building of irrigation canals for example; but we know that this is not true, that gods showed us how to build them. Or, yes these cave paintings of hunting buffaloes depicts a real event, but the one right next to it that depict hunters looking upwards at what can only described as flying saucers is not considered as representing a real event. Perhaps this is true, but that reasoning is unacceptable.

SECTION III:
CRYPTOZOOLOGY

1

APEMEN

A THEORETICAL DISPERSION OF BIPEDAL PRIMATES

In movies and popular consciousness alike, Tarzan was raised in the jungle by apes, or more precisely gorillas. We've all seen some version of the story, whether it be the original black and white movie or the more modern Disney rendering; I myself like Tarzan's Greatest Adventure, which includes Sean Connery as a diamond hunter. The thing is, in the original books Tarzan wasn't raised by gorillas at all. He was raised by man-like apes, resembling relic Hominids. The books clearly differentiates between traditional apes and Tarzan's more human like apes. A work of fiction, yes; but Burroughs apes were based on something real. Something natives in central Africa call the Lion Killers; and those were the thoughts that were going through by head as I sat in a small seat, in a small plane, over a very large forest.

We were flying low, over the Pacific Northwest's rain forest, and all you could see for an indeterminate amount of miles was green. It was easy to see how things could hide here.; it's our North American jungle. Planes have crashed here and never been found. And since I have some time left on this plane; let me tell you a story, if you can hear me through the sound of the propellers.

Four million year ago a small group of hominids with names like Australopithecus and Paranthropus emerged in Eastern and Southern Africa. They were the first walkers; but only to be replaced a couple million years later by a more adaptive hominid, the first of the tool users. Let's imagine for a second that a small population survived, hidden in the forests of Africa where four million years later they would be given new names; Agogwe, Sehite.

In time, a few would walk better than others, evolving a more efficient walking style. They would leave Africa through Europe and on to Asia where the deep jungles and forests evoked vestigial memories of their African origins. On the way a few would stay in the foothills of the Himalayas, adapting to a new environment; fooling later Homo sapiens, making them think that they lived and roam the mountain peaks. In truth, they were safe and sound in the valleys below.

But evolution does not stand still for any of its children; in time the majority of the specie would be pushed back by an increasing hominid presence that was bigger and smarter. They were guided by survival into the jungles of South Eastern Asia.

New species of hominids and apes that may have pushed them out of Europe and Asia were Homo erectus, Home ergaster and Gigantopithecus respectively. In certain places such as the Tibet, Nepal, the Caucasus, Mongolia, Siberia and parts of Central Asia, these larger species made a home and some of them would one day be known as Yeti and Almasty. A small population would even flourish around Vietnam where they would become known as Nguoi Rung. The largest specie, would settle comfortably along the mountain ranges, in Tibet, and further eastward; waiting patiently for a land bridge to a new land. This mysterious creature would become very successful, yet remain elusive until one day one was filmed in the forest of California in 1967.

BIGFOOT

There are officially no apes on the American continent. While that statement in inherently true, it is also completely misunderstood. What it really means is that there are no native ape specie on the continent. In other words, the North, and South American continent for that matter, never originated an ape specie. It says nothing about an ape or primate specie migrating here.

Bigfoot or Sasquatch as our Canadian neighbors prefer, is not a recent addition to the American fauna. This animal is well represented in native American lore. A Sasquatch mask can be found at Harvard's Peabody Museum dating from the 1800's. It belongs to the Tsimshian nation of British Columbia, which is the modern epicenter of modern Bigfoot sightings. I cannot in all good concious venture a guess as to the number of Bigfoots out the wild; but the Pacific Northwest mountain ranges and forests can easily hold a thriving population. Bigfoots are reported consistently every year, mainly from British Columbia, Washington State, Oregon and northern California. What all species need are room to reproduce, shelter and access to water and food. This area meets all the criteria above.

A case can be made for the extension of the specie towards the border of California and into Arizona. The Desert Sasquatch they call it. There are some well documented sightings in these areas, but whether the environment can support Bigfoots and keep them from discovery remains to be seen.

It is estimated that the average height of a male Bigfoot is 7 ft 8 inches and 6 ft 6 inches for a female of the specie. The average weight of a male probably around 800 pounds and 500 pounds for a female. The difference I believe, is due to sexual dimorphism which is common among higher primates. The body is covered with thick hair, except for the palms and soles. The hair is also much shorter in the facial area and on the back of the hand. The neck is very short and extremely muscular, giving the impression that Bigfoot has no neck. Enhancing this effect are the height of the shoulders and slight prognathism of the lower mandible. if viewed from a frontal position, the majority of the face will sit below the top of the shoulders. The nose is fairly broad, the mouth apparently without lips and the eyes deep set. The later, a reflection of a prominent brow ridge.

If Bigfoot were to be a hoax, it would prove to be a full time occupation with a work force of thousands to keep up with the number of sightings and footprints found each year; a great majority in remote areas. Thousands of tracks have been found since the 1950's with only a small percentage proven to be fake. Certainly there are more hoaxes that we are aware off, certain tracks considered as the real thing may have been hoaxed or misidentified. That been said, many tracks go on for miles, often in snow. The stride is so far apart that if it were a man with fake Bigfoot feet, he would have to be at least 7 feet tall; and, in some cases, judging from how deep the ground is indented, he would have to carrying anywhere from an extra three hundred to five hundred pounds on his back. Due to the number of tracks up and down the Pacific northwest found though out the years, there would have to be a well organized army of these guys. The tracks also show a flexible foot with dermal ridges, which represent yet another challenge to our hoaxers. On some of the clearer tracks the weight distribution and an extended heel show that the ankle is moved forward, that is compared to man. This is an important point and physiological advantage for an extremely heavy bipedal animal. Then, there are the tracks that accompany a visual sighting of a Bigfoot, which are consistent with height and weight of the animal. Are there a large number of hoaxes and mis-identifications? Yes, but If all the tracks were hoaxed, it would be the conspiracy of the millennium. Who's paying these people?

One of the main debate in the field of Bigfoot research is establishing a taxonomy for the animal. Humans and the great apes belong to the superfamily Hominoidea, also referred to as hominoids. This includes hominids (modern man and direct ancestors) and the aforementioned great apes. The corresponding family for the apes is called Pongidae, more commonly called pongids. The actual split of the hominid and pongid lineage occurred somewhere between 10 and 5 million years ago. All this brings us to the all important question, which side is Bigfoot on, man or ape.

If Bigfoot comes from the hominid lineage and is thus more closely related to man, it means a common ancestor no older than 4 to 6 million years old, in line with the appearance of the hominid line in the fossil record. It has to be remembered that dates are based on fossils that are found, these are not absolutes. Dates get moved back or up as new fossils and species are discovered. The process of fossilization is the exception and not the rule. The great majority of bones are never fossilized, depending on the environment and local predators. Primate bones are especially problematic due to the fact that primates tend to live in humid and forested environment, where bones disappear very quickly.

The first Hominids suitable for are purpose of discussion are the Australopithecine. Two types existed between 4 million years ago and 1 million years ago. There were a more gracile form who 2 million years ago led to the first line of Homo; and eventually modern man. The second type, the robust Australopithecine co existed with ancient man till about 1 million years ago. More commonly called Paranthropus today, this specie is thought to have been out competed for resources by the more intelligent Homo ergaster and Homo erectus, and as a result became extinct.

Paranthropus was much smaller than Bigfoot in height, probably no taller than 4.8 ft. Yet they shared many similarities with what we know of Bigfoot today. Despite their small height they were extremely muscular, with very large jaw bones and a very distinctive sagittal crest. The later may be very telling as the sagittal crest sits on top of the cranium and is an attachment for jaw muscles. It is present in male modern gorillas as well. What is interesting here is that Bigfoot and its counterparts in Asia are described as having coned shaped heads, which clearly indicates a sagital crest on top of the cranium.

Theoretically, Paranthropus could have continued to evolve in a robust direction leading to a modern equivalent in Bigfoot; on its way to the North American continent through Asia where related species to Bigfoot exist today. The main problem with this hypothesis is that there is no fossil evidence to support it. This doesn't make it an impossibility because the fossil is rather scarce to begin with; but no Australopithecine fossil, robust or otherwise, has ever been found outside of Africa. We have to look at more recent species in my opinion. We'll get back to the Australopithecine when we discuss Africa's Agogwes.

A second hypothesis is that Bigfoot descends from Homo erectus or any Hominid specie post Australopithecus and pre Neandertal. Homo erectus and related species ventured out of Africa and were well represented in Europe and Asia. This specie appeared about 2 million years ago and went extinct, at least officially, around 100,000 years ago. One of the problems associated with this hypothesis is that Homo erectus used stone tools; Bigfoot and the Yeti for that matter do not seem to possess that skill. Stone tools were a catalyst for the development of culture. The making of stone tools had to be learned; there has to be a student and a teacher, a social interaction. Eventually leading to the development of language. It reduces the emphasis on heavy musculature and increases the usage of the brain. Evolutionary speaking, it then becomes advantageous to be intelligent and to be able to communicate, in turn decreasing the need and reliance on brute force and ergo, a heavily build body. This is the way Homo erectus led to Homo sapiens. Bigfoot seem to have gone in the other direction. While it is premature to discuss this specie cognitive abilities, but whatever evolutionary link Bigfoot and the Yeti have, they evolved in a very robust direction.

This is not to say that Bigfoot couldn't have branched out from any of the Hominid specie prior to the Neandertal; but we so far do not see that in the fossil record. As we will see however, reports of the Almasty in Russia and central Asia may be more relevant to the preceding hypothesis.

Other proposed candidates such as Neandertals and some form of archaic Homo Sapiens are even more unlikely. Even though a case as been made for surviving Neandertal in Russia and again central Asia, I do not see them as possible candidates for Bigfoots. They weren't quite as hirsute or primitive, and had a well developed culture. They would have to have undergone severe reverse evolution in a short amount of time in order to fit the model for Bigfoot, or the Yeti.

As a different argument to the Hominid theory put forward in the introduction, the following candidate is the most popular with modern Bigfoot researcher, and is called Gigantopithecus. Gigantopithecus is possibly the largest primate to have ever existed, but with a poor showing in the fossil record. All that has ever been found are a handful of incomplete jaws and around a thousand teeth. This primate lived in Asia and became extinct a mere 300,000 years ago. The size of the jaw indicates that this animal weighted up to 900 pounds, which is comparable to Bigfoot's estimated weight. The geography also makes sense, especially if Bigfoot and the Yeti belong to the same specie. Gigantopithecus occupied areas that today is rich in Yeti lore and sightings, and could have made its way into North America the same way Homo sapiens did, though the Siberian land bridge. The extinction date of 300,000 thousand years ago is given because that's the date of the latest fossil that we are aware off.

If Bigfoot did not exist, and the Yeti did; Gigantopithecus would be the perfect candidate. It lived in the same geographical area as the Yeti, and 300,000 years is fairly recent. Furthermore, the Yeti has been reported as at times moving in a very ape like manner, on all fours. This is something you do not see for Bigfoot. I initially assumed this to be a problem in linking Yeti to Bigfoot, but in truth it may just be quite the opposite.

The Yeti is one hundred percent capable of walking upright, but may have retained some quadrupedal locomotion from his ancestor Gigantopithecus. A trait that would have been abandoned if the specie were to migrate a considerable distance. Walking upright is by far the more efficient way to travel for an expanding specie. Thus, there would be no advantage for Bigfoot to have retained that ability.

THE BEAST OF BOGGY CREEK

Bigfoot researchers don't always agree on a variety of issues. The field is riddled with differences in opinions, on the nature of the beast, on what constitutes evidence, on whether it is man or ape, on whether Bigfoot should be shot, and everything else in between. There was even a fist fight once at a Bigfoot conference over a difference in opinion; over shooting a Bigfoot I believe. Oh how I wish I could have been there.

In any case, what almost everyone in the field do agree on is the Impact of the 1972 docu-drama, "The Legend of Boggy Creek". In many ways, the Bigfoot field would be a vastly different place today, if that filmed had never been made. I first saw it in the early 1980's on late night television, long before I new what a docu-drama was, and while my interest in Bigfoot was already in bloom, now I was obsessed, enthralled. I suspect it started quite a few careers in Bigfoot research; the sequels though, not so much.

The Beast of Boggy Creek is really about Bigfoot sightings and in this case an attack, near the small town of Fouke, Arkansas. Most associate Bigfoot with northern California, Washington State and British Columbia. The largest population of Bigfoots today are no doubt in those areas. However, if you were to ask me what may be the best place to obtain evidence of Bigfoots? I might very well answer the four States area, of Arkansas, Texas, Lousiana and Oklahoma. While I seriously question reports in certain States, the southern Sasquatch is real.

Today, Fouke is a little more modern than it was in the 1970's, and the sightings have moved deeper in the swamps, most notably in the Sulphur River bottoms. The geographical area that covers the borders of all four states is filled with deep woods and swamps; and a large number of eyewitnesses sightings of the beast each and every year. Oklahoma was featured recently on a Bigfoot documentary called "Bigfootville", Texas has quite a few reports from the Big Thicket area, and not to be outdone, Lousiana has the Honey Island Swamp Monster. I've personally received a number of very credible sightings from other regions in the Southern United States. These are very recent, and involve local hunters and law enforcement personnel.

What differentiates the Southern Sasquatch from its Pacific Northwest counterpart is the occasional presence of three toed tracks. This is a problem, because no primate specie has three toes. This has lead many to completely discount the southern Sasquatch; prematurely in my opinion.

Logic would dictate that the Bigfoot population in southern states is much smaller then in the Pacific Northwest. I am basing that assumption on the fact that we are dealing with a smaller geographical area, where a population needs to remain manageable in order to stay hidden and have access to sufficient resources. This creates a smaller gene pool, where inbreeding and mutations are more likely to occur. This is called a bottle neck effect.

Case in point, the Doma people of Zimbabwe; who are known as the ostrich people because their feet only have two toes. Due to a mutation as a result of a small gene pool, the three middle toes are missing, and the outer toes are fairly large and turn inwards. This is not a handicap, this is a dominant condition; they are fully functional. Very few mutations are beneficial; and most result in a disadvantage, and usually death. In the southern Sasquatch, we may be seeing another exception to the rule.

SOUTH AMERICA, THE UCUMAR AND THE MONO GRANDE

Central and South America have their share of Bigfoot reports as well, but the picture is somewhat muddled due to the onslaught of names and the lack of on site research. The majority of Central American reports are identical to Bigfoot; called Sisemite in Belize and Xipe in Nicaragua, just to name a couple regional versions. Its range starts in lower Mexico, extends through Belize, Nicaragua, Costa Rica, Panama and parts of Northern South America. This simply appears to be a southern expansion of the specie, following the mountain range into South America.

Stories have emerged out of Brazil as well where the animal is referred to as Mapinguary. The problem with Brazil is that the term Mapinguary is also used to describe another unknown cryptid which may or may not resemble a giant sloth. I think, from any cryptozoological standpoint, Brazil should not be overlooked. Both the Mato Grosso and the Amazon basin can sustain a number of uncatalogued organisms.

One very promising area with a long and rich history of sightings are the Andes; notably on the Argentinian side where Bigfoot is called Ucumar. Not much has been written about the Ucumar, but this is a story I've been following for some years. The descriptions for the Ucumar is identical to Bigfoot, from its height to the footprints left behind. It's behavior does appear to be slightly more aggressive, with cattle as the Ucumar's main antagonist. The Yeti in Tibet and Nepal seems to have the same tendencies towards yaks. Yetis have been known to break the neck of yaks. In Argentina, the Ucumar is said to have a habit of pulling out the tongue from the mouth of cattle. There are quite a few cases of the later, indicating that the Ucumar isn't afraid to venture close to human habitation.

There is yet another creature reported in South America which I believe differs from Bigfoot; the Mono Grande. Often grouped with reports of Bigfoot like creatures; this animal is in my opinion a new world monkey. It's range is upper South America, deep in the jungles of Ecuador, Columbia and Venezuela. It appears to resemble a howler or spider monkey, only larger in size. Vocalization attributed to the Mono Grande is similar to both howlers and spider monkeys. Continuing with the monkey hypothesis gives us two options in identifying the Mone Grande. The first one is that it represent an undiscovered larger relative of the howler or spider monkey. Two, that the Mone Grande is related to an extinct specie such as Protopithecus. Protopithecus was a South American monkey who appears to have died out about 10,000 years ago. It was easily twice the size of howler or spider monkeys, but otherwise similar to both.

ORANG PENDEK

In 2003, bones were discovered on the Indonesian island of Flores of a primitive small specie of human, named officially Homo floresiensis. The bones gave us a date of 12,000 years ago. Some 10,000 to 20,000 years past the extinction date of Neandertals and Homo erectus.

Homo floresiensis stood between three to four feet in height, with a receding forehead and a lack of a chin. All primitive traits floresiensis shared with earlier hominids. Bone analysis seem to indicate that Homo floresiensis was more similar to Chimpanzees and the Australopithecine than modern man. This is a point of contention for some anthropologist, which clearly demonstrates that even with fossils, identification can remain elusive.

Man's evolutionary line is fairly convoluted, with numerous offshoots and several species coexisting at the same time. In fact, omitting floresiensis, the last 20 to 25 thousand years is the only time in our evolutionary history that man is the only official bipedal Hominid on the planet.

The original biped Australopithecus is a direct ancestor of man and officially went extinct 2 million years ago, and as late as 1 million years ago for the more robust version. The later is not thought to be an ancestor to modern man. The reason I bring this up is that weighing at around 55 lb. Homo floresiensis is comparable to the Australopithecine who as far as we know never ventured out of Africa. Homo erectus did and survived until about 25,000 years ago on Java. Java is situated between Flores and Sumatra. Could floresiensis be a late surviving small version of erectus? The problem is that the brain capacity appears to refute that hypothesis. The brain size is actually more in line with a chimpanzee brain or once again Australopithecus; all considerably smaller than in erectus. Now, with all that out of the way, let's vacate the past and head to the present.

Using all available data and criteria for determining the possibility of a cryptozoological specie to exist; the Orang Pendek is a certainty. With sightings dating back to the Dutch colonial period in the 1700's; Orang Pendek is Indonesia's version of Bigfoot in miniature. Orang Pendek is reported from the island of Sumatra and seems most abundant in Kerinci national park. Kerinci national park is 15 000 square km; and one of the most remote rain forest in the world, It is home the Sumatran tiger. The tiger is endangered and one of our most reliable Orang Pendek sightings come from Tiger conservationist Debbie Martyr: «It walked straight across the valley in front of me, thirty meters away. So Close! I didn't expect it. I certainly didn't expect to see it so clearly. It was walking between two trees, vegetation to about hip level. This gorgeous, graceful, very strongly built primate, a big ape, walked out of a legend and into broad daylight, lit up by the sun. If I'd seen it concealed in undergrowth, I could have said, well I saw something. But I didn't see something. I saw an orang pendek».

Orang Pendek is between 4 and 5 feet in height and extremely muscular. The fur color ranges from black, to brown to a dark red. In comparison to its large torso, Orang Pendek has relatively small legs. Close up sightings indicate that when threatened Orang pendek shows its teeth which has very broad incisors and long canines. Bipedal at all times, it is also an excellent climber. Sumatra is also home to the Orangutan, which is the skeptics favorite explanation for Orang Pendek. Orangutans are not bipedal, and more importantly are not found in Kerinci where the Orang Pendek is reported.

Long before the discovery of Home floresiensis, tales of a mysterious small bipedal hominids existed throughout out the jungles of Flores, called the Ebu Gogo. Identical in description to Orang Pendek, the Ebu Gogo was once upon a time tolerated by the people of Flores. However, the Ebu Gogo was fond of stealing crop and food from people and even of attacking children. As a result they were hunted to extinction during the 19 th century.

AN AFRICAN CONNECTION

In 1937, Discovery magazine ran a story about Captain Williams Hichens who was lion hunting in what is today Tanzania. While waiting for a potential kill in a forest glade Hichens saw two «little furry men « briefly walk out of the forest. His native guide informed him that they were called Agogwe and were extremely rare. Hichens described them at 4 feet in height, covered in brown fur and completely bipedal.

The story caught the eye of a British Officer by the name of Cuthbert Burgoyne who wrote to Discovery about his own sighting of the Agogwe in what was then portuguese East Africa and today Mozambique. Mozambique is just below Tanzania. His sighting came from aboard a cargo boat where he witnessed two Agogwes on the beach. His description matched Hichens.

Aside from east Africa, modern day report have also surfaced from western Africa and central Africa. In parts of the Congo, these primates are called Kakundari, and are not to confused with the Bili ape which I'll discuss shortly. A kakundari was briefly caught in the late 1960's by famous animal collector Charles Cordier. Cordier was regularly hired by zoos and museums to obtain various specimens; and a kakundari was briefly caught in one of Cordier's bird snare. As a result Cordier had ample time to obtain a detailed description wich matched the physical description of the Agogwe. According to Cordier, the kakundari fell face first, reached down to entangled himself and walked away on two legs. On the west coast these hominids are called Sehite and appear to belong to the same specie as the Agogwes.

In 2008, over 100,000 western lowland gorilla were discovered in the Republic of the Congo. Next door in the Democratic Republic of the Congo, lives the Lion Killers or Bili apes. Until the mid 2000's, this animal held the same status as Bigfoot in the United States. It was considered mythical by most biologists. Except that it was real, and turned out to be giant chimpanzees, the size of gorillas. Watching footage of this animal is disconcerting in many ways. Chimpanzees are so similar to man and so close genetically, that the first time I saw this animal on film I felt like I was watching footage from millions of years ago, and that I was looking at something primitive. As far as the Sehite, Agowe and Kakundari are concerned; ape or primitive human remains to be determined, but now the existence of such a specie is no longer anathema to biology and reality.

Thus there's only two ways to look at this. One is that these creatures are simply bipedal apes, and ergo not related to Homo floresiensis. From an evolutionary perspective, bipedalism is an adaptation like any other. A bipedal ape does not violate any biological rule, if it becomes advantageous for that organism. A theory I still feel more comfortable with when it comes to Orang Pendek; but, since the discovery of Home floresiensis, the possibility that Orang Pendek is closely related to man has gain some ground.

The reality is that without DNA analysis, it is somewhat premature if not irresponsible to speculate, which obviously is not stopping me. A descendants of a smaller version of Home erectus or a relative of the australopithecine is a tantalizing hypothesis. The Agogwe and Sehite are extremely similar to the australopithecine's, who are extremely similar to Homo floresiensis, who is nearly identical to the Orang Pendek. Let's go from there.

X

Mankind was partly birthed in east Africa. The earliest Australopithecine fossils are from east and south Africa. Mitochondrial eve has also been traced back to eastern Africa. Y-chromosomal Adam is not; he was most likely from central

Africa. In fact, mitochondrial eve and Y-chromosomal Adam never met. They were actually from different time periods. In any case, east Africa today is a far cry the Africa of our ancestors. It is not the deep jungle Africa of our quixotic imagination. It is not a place one would expect to find unknown Hominids. But, Africa has a sense of the poetic and history, and thus comes a Hominid called X.

Kenya is known for it's mountains and is in fact named in honor of mount Kenya. Between its mountains are forests, and here are where the stories of X originate. The name X was coined by Jacqueline Roumeguere Eberhardt; a french woman who spent quite a bit of time in Kenya and who wrote and spoke about X internationally. She wrote about five versions of X which has created a great deal of confusion and misconceptions. There are not five species of hairy upright primates walking around east Africa.

Adding to the confusion, she labeled them X1, X2, X3, X4 and X 5. Three of the five refer to Homo sapiens whose tribes are unknown. These are sightings made by natives and several outsiders of members of an unknown tribe or a hunter scavenger culture that have yet to be documented by anthropologists. These are no less fascinating, but are regular members of our specie; perhaps "stuck at a stone age level of technology. We know this because artifacts have been recovered, specifically bows and arrows. The bow and arrows are different in style to any of the known tribes in eastern Africa. This group if known from Kenya and is taller and lighter skin than other ethic groups in the region. The air of mystery surrounding them have led to some confusion and grouping with unknown hairy Hominids in the region. On a peculiar side note, they remind me of some of the sightings of similar people in central Asia which have also been grouped with reports of their version of Bigfoot called the Almasty.

The other X is extremely rare and appears to be the same creature as I discussed above for the Congo. This diminutive Hominid is apparently extinct in east Africa. There are no modern reports that I'm aware off.

X 1 is the creature most often reported in the forest's of the region. He is described as ranging from just below 6 feet to 7 feet in height, extremely muscular and hairy all over.; less so in the hands and facial area. Very rarely aggressive towards man, but very fond of buffalos. Great news for man, but not so much for the buffalo.

Stories of X attacking and eating buffalos are very similar to the Yeti attacking yaks and similar to the Ucumar attacking cattle in the Andes. The one known difference is that X has been known to use a sort of club in his attacks on the buffalos. This is something we don't see in the rest of the world; with as we shall see a potential exception with Siberia's Chuchunaa.

ALMASTY

Second only to Sumatra and the Orang Pendek, the most likely place in my opinion to discover a new specie of bipedal primate is Russia and Central Asia where this creature goes by the name of Alma or Almasty. The Almasty's range includes the Pamir mountains with activity extending across the border into China. Sightings are also common in the Altai mountains, in the Caucasus, Mongolia; and also in Siberia. Some reports have also emerged out of Iran and Pakistan. Nothing recent for Iran and Pakistan, but you know, they've been busy with other things over there.

What is immediately apparent about the Almasty's geographical distribution across Asia is that this specie follows the mountain ranges across the regions mentioned above. Taking the mountainous area between the Black sea and the Caspian sea as a starting point and heading south east in to Pakistan, you find this creature called Barmanu. From here on, if you follow the mountains north east to Mongolia you find yet more reports; as well as north into Siberia. Continuing east and a little bit south from Pakistan into Tibet and Nepal you get the Yeti. Further east and a little north into mainland China you find the habitat of the Yeren. You get the idea.

From this, logic would indicate that we are dealing with one type of animal with superficial morphological differences, or just cultural descriptive differences. It can then be assumed that a common ancestor exists. It can also be hypothesized that at some point into its history, after establishing itself in Asia and eastern Europe, the ancestor to the Almasty followed the mountain ranges into Siberia and subsequently across the land bridge into Alaska; most recently 12 000 years ago during the last ice age; and showed up into Canada and the United States.

This is a very clean theory, but unfortunately the Almasty creates a little bit of a problem to this hypothesis. Sightings appear to indicate two different types of creatures; one being the standard Bigfoot type creature that we have mostly been discussing until now, and two, being a more «human» creature that some Russian scientists have speculated as surviving Neandertals. Reports from the Pamir mountains indicate the standard Bigfoot like creature. The footprints are similar to Bigfoot in both size and shape. The creature exhibits a cone shaped head, a trait also shared with the larger Yetis. They appear to have no neck as in Bigfoot and are covered entirely with hair minus the hands and facial area. The hair color is described as reddish brown to black, similar to both the Yeti and Yeren.

Reports emanating from the Caucasus mountains seem to indicate an all together different creature. Casts of footprints coming from this area are definitely more human looking, but are longer and wider than human footprints and lack an arch. The height of these creatures is on the average 6.5 feet with no apparent sexual dimorphism. They are covered with reddish to brown black hair, they have short necks, large shoulders, short thumb, projecting brow ridges, retreating forehead, flat braincase, large face, wide nose, wide mouth, retreating chin, slight prognathism of the jaw and slanted eyes. Some of these traits are comparable to the Neandertals, but most are more primitive.

Russian scientists are quick to point to the possibility of surviving Neandertals; but in my opinion there are considerable problems with this hypothesis. The Neandertals had very large rounded brain cases which isn't the case with the Almasty. The Almasty's nose is flat while the Neandertal nose while large and wide was projecting, not flat. Furthermore, there are no reports of culture among the Almastys, no stone tools. Neandertals whom occupied this region as recently as 30,000 years ago, were famous for their stone tools. There would seem to be no reason for them in 30,000 years to abandon tools. Neandertals were considerably less apelike than the Almasty. They were skilled big game hunters. The later means that they probably perspired as anatomically modern humans do which restricts the amount of hair on the body. Yes, they were a little hairier and much more robust than modern man, but certainly not to the extent attributed to the Almasty. A more primitive Hominid would be a better fit in this case.

Another issue to consider is the question of hybrids. Many anthropologists feel that a considerable amount of breeding took place between Neandertals and anatomically modern humans. A recent find in Portugal dated at 25,000 years ago shows a boy who has both Homo sapien sapien traits and Neandertal traits. The question on inter specie breeding has always been controversial, and has created problems when it comes to definite specie identification through the fossil record. This issue goes as far back as when the lineage of man and chimpanzee split, interbreeding between the two may have continued for a million years or so. There is no question that breeding between Homo erectus or Homo ergaster and emerging Homo sapiens would have produced viable offspring. The question of interbreeding and viable offspring between primate species and Homo sapiens is complicated and very taboo. Russian scientists, as recently as the 1930's attempted to breed human-ape hybrids.

Zana was the name given to a female Almasty captured in the late 1800's in the Caucasus. She was kept in captivity for years, but remained animalistic. In time though, she became dependent on whoever fed her, and when allowed to roam always came back. She was in the habit of creating primitive stone tools, but would only use them as projectiles, usually towards dogs.

Bordering on extreme deviance by her captors, she became pregnant on several occasions; confirming her hominid lineage? Many of the children died right after child birth when she attempted to wash them in the river. The known surviving children were human looking except that they were very robust with dark skin. Zana's remains have never been found but the skull of her youngest son has. Anthropologist Grover Krantz, examined the skull, and feels that the skull is within human parameters; but Russian scientists feel differently.

Zana died sometime in the 1890's, and we know that the children existed. We have official record of their birth and marriages even. What we don't know is whether Zana really was Almasty or just a normal "wild" woman living apart from society, maybe suffering from a psychological condition?

YETI

At age 10 I was well aware of the real stories behind Bigfoot, but at the time had no idea that half way around the world Bigfoot had a cousin. That was until I saw the Yeti on "In Search off" with Spock. I was blown away, speechless; it was like going from 2D to 3D, and right then I started dreaming about these far away cold mountain peaks.

The Yeti, more commonly referred to as the Abominable Snowman, is native to the forests around the Himalayas of Tibet, Nepal and Bhutan. Locals use three different terms in relation to the Yeti. Teh-Ima is described as 3 to 4 ft in height and lives in the lower valleys of the Himalayas. Meh-teh is about 5 to 6 ft in height and lives in the upper forest, but often travels across the mountains leaving the now famous tracks. Dzu-teh is over 8 ft in height and resembles Meh-teh.

It has been proposed that the three terms is an indication of three separate specie of Hominid living around the Himalayas mountain range. I do not believe this to be the case. Nonetheless, a case may be made that three types of undiscovered bipedal primates, exists in the world today, with a yet to be determined genetic relationship. In turn making this region of the world ground zero, if you will, for the expansion of these three types of potential Hominids. Following that logic, the smaller Yeti may be related to the Orang Pendek. Some descriptions mention a tail which points to an ordinary monkey. Another possibility is the Teh-ima is a term used to describe a juvenile Yeti. In all honesty, the Teh-ima is most likely a combination of the later two, a local monkey specie and juvenile Yetis. The Teh-ima which is said to only be seen in the lower valley, may indicate that this is where female of the specie give birth and raises their offspring. The temperature are more temperate and there's plenty of food, water and shelter to raise their young.

The Meh-teh and the Dzu-teh do not seem to differ enough to warrant two different species either. Accounts do vary in size, from a 6 ft creature to a giant creature of over 8 ft, but this disparity is not uncommon in Bigfoot reports either. It may just be a case of sexual dimorphism where the male is larger than the female; which is a common trait among upper primates. If we are dealing with two different animals, they are most likely very closely related; such as the low land gorilla and the mountain gorilla, different in size but still both gorillas.

The protocols for naming an animal in many cultures are different from ours. We name species based on their evolutionary and genetic history while many other cultures name their animals strictly on physical differences, such as size.

The great majority of sightings and footprint size point to a creature comparable to Bigfoot. As such the Yeti stands between 5 ft and 8 ft in height, very muscular, long arms that reach down to the knees, a conical head, reddish brown and black hair, and has five toes with a most prominent second toe. Tracks indicate a second toe that is the longest of the five, with the first toe almost as long. The last three toes are bunched together and are spaced a little apart from the second toe. In Bigfoot prints the toes point forward, but in many Yeti prints the big toe points to the side. All other aspects of the Yeti resemble Bigfoot closely which still leads us to assume that we are dealing with the same specie, or at the very least the sharing of a common ancestor. The big toe divergence may be an evolutionary adaptation for the Yeti's ecological niche, which differs from Bigfoot.

Female Yetis have large breasts which natives say can be swung over the shoulders. Most likely an exaggeration but the same is said of female Bigfoots by native Americans. What is a very pronounced characteristic of the Yeti and Bigfoot is the conical head. The conical head is interesting because it would indicate the presence of a sagittal crest, also found in the Gorilla. The sagittal crest is an attachment for muscle pertaining to the jaw. It signifies a very strong jaw. Traditionally male primates have a sagittal crest while females do not.

One of the most tantalizing peace of evidence concerning the Yeti comes from a mysterious severed hand said to belong to a Yeti. The hand originated in a monastery in Pangboche, Tibet, where Peter Byrne and Tom Slick were able to obtain the thumb and the phalanx of the index finger of the mummified hand. He switched parts of the hand with human ones and smuggled the parts out of Asia through India. To get them out of India he entrusted the pieces of the hand to Jimmy and Gloria Stewart who hid them in one of their suitcases. At any rate, the thumb and the index phalanx along with skin samples were analyzed by Professor Osman Hill at UCLA. At first he thought that the bones were human, but upon further analysis changed his mind. Other scientists conducted an analysis of the bones and the final verdict was that the bones were from an unknown primate. The skin was analyzed by zoologist Charles Leone who couldn't identify it. All he could say was that it is not human, gorilla, monkey, pig, goat, horse or bear skin. In 1991 the NBC show Unsolved Mysteries contacted Dr George Agogino who had kept a segment of skin of the Pangboche hand. They analyzed the sample once again and found that it was not human but close to human. Following the broadcast, the actual Pangboche hand was stolen from the Pangboche monastery. Its whereabouts today is unknown.

I was able to meet with Peter Byrne some years ago. He actually lived ten minutes away from me at the time, where he was indeed able to confirm the story over a cup of tea, quite the gentleman that Peter Byrne.

YEREN

On the other side of the Pamir mountains into China, and also in the Hubei region are pockets of Almastys or Yetis called Yeren by the Chinese. Chinese scientists take this creature very seriously, and numerous expeditions have been sent out by the Chinese Academy of Science. They have concluded that the Yeren stands between 6 and 8 feet tall, covered with reddish or brown hair, has wide shoulders, slopping forehead, roundish nose, big ears, large teeth, protruding jaw, short hair in the facial area with long flowing hair over the shoulders.

Several hair samples have been analyzed by several Chinese scientists. One particular hair sample was found on a tree, where it was thought the Yeren had scratched itself. The samples were sent to the Tongji Medical University's forensic biology department. Their finding was that it belonged to a primate, closely related to man. Further set of samples have also shown a primate origin, and a close morphology to human hair.

Several strands of hair recovered by a British expedition show a very high iron to zinc ratio, fifty times higher than in man. They also contained more calcium, copper, strontium, cobalt, chromium and magnesium than any known primate and human hair. The hair was also reported to contain 16 amino acid which is contrary to the 17 found in all mammals. Due to the unusual nature of the hair samples brought back by the British, the consensus is that the sample was contaminated. I have to agree.

Chinese scientists have also speculated that the Yeren sleeps in ground nests. Several of these nests have been found, notably in the Hubei province. Nests have also been found in the United States in relation to Bigfoot. What they are is essentially branches and vegetation matted down on the ground forming a sort of bed. I've personally received reports by hunters of these nests, deep in the forest. These are individuals used to the outdoors, but were somewhat unnerved by the nests as they could not identify what animal was responsible. This is indicative of primate behavior. Gorillas in Africa make similar nests on the ground.

NGUOI RUNG

The Almasty and Yeren may have a relative in Vietnam, called Nguoi Rung or Batutut. Relatively unknown to the world at large., first reports of "L Homme Sauvage" came from French colonists, who were most likely wondering what kind of hell were they colonizing this time. Further reports of these creatures emerged during the Vietnam War when soldiers came home with stories of these strange upright apes from the jungles of southeast Asia. They called them the Rock Apes.

In 1975, Dr John Mackinnon wrote "In Search of the Red Ape", which was an anthropological study of Orangutans. In that book, Mackinnon mentions tracks in the jungle of a bipedal nature that he could not identify. He felt that an unknown Hominid similar to Meganthropus, now known as Paranthropus, was responsible. Local description for the Nguoi Rung places its height at around 6 feet, with hair color from black to brown with some occasional gray. They can be aggressive towards man as reports of them attacking and killing man do exist. Unlike Bigfoot and the Yeti, they are sometimes seen moving in groups.

In a rather unusual turn of events the best evidence for the existence of the Nguoi Rung may have once been found in Minnesota where the body of an «apeman» surfaced in the 1960's. The Minnesota Ice Man was analyzed for three days by Ivan Sanderson and Bernard Heuvelmans while frozen in ice;

the body was frozen, not Sanderson and Heuvelmans. Later, the story would take a turn for the bizarre as the body was apparently exchanged for a fake. Heuvelmans felt that the owner was worried about legal ramification of having a human like dead body on display. This lead to many calling the entire affair a hoax. Unfortunately Heuvelmans notes and subsequent book has never been translated into English, thus limiting people access to the original data. I have read the original analysis as written by Heuvelmans and seen the pictures taken by both investigators; it is impressive.

Both Sanderson and Heuvelmans have stated that they could smell the putrefaction of the body, see blood in the ice, see speckles of dirt between hair follicle and even see the broken ulna sticking out of the left arm. In any case, the body while certainly hominoid does not fit the profile of an adult Bigfoot. It was obviously male because the genitals were visible. The body itself was about 6 feet in length and gracile. Thus, two possibilities exist; that it was an juvenile Bigfoot, or another type of hominid.

Likewise, two stories exist on its origin; one that it was shot in the woods of Wisconsin, and two that it originated in Asia. Both stories have reportedly originated with Frank Hansen, the man responsible for showing the body at various state fairs and the man responsible for switching the body for a fake. Heuvelmans thought that the body was of Asian origin, but no substantial proof exists either way. Pictures of the iceman do appear similar to physical descriptions of the Vietnamese Nguoi Rung.

For now, this is where the evidence leads. It may turn out differently once DNA is obtained. If I've learned one thing from Sir Arthur's Conan Doyles, it is that you go where the evidence leads, no matter how improbable it may initially appear, and a solution will present itself.

YOWIE

Australia may seem like an unlikely place for a Bigfoot type animal, with very few placental mammals to speak off. A stretch in believability perhaps, but the evidence in terms of eyewitness accounts and footprints equals North America. All accounts of the Yowie are indistinguishable from Bigfoot and Yeti descriptions; this includes facial and cranial traits, fur color, height, weight as determined by footprint indentation, vocalization and smell. Obtained hair samples have also been compared to Bigfoot hair sample, and are similar, if not identical. This is based on hair morphology; not DNA analysis. Behavior is also similar to Bigfoot, from aggression towards dogs to the throwing of rocks when man presumably gets to close. One extremely intriguing similarity is the occasional three toed Yowie tracks, which we have seen with Southern Bigfoots.

Oral Aborigine traditions are rich with Yowie lore; also stating that he preceded them onto Australia. These stories are depicted in various rock carvings depicting encounters with the "big hairy man". There are also Aboriginal stories of "wars", if you will, with the Yowie; due to competition over resources. The early colonials of Australia were also familiar with the "Hairy Man", which appeared to have been greater in numbers in those days.

When it comes to cryptozoology, and other strange phenomena for that matter, Australia is an untapped resource. There are some excellent Australian researchers, but their findings are largely unknown in this part of the world. Furthermore, Australia's interior is very sparsely populated, with an enormous amount of outback, forests and mountain ranges potentially filled with things that we are told cannot exist.

But they do, especially in the Blue Mountains where a large number of modern Yowie sightings have taken place. The Blue Mountains are actually similar to the pacific Northwest in terms of landscape. Other areas of interest for a potential Yowie population are the south coast of New South Wales and the Gold Coast Hinterland (Healy and Cropper, 2006)

CHUCHUNAA

Siberia conjures up images of a frozen tundra, Arctic species and once Soviet dissidents; not at all a place you would expect to find an ape like specie either. But in remote areas in such places as Yakutia which appears to be an extension of the Almasty's range, are tales of the Chuchunaa. Very little research has been conducted in regards to the Chuchunaa. This is highly unfortunate, because this creature is of particular importance. Researchers are often divided upon whether unknown hominid worldwide are closer to man or apes. The Chuchunaa sits at the threshold of that hypothesis. Logic would dictate that this creature would be an extension of the Almasty, only at its extreme Eastern range. Yet it is somewhat differentiated by reports of the occasional fur clothing; and thus resurrecting the old surviving Neandertal argument. An argument I was never in favor off.

Chuchunaa means outcast, and were first talked about by the various tribes and nomads across Siberia. It wasn't until the 1920's that science became aware and interested in the Chuchunaa, as the Russian started sending out scientific expeditions in order to seek out and study these creatures. They are described as 7n feet in height, covered in hair with a broad flat nose and a prominent brow ridge. Some of the other descriptions such as the amount of hair, the broadness of the shoulders and the fact that the head sits low on the torso giving the impression of a lack of neck is comparable to Bigfoot and Yeti. Obviously if the report of it wearing clothing is accurate, it represent a considerable cognitive leap from Bigfoot or the Yeti. I think due to the scarcity of information available for the Chuchunaa, and quite frankly resting on just a handful of sightings of it wearing fur clothing; additional data is needed to formulate a proper working hypothesis. On a completely unrelated side note, you may see a similar conundrum on Mykonos as well; trust me I've been there.

FURTHER EAST

Here is where we come full circle, at the edge of a continent. Beringia, better known as the Bering land bridge is where man first came across into North America from Siberia, and presumably any other bipedal primate specie. The later, a population whose decedents are now established in North America; and with a small pocket in far eastern Siberia. Further east means the Chukehi Peninsula facing Alaska and the Kamchatka Peninsula. At this point we are talking about species that can survive near the Arctic ocean, a very cold environment for any type of primate. But sightings do occur, even with the lack of any sizable human population to speak off. Most of these reports eminate from rugged outdoor men and hunters who know their wildlife quite well, and I would assume would be able to differentiate between a bipedal ape like creature and a bear.

Years ago I spoke to man who found himself on a unmanned island above Canada in the Arctic circle. The island was only accessible by sea plane. I cannot quite recall what he was doing there, but he told me one day while walking on the beach he saw these footprints. Footprints that belonged to a creature walking barefooted but also a creature that had to be at least 8 feet in height in his estimation.

Already well versed in the Bigfoot phenomenon, I was somewhat skeptical of the ability of a primate specie to survive that far north. Nonetheless sightings in these areas do exist on both side of the Bering strait. A pattern that stands out in these sightings is that as you go further north, the Bigfoots seem to be getting bigger. Whether this is a flaw in the data or a particular adaptation remains to be seen.

2

PRIMITIVE

PART I

DINOSAUR

I saw a dinosaur once; of sorts. It was 1982, I was twelve and I was in Australia. At the Sydney zoo to be exact, I stood for forty five minutes staring at a primordial beast; a rather large komodo dragon. I was transfixed. It's movements appeared so primitive, it was like looking back 65 million years.

Komodo dragons weren't discovered until 1910 on the Indonesian island of Komodo. Tales of these animals were considered myth prior to that date. Out of myth and into science, fossils have indicated that Komodo dragons migrated to Indonesia about 15 million years ago out of Australia. It has also been recently discovered that dragons can reproduce parthenogenetically. This is the virgin Mary syndrome; its not actually called that by the way; where certain reptiles can reproduce without a male.

This ability can be advantageous when there is a limited amount of available males due to a reduce population. This ability would certainly benefit a theoretical hidden living population of large animals. It would help sustain a population that needs to remain small in numbers in order to survive by remaining undisturbed. Back in 1982, all that I knew was that I saw something primitive, and I wanted to see it again.

Evolution is a response; a response to outside forces. But, what happens when there is little outside pressure? What happens when for millions of years very little environmental pressure is exerted upon a specie? Central Africa is where the past resides, home to the Leaf Nosed Bat, little changed in 60 million years; the Mouse Deer, unchanged in 30 million years and the African Finfoot, a primitive bird with claws on its wing. The Congo is also home to the lungfish, so named because ot its ability to breath in and out of the water. This fish can grow up to 7 feet in length and belongs to a primitive group called Crossopterygii; a group from which terrestrial animals have evolved. The lungfish can also be found in South America and in Australia; two locations in play in our scenario. And then, there's Mokele-mbembe, dinosaur of the Congo and my personal white whale.

MOKELE-MBEMBE

Mokele-mbembe is well known to the inhabitants of the Likouala region of the Congo. In recent years sightings have certainly diminish in the region, with in my opinion the specie retreating westward. Once abundant in the Lake Tele area and in rivers near remote villages, the animal is only seen a couple times a year by fishermen that wander just a little further than the time before. Still, the stories keep coming of this animal whom is rarely seen on land, and uses the river system to get around. The majority of sightings happen early in the morning when Mokele-mbembe feeds on the Malombo plant, that borders the rivers of the region. This is Mokele-mbembe's favorite food according to locals. Mokele-mbembe does not appear to be an aggressive predator, but has shown a certain amount of aggressiveness towards man. It has at times attacked dugouts that come too close, coming up from below and slashing at the overboard man with its tail. Mokele-mbembe, while a quadruped, is an excellent swimmer and seems to spend a great deal of time under water.

A SMALL SAUROPOD?

Now comes the uncomfortable part, the identity of these animals. There is no way around it, it resembles a small sauropod dinosaur; between the size of an elephant and hippo, 30 feet in length with a long tail. The body is thick with a long neck and small reptilian head, reminiscent of apatosaurus. Apatosaurus is a sauropod dinosaur once know as brontosaurus. This reported morphology has been very consistently described, from early missionaries, native tribes, pygmies and modern eyewitnesses. A great majority of the Cryptozoological community, and in turn the accompanied literature, assumes that Mokele-mbembe is a dinosaur. From a morphological standpoint, the small sauropod identity is compelling. This is not stating that this animal has remained completely unchanged in 65 million years, and dinosaur descendants aren't unheard off. They are called birds.

The Sauropoda family was relatively successful extending from the middle Jurassic to the late Cretaceous. It was once thought that Sauropods like crocodiles, which are a bona fide pre-historic specie, lived in a semi aquatic environment which would increase the Mokele-mbembe sauropod link. However, the semi aquatic hypothesis for the Sauropods has been discarded by many scientist in preference for a dryer environment. This is not a view shared by all, and truth be told they may both be correct. Some sauropod specie may have preferred a dry environment while others a more aquatic environment.

For now the sauropod hypothesis remains viable. If crocodiles managed to survive the end of the cretaceous, why not a sauropod in an environment like the Congo which hasn't really changed in 65 million years. Sauropods were herbivores which is consistent with what we know of Mokele-mbembe, with the assumption that it eats fish as well. The physical description fits, and when eyewitnesses have been shown pictures of various animals that are thriving today and extinct animals, in all cases they have designated the sauropod as Mokele-mbembe.

There have been various attempts to assign a more conservative reptilian or mammalian identity to Mokele-mbembe, with little success. No mammal or reptile currently living or known from the fossil record resembles Mokele-mbembe. That by no means excludes that possibility however. A case of convergent evolution should be seriously considered. Convergent evolution is when unrelated biological organisms develop similar adaptations. Wings on birds and bats would be a good example of this mechanism at work. When a niche is open, nature will fill it. A theory that has gained ground with me in recent years, despite the lack of fossil evidence for a mammal or reptile having acquired sauropod traits.

The term misidentification has been thrown around quite a bit, usually mentioning elephants and hippos as possible sources of Mokele-Mbembe sightings. Mokele-mbembe tracks differ from both elephant and hippo tracks as they appear to be clawed. Misidentification cannot explain close up sightings, and hippos are not found in regions where Mokele-mbembe types are said to dwell. Both these animals seem to occupy a similar, if not identical ecological niche, and thus stay well clear of one another. Even if the dinosaur hypothesis turns out to be erroneous, I believe that we are still left with a mystery animal in the Congo and perhaps elsewhere. let me rephrase that last sentence; Mokele-mbembe exists, it is there.

HISTORICAL SIGHTINGS AND GEOGRAPHY

Ever since westerners have entered the Congo there have been tales of large unknown beasts in the region. Missionaries in the 1700's were mystified to find these large clawed tracks that didn't seem to belong to any known animal. These tracks were first reported by the Abbe Lievain Bonaventure Proyart and his book with a title even longer than his name; "Histoire de Louango, Kakongo, et autres royaumes d'Afrique, redigee d'apres les memoirs de prefects apostolique de la Mission Francoise".

These strange tracks were also observed by Alfred Aloysius Smith, better known as Trader Horn. He was given a physical description of the animals responsible as well as shown cave drawings of animals identical to modern day accounts of Mokele-mbembe. The later occurred in Gabon which also seems to harbor a population of these animals. Modern tales out of Gabon and Cameroon also emerged in the late 1970's when herpetologist James Powell spent time in the region studying crocodiles. He heard about these animals from locals who had seen them, but never saw one himself.

Mokele-mbembe's range does appear to be shrinking which may indicate a reduction in numbers. Around 2000 and 2001 I was told by various sources within the region that the animal can be found west of lake Tele in various pools connected by a river system. In fact, since I received those reports, sightings appear to have shifted even further west towards the border and across into Cameroon. The animal is larger in Cameroon with reports of dermal spikes whereas within the Congo and lake Tele area the animal is described as smooth. A very important distinction in my opinion, which we'll get to shortly.

Back into the Republic of the Congo, the Likouala region alone is 55,000 square miles of mostly unexplored swamps and rain forests that has only been mapped from the air. This place almost necessitates the presence of strange creatures, of Mokele-mbembe. This is a region, along with parts of Cameroon, Gabon, the Central African Republic and parts of southern Chad, where the climate and geography have undergone minimal changes in 65 million years. This is a center of endemism, meaning an area that acts as an island where due to a specific environment, species become isolated; where we would expect to find unique organisms.

It can be both a refuge and a force for the development of new traits in established species. Within a center of endemism a bottleneck effect may occur, where a specie receiving no genes from the outside is forced to reproduce in a smaller gene pool; and can evolve very quickly and very differently from the same specie living outside of the center of endemism. Imagine 65 million years of this.

On a more stable note, certain organism, such as the primitive species I mentioned in the introduction, plus the crocodiles, can thrive and remain unchanged for millions of years. Mokele-mbembe, in theory, could belong to either of these two paradigms. I would be surprise if Mokele-mbembe is the only large biological surprise in this region. And indeed, other unknown animals such as the Chipekwe has been described in this area. This is the Lost World, 55,000 square miles of it, and it's on the move into Gabon and Cameroon.

INTO GABON AND CAMEROON

With sightings possibly diminishing in the Congo region, the specie may be retreating westward into the deep swamps and across the border into Gabon and Cameroon. It may also be a case of focused research in these countries of late, due to the difficulties in research in the Congo due to continual instability and wars.

Whichever the case may be, once abundant in the Lake Tele area and in nearby rivers, the animal is now seen perhaps a couple times a year. The other possibility is that the animal as it matures heads west towards the Cameroon border. Aside from rare sightings of juveniles, specimen sighted around the Lake Tele area are about the size of hippos or small elephants with a smooth body. A frill is at times seen on the top of the head which may be do to sexual dimorphism. Animals seen towards Cameroon and Gabon are much larger and sometimes endowed with dermal spikes on their backs. Now, granted that we are dealing with a relatively small pool of reports, but in my opinion this could be a case where the animal in Cameroon and Gabon is of older age. Perhaps, the animal doesn't develop dermal spikes until he attains a certain age. This may be an example of migration, where the animal gives birth in the Congo and heads west as it matures.

Gabon actually has a fairly long history of these animals. As I already briefly mentioned, Alfred Aloysius Smith had seen and written about strange tracks in the region. Upon asking locals what animal the tracks belonged too, he was given a physical description as well as shown cave drawings of animals identical to modern day descriptions of Mokele-mbembe.

CHIPEKWE

Emela-ntouka or the Chipekwe is the second most talked about mysterious animal in central Africa. The name means killer of elephants and like Mokele- mbembe is semi aquatic. It obtained it's name because it has been known to dismember elephants or any other animal foolish enough to venture into a river where the Chipekwe is bathing. It accomplishes this feat with it's powerful horn on top of it's snout. This animal is more aggressive than Mokele-mbembe but is not a carnivore either. Natives are adamant about the fact that it does not eat it's victims; but one has to wonder how often eyewitnesses have stuck around to observe the animal's dietary habits. This animal is about the size of an elephant with a bulky body, four equal size limb, short neck and a long tail. Footprints seem to indicate three toes with claws. Keeping in mind certain descriptions have most likely been confused with descriptions of Mokele-mbembe. The more reliable sighting describes this animal as resembling a Ceretop or a Rhinoceros; in fact it has been described as a water Rhinoceros by some that are familiar with the animal.

As a result, it has been suggested that this animal is related to the rhinoceros family. While certain physiological traits in Chipekwe contradicts this hypothesis, I don't believe it should necessarily be discarded.   At the very least the possibility that this animal belongs to the mammalian family should be explored.

Some of the differences with the rhinoceros are reports of a long tail, which does not appear in any rhinoceros alive or in the fossil record. The rhinoceros horn is made up of tightly weave hair which cannot support anything overtly heavy. In contrast Chipekwe's horn is described as a real horn capable of withstanding great force such as exhibited in the killing of elephants.

So, again we are left with a hypothesis involving a surviving member of the dinosaur family, quite possibly of the ceratopsian family which includes the famous triceratops. The triceratops was endowed with three horns which eliminates it from consideration due to the Chipekwe's solitary horn; but some of it's relatives correspond to Chipekwe quite well. Again, however we are are treading in uncertain waters as some have reported the animal with additional smaller horns.

If we are to entertain the ceretops hypothesis as proposed by Roy Mackal, the two leading models could be Monoclonius and Centrosaurus (Mackal, 1987). They were both approximately the same size as Chipekwe and vegetarians. They were both endowed with a heavy tail and a true horn. Furthermore, the first toe and the fifth toe were greatly reduced thus giving a three toe impression in footprints. Centrosaurus lived near rivers and swamps with a large population in what was then Canada. It was about 20 feet in length and officially survived up to 75 million years ago.

Here is the primary problem with the preceding hypothesis. The physiology matches but unlike Mokele-mbembe the geography does not. The Ceratopsians were active in North America and in north western Asia. No fossil has ever been found in Africa. The fossil record indicates that the Ceratops thrived in a swamp semi aquatic environment which is consistent with the Chipekwe, and at the end of the Cretaceous swamp areas around the world were been replaced by dry areas. A phenomena many scientist attribute to the demise of the dinosaurs. However, two areas of the world maintained their wet climate much as it is today. These two places were South America and Africa, including the Congo basin region. Could the Ceratops have made their way into Africa so long ago in order to flee the increase desertion of their environment? Perhaps it is no coincidence that this region of the world accounts for so many creatures resembling extinct species. Central Africa is one of the few region of the world which could have provided a refuge from extinction at the end of the cretaceous Again we are left no fossil to support that hypothesis The survival of the ceratops is an exciting proposition but as a viable working hypothesis, I feel that we should consider a mammalian origin to these sightings first.

TASEK BERA

Taking an environmental approach to the possibility of prehistoric survival, South America would be the next logical location. From the Amazon to Patagonia there are plenty of unexplored forest and swamps with similar environments to the Congo Basin. The evidence however isn't quite as compelling; at least when it comes to the Mokele-mbembe specie.

Malaysia may be a different story however, home to a creature whose physiology is remarkably close to Mokele-mbembe. This animal is called the Ular Tedong and it can found in and around the Tasek Bera swamps, lake and river system. The Ular Tedong is described as possessing a reptilian head with two small soft horns on top of the head, a long neck attached to a bulky body that usually remains hidden under water. The soft horns are puzzling as it is usually a physiological trait associated with lake creatures such as Nessie. These may in fact be some form of breathing apparatus. An adaptation either developed recently, as to permit the animal to stay hidden under water and still been able to breath, or might just be an unknown sauropod adaptation due to the fact that these wouldn't survive the fossilization process. I hesitate somewhat to draw to close an association with Lake Monsters such as Nessie which may turn out to be mammalian. That been said, mammal, reptile or dinosaur may not matter; at least at the moment. That is a question that will be answered in the future once DNA evidence is obtained. In the Lake Monster section of this book, I address sightings of an animal called the Patagonian Plesiosaur whose behavior and morphology is in many ways an amalgam of Nessie and Mokele-mbembe. This brings up a rather radical possibility of all these animals are related species, differentiated by evolved adaptations based on their current environments.

Whatever the case may be and in light of the physical descriptions attributed to the Ular tedong, it is in all likelihood related to Mokele-mbembe. Ular tedong is also said to echo a large booming sound not unlike an elephant. Another similarity between both creatures is that the Ular tedong is also vegetarian. Native reports say that the animal extends it's neck out of the water to munch on nearby vegetation.

North east of Tasek Bera lies another fake called Lake Chini where reports of similar creatures are also heard. Semelai stories say that these animals are born at a north east mountainous site called Gunong Chini and that they migrate to both Lake Chini and Tasek Bera through mountain streams (Shuker, 1995). The eyewitness sightings for the Ular Tedong isn't nearly as impressive as it is for Mokele-Mbembe. I think that more data is needed in order to assess the Ular Tedong relationship to Mokele-mbembe, and more importantly whether this animal does in fact live in the Tasek Bera today.

COLONEL FAWCETT AND SOUTH AMERICAN DINOSAURS

Occasional modern reports do emerge out of South America, but on a considerable lesser frequency than Africa. Yet, areas like the Mato Grosso remain little explored, and jungles in Bolivia, Brazil, Peru, and further up in Columbia have had sightings of strange large animals; some resembling Mokelembembe. Reports of the later were almost routine in the early days of the 20 th century; leading me to believe that if there were a thriving population of these animals one hundred years ago, they have been considerably reduced in numbers by now. On the other hand, reports of plesiosaur like animals resembling Nessie are fairly common on the South American continent, especially in Patagonia. I will discuss these later in the lake monster chapter.

A word of caution though when it comes to stories of living dinosaurs one hundred years ago; they can be a little suspect as tall tales inspired by newspapers were common back in those days. I've had to make a judgment call on some of the sightings. I've omitted from consideration several of them that I feel are in all likelihood malarkey. With that in mind, the more credible reports come from the borders of Peru, Bolivia and Brazil.

In the swamps near the Acre river natives tell of gigantic tracks of unknown animals that live semi submerged in the water. Some years ago I had dismissed reports of Mokele types outside of Africa. Yet, this area between Brazil and Bolivia wont quite go away. Reputable explorers such as Lieutenant Colonel Percy Fawcett spoke of these animals, before his much public disappearance. Fawcett, an officer of the Royal Engineers, British Army, was charged with delineating the border between Brazil, Peru and Bolivia. East of the Ucuyali in the Beni swamps of Madre de Dios and near the Madidi river across the border in Bolivia is where Fawcett initially heard native tales about these gigantic dinosaur like animals. The stories were of large animals with long necks and small heads that would emerge out of the water in order to feed. They were known as fairly aggressive, especially towards canoes that came to close. Fawcett himself saw numerous large tracks and even had one up close sighting of one of the creatures emerging briefly out of the water.

These stories were confirmed by his son and later explorer Leonard Clark. Clark was a former OSS agent and retired Army Colonel who spent some time in the region starting in the late 1940's. He heard the same tales and description from the natives around the Madidi river region. The other regions of South America with sightings include the Amazon basin and Patagonia; but these animals are different. There are certainly undiscovered species in those areas, some may turn out to be spectacular, but most likely not related to Mokele-mbembe or dinosaurs; probably.

THE OUTBACK

And now, we come full circle and back to Australia. In the far north are stories of gigantic reptilian animals and some very strange tracts. Aboriginal oral tradition supported by cave paintings tell of great warriors back in the dreamtime that hunted great beasts. Modern Aborigines say descendants of these great beasts can still be found in remote places; called the Burrunjor in the north and Kimamsisla in Victoria.

But accounts do not reside with the Aborigines alone. In the 1950's cows and horses near Burktown were been attacked and found half eaten. Local cattlemen became increasingly concerned, and in response, they organized a hunt to find the culprit. They found huge tracks which they followed until they reached a swamp area. These might have been courageous men but the thought of chasing a large aggressive animal which easily dismembered their livestock into the swamps was becoming less and less appealing. Many turned back, but a couple of men went on by foot since the horses had refused to go any further. Upon their return they claimed to have seen a reptilian creature in the distance whom looked to be about 30 feet long. They, like the others decided to turn back (Gilroy. 1995)

Due to the fact that we have to take the words of two men with no proof at face value, the preceding story as any kind of evidence is questionable. However, in 1974, possible supporting evidence showed up. Large reptilian tracks were found in mud stone which weren't completely fossilized. Paleontologist who examined these tracks acknowledged that the mud had only dried up in the last century. Since no living creature could be assigned to the tracks, paleontologists decided to ignore the whole episode.

They are some intriguing reports deep in the outback of a what appears to be a bipedal reptile, looking somewhat like a smaller T Rex. I am not saying that there are T Rex's running around in Australia, but I've seen several interviews with native guides that claim to have seen something; an animal they call Burrunjor. Aborigines and guides aside, rare visitors to this area have also seen this animal. Furthermore, there are several early Aboriginal paintings on rock that depicts a large bipedal reptile. I have yet to formulate a working hypothesis for Burrunjor, but it comes to half eaten cattle; I think we need to look a little closer in time.

The Australian monitor lizard is one of the largest lizards in the world at a maximum of 10 feet in length. It is eclipsed only by the Komodo dragon and the New Guinea Salvadori's monitor. In fact, not counting Burrunjor sightings, eyewitnesses points to an animal resembling a monitor lizard, but much bigger, up to 30 feet in length and extremely fast and aggressive. Even accounting for an abnormally large monitor and considerable exaggeration, 30 feet in length or even 20 feet is a stretch for a known monitor.

There once was a lizard of that size that lived in Australia until about 40,000 years ago. It was called Megalania. At the very least, the original inhabitants of Australia may have been contemporaries of Megalania. Tracks found seem to support the giant lizard hypothesis. While the cryptozoological evidence isn't quite as strong in Australia as it is in Africa, I do believe that it worth looking into. At least with a working hypothesis of a relative of Megalania or perhaps a bigger version of the Komodo dragon.

BEL AND THE DRAGON

There's a narrative called Bel and the dragon in the Apoc-
rypha's book of Daniel. In the story King Cyrus of Babylon had in
his possession an animal described as a great serpent or dragon,
that he recognized as a God. Daniel who wasn't a big supporter
of alternative Gods was told by Cyrus, or Nebuchadzzar in some
versions, to worship this beast because it was a god that lived,
ate and drank, and thus much more alive than the Hebrew God.
Cyrus argument doesn't rank as one of the most convincing in
history since Daniel preceded to poison the animal.

A depiction of this "dragon" can be seen depicted on the
Ishtar gate right along side with lions. and rimis which are wild
oxen. The animal is called the Sirrush and is represented in the
same context as the lions and oxen, thus indicating that it was
thought to be a real animal. To be fair, only potions of the Sirrush
appears reptilian in the Ishtar gate representations; the body is
a little to sleek, but the tongue is definitely forked. The animal
is a quadruped though.

The first mention of this animal may have been in the bible
where it is called Behemoth. Scholars feel that the Behemoth is
meant as a real animal, but no identity has been put forward.
In Job 40 the Behemoth is described as an enormous animal
with a big tail. He is very strong, a vegetarian and lives in the
swamps, partly submerged in water. We cannot be certain that
the Sirrush and Behemoth refers to the same animal, but we do
know that the Babylonians ventured into Africa.

A SCIENTIFIC DEBATE

It is accepted as fact that dinosaurs went extinct about
65 million years ago. A great cataclysm occurred and the majority of life on the planet subsequently died out. However, that
premise has its problems. Most life went extinct, but many

survived, such as crocodiles, various forms of sea life and certain mammals that would eventually inherit the planet.

The creatures that adapts best to a changing environment are the ones who survives. The ones who adapted to night for three years and great earth changes caused by the asteroid lived on. What creatures were more diversified than dinosaurs. There were reptilian like dinosaurs, bird like dinosaurs, some were endothermic while others ectothermic. There were herbivores, carnivores; many lived on land while others preferred the water. Yet it is believed that every single specie of dinosaur died out by the end of the Mesozoic while several reptiles, birds and mammals lived on. That premise bothers me.

Between the Mesozoic era and the Cenozoic era; or more precisely between the Cretaceous and tertiary period; lies the KT boundary. The KT boundary is marked by a layer of red clay which contains an abnormal amount of iridium. No dinosaur fossil has ever been found above this layer, according to text-books. Meaning that no dinosaur survived past the 65 million year mark. Actually, that is not entirely true. A handful of fossils have been found from the Cenozoic, but paleoanthropologists feel that the fossils must have slip in the sediments from the Mesozoic era. This can indeed occur, and also some specie may have taken a while to go completely extinct, into the Cenozoic.

Iridium is very rare on earth and can only be found in such quantity during volcanic eruptions. Since the iridium layer is a global phenomena, another source had to be the culprit. An asteroid was to be the suspect. Today the history books tell us everything was all and good until the asteroid hit and created the last great mass extinction. In reality the picture isn't quite as clear, enter the micro paleontologists.

Micro paleontologists study micro fossils which are much more abundant than regular fossils and thus can give a better understanding of what really took place so long ago. While it was found that many Micro species also died out by the end of the Cretaceous; it was found not to have been as sudden event as established dogma had it. Extinction actually started

3 000,000 years before the end of the Cretaceous and continued for 2 000,000 afterwards (Paul Chambers, 1998). To further complicate matters some micro fossils were completely unaffected.

As far as the dinosaurs were concerned they too seemed to have begun to die out way before the asteroid impact. Judging from fossils it appears that only 12 genera of dinosaurs were still roaming by that time. It now becomes apparent that the mass extinction was gradual. Does this reinforces the idea that some specie of dinosaurs survived to the present day? No, but this model points out that the extinction of the dinosaurs isn't as a clear cut issue as most believe. But, you can make a case where nature was trimming down its various organisms into more manageable numbers, and earth changes certainly played a part in this mechanism. The question is, was this mechanism specific enough to target all dinosaurs, while sparing a number of other organisms?

TERROR BIRD

Another issue to consider is the evolution of dinosaurs into birds. Birds and certain dinosaurs share many traits which include the wishbone and cavities in certain skull bones. The later, a trait shared with crocodiles which are thought to be the closest living relatives to dinosaurs; outside of birds. Fossil evidence indicates that 145 million years ago a little dinosaur not unlike the velociraptor gave way to creatures that bore wings and took to the skies. This is not the pterosaurs by the way. Pterosaurs which includes the famous pterodactyl are actually reptiles.

When is a bird a bird, a dinosaur a dinosaur; and when is a bird a dinosaur and vice versa? Many will tell you that's easy, but their answers will be based on assumptions. An assumption that species are separated by certain traits that are inclusive to one and exclusive to the other. One animal however refutes these assumptions. A creature that stood at 6 feet in height, weighs in at over 300 pounds, a head 2 feet in length, of which the majority was beak, and sharp claws that were 4 inches long. This animal was bipedal, fast and a furious predator, and they were still around a mere two million years ago. This animal was called Titanis the terror bird. These animals had arms that were used to hold their prey down while they ripped through the flesh. Fossils have showed that Titanis had bones made up of hard tissue and not hollow like regular birds. The only things that separate this bird from dinosaurs is a short tail, a fused hand and a lack of teeth.

It lacked some dinosaur traits but it also lacked some bird traits. So, it isn't so farfetched at all to think that other creatures today may be related to dinosaurs. Maybe lacking certain characteristics, but how many of those do you need to call it a dinosaur. Perhaps, it becomes more believable to the layman and scientist alike to think that the reports of living dinosaurs are creatures actually closely related to dinosaurs and not bona fide dinosaurs. Like birds, they may be evolved dinosaurs; but until a body shows up speculation becomes an exercise in futility. What is apparent though, is that something is out there.

PART II

THE GIANTS

Size for certain species is determined by their immediate environment. Anacondas for example will keep growing as they age, with limits set by the amount of food available and space. Other organism, such as spiders are limited by their breathing apparatus and by their exoskeleton, with some modern spiders developing a unique breathing apparatus in order to get around these limitations.

Eighty feet snakes in the amazon and five feet in diameter spiders in the Congo may sound like science fiction today; but giant versions of animals that thrive in today's environment once existed. Biology does not prohibit giant versions of organisms, or the expression of a vestigial trait or gene expressed in a modern population. Sure, certain environmental factors and biological necessities for survival and reproduction need to be addressed and overcome; but nature has a tendency to find a way. Case in point, in 2012 scientists found a giant shrimp in the Kermadec Trench off new Zealand, ten times larger than previously known for that particular specie and three times larger than any close relative (Fox News 2012).

SUCURIJU GIGANTE

Tales, rumors, stories, sightings of giant snakes exceeding 40 feet in length and reaching almost a 100 feet have divided herpetologists for generations. With a well define geographical location in South America and deep in the amazon river system, these snakes certainly are a tantalizing possibility. One important quality to the sightings is that they overlap with the anaconda's range, within Brazil and Bolivia more specifically; leading to speculation that these animals called Sucuriju Gigante are giant anacondas.

In the Amazon river and its tributaries, the largest snake is the green anaconda whose official size limit is about 27 feet. Some larger numbers have been thrown about from time to time, only to be taken back due to lack of proof; and here lies the problem. The anaconda lives in water, due to it's extreme size and weight; with its size only limited by space and availability of food. Alive and in the wild, as you could imagine, these animals are nearly impossible to measure. The majority of measurements come from zoos and from dead specimens.

Within a proper environment such as an aquatic environment that can support it's mass, a limitless food supply and essentially been left in peace, the anaconda can theoretically grow much larger. Room within its aquatic environment is the key, as a snake that size cannot support itself out of the water. Except for maybe in Anaconda the movie which I maintain, among strong derision from my peers, is extremely entertaining. If only for the biggest case of overacting by an great actor, John Voight, in cinema history.

The amazon fulfills all of the above criteria. The question then is not whether the Giant Anaconda can exist, but whether it does and if so, how big are we talking about. Stories of the Sucuriju Gigante began with the earliest colonist who either saw the animal or heard about it from natives. But, these animals hit the mainstream press when in 1907 Col. Percy Fawcett shot a giant anaconda he measured at 62 feet. In his writings, Fawcett, who was hired by the Royal Geographical Society of London to survey the Amazon basin, mentions that the Brazilian Boundary Commission had measured an 80 feet specimen as well.

In 2009, 28 fossilized snakes were found by scientists in Columbia. Alive these snakes would have measures 40 to 50 feet in length and weight over 2000 pounds. Named Titanoboa, this to date is the largest snake fossil ever found and dates from 60 million years ago. What Homo Floresiensis did for the Orang Pendek, Titanoboa did for the Sucuriju Gigante; all of a sudden it became just a little more possible.

As a result, the Giant Anaconda theory was reassessed. What if Sucuriju Gigante was not an anaconda, but another type of snake? Pictures taken of the supposed Sucuriju Gigante are also inconclusive. While some photographs undoubtedly show a large snake resembling an anaconda, it is impossible to determine size from these photographs. One telling aspect of the Sucuriju Gigante distribution of sightings is that they haven't diminished over time. There aren't an overwhelming amounts of reports, due to the remoteness of the environment, and locals that don't twitter; but these animals do not appear to be decreasing in numbers. The size estimation from modern reports, both from natives and explorers, are between 40 feet to 80 feet on average. Furthermore, the areas reported in modern reports haven't deviated since the time of Fawcett; all deep in the dark rivers and jungles of Brazil, Paraguay, Peru and Bolivia.

The Sucuriju Gigante is at times confused with another mystery South American snake or worm like animal called the Minhocao. Whiles they do overlap in niche, the Minhocao is clearly not a snake, and appears to spend the majority of its time underground. While it's size is comparable to the Sucuriju, it is black with a segmented worm like skin, with two "antennas" on the top of its head. Minhocao means big earthworm in Portuguese which has lead to the speculation that this animal is a giant earthworm. While a worm of that size is unlikely, other possibilities have been put forward by various cryptozoologists. The leading candidate in my opinion has been proposed by Karl Shuker; and that's a giant caecilian, which would explain the antennas. Caecilians who are amphibians are endowed with feelers or tentacles on top of their heads in order to enhance their sense of smell. They are a South American specie, but generally do not exceed 5 feet in length. Disregarding the size issue, and it is very probable that the size in Minacao sightings are somewhat exaggerated, caecilian are a perfect fit. They resemble worms and snakes, and they spend most of their times underground.

One more animal that I do want to mention in the snake worm category is the Mongolian Deathworm, the Olgoi Khorkhoy. Aside from having the greatest nickname in cryptozoology and being the deadliest thing in Mongolia since Genghis Khan, this animal is described as a blood red worm about 2 to 5 feet in length and very thick. It is very rare and lives in the more remote parts of the Gobi desert. Its a relatively unknown cryptid to the world at large, even if it did have a low budget movie called "The Mongolian Death Worm" air on the SyFy channel in 2010. At the time of this writing, for unfathomable reasons I have yet to see this movie.

There's a fair amount of local sightings for this animal, and quite a bit of fear associated with it. The fear, probably increased by its blood red color, is otherwise due to the fact that people have reportedly been hurt and even killed by this animal. The Death Worm has the ability to kill at a distance, reportedly by spewing venom or by electricity conduction, like an eel. Sightings tend to occur after rains, or when the animal is feeding on its favorite food, the goyo plant. It does appear to spend more time over ground in the months of June and July.

J'BA FOFI

There are certain physiological limits in biology. For example, insects can only grow to a certain size due to the fact that too large and nerve impulses would become to slow for proper functioning; not to mention size limits imposed by an exoskeleton. Spiders have another issue related to size, and that is their book-lung respiratory system. A book-lung is an organ located on the abdomen of a spider which is responsible for oxygen transference. It only works up to a certain size organism. If the spider becomes too large, the book-lung becomes insufficient in carrying oxygen. Many of the larger spiders today have gotten around this problem by a book-lung trachea combination which increases blood flow, and also increase speed and stamina; but only to a certain extent. So the question is; how big can spiders really get?

The answer may lie deep in the Amazon rain forest and in darkest Africa; and more precisely in Venezuela and in the Congo along with neighboring central African nations. By giant spiders, I don't mean "Food for the Gods", but as large as five feet across. In the Congo this monster has a name and it is called J'Ba FoFi.

These animal already familiar to natives, with the first story to reach outside of Africa occurred In the 1890's in Uganda. Arthur Simes was an English missionary on expedition near the shores of Lake Nyasa when in horror movie fashion several of his porters became entangled in a web that stretched out between two trees. According to Simes, giant spiders preceded to quickly descends upon the porters and bite. The results were not great, swelling of the extremities, fever and eventually death for the men followed.

Almost fifty years later, In 1938, a British couple was driving in what was than the Belgium Congo when a spider that they estimated to be three to five feet in circumference walked across the road. The spider was so large that they initially though that it was a cat. They were told that these animals were rare but not unknown, and dangerous to men.

Pygmies living in the forest describe the spider as brown and purple and about five feet across. They are described as similar in behavior and appearance to tarantulas, and seem to build web nests similar to that specie. They generally prey upon birds and small monkeys, but not adverse to attacking man if the opportunity presents itself.

The only other places where this specie has been reported is in the Amazon Basin and less likely in Cambodia. The Asian reports are essentially made up of rumors represented by the following story. In 1970 a Green Beret claimed to have seen such an animal at close range, about ten feet in front of him, and that's pretty much it. I wouldn't put too much stock in the Cambodian data, especially in light of no recent sightings that I'm aware off.

Reports in the Amazon basin are centralized near remote villages in Venezuela. Similar in size and behavior to the African reports; obliging one to assume that this is a related specie. These spiders are described as five feet in circumference, including the legs. The abdomen is about two to three feet in length. When the animal stands up with it's legs up in the air, a defensive position for certain spiders such as tarantulas, these animals can also reach about five feet in height. In fact, on rare occasions children have been attacked, and disappearances of adults especially at night are at times attributed to these spiders. While these tales may or may not be true and given a certain amount of size exaggerations, a spiders of three to four feet across would have no problem in taking down chickens or dogs. These two are indeed the victims of choice in both Venezuela and Central Africa, according to locals. As far as physical descriptions go, the Venezuelan specimens are brown and hairy, again resembling tarantulas.

Physical descriptions as well as their behavior certainly point to a undiscovered relative of the tarantula. Tarantulas are members of the Theraphosidae family with approximately 900 species. The largest is the goliath tarantula, largest spider on the planet at 10 to 12 inches across. A far cry you say to the reported five feet monsters; but there are 50,000 specie of spiders on the planet with an estimate of at least 200,000 more to be discovered. Within that number, may lie a much bigger relative, rare, but native to the Congo and Venezuela. The Amazon rain forest is over 3 million sq. miles and the Congo basin almost 2 million sq. miles; imagine the possibilities.

Jaekelopterus rhenaniae lived 390 million years ago. It was the size of a large crocodile and was an arachnid, more precisely a sea scorpion. Arachnids grew to spectacular sizes in those days do to the fact that the environment contained 65 % more oxygen. As the oxygen decreased in the environment and nitrogen increased, arachnids shrunk due to their book lung issues I've priorly illustrated.

Furthermore, the fossil record is an anomaly; very few specimens fossilize. We are unaware of over 99 % of species that have populated our planet; especially when in comes to Theraphosidae. Only two extinct members are known from the fossil record. The number of giant arachnids, spiders and relatives in the past is unknown; but we do know of jaekelopterus rhenaniae. We also know that spiders the size of large crocodiles is impossible today; not enough of a concentration of oxygen in the air. So, back to the original question, how big can spiders get in the current environment? We know the improvement to the book lung organs in species such as tarantulas. Furthermore we can tentatively assume that based on anatomy and behavior that if the giant spider of the Congo and Venezuela exists, it is in all likely hood a relative of the tarantula. I can conclude within then, let's say, 75 % of spider specie yet to be discovered, exists some very big relatives. Ergo, three to five feet specimens living in the jungles of the Amazon and Congo basin is by no means a zoological impossibility or even an improbability.

4

SURVIVAL OF THE MEGAFAUNA

TIGRE DE MONTAGNE

Le Tigre de Montagne is the name given to a large cat that inhabits the Ennedi mountains of northern Chad in Africa. The first descriptions surfaced in the 1960's from hunting guide Christian Le Noel, who heard about the animal from the Zagaoua tribe. They described it as large as a lion, very strong, short tail, red fur with white stripes. They also added that it had a pair of huge teeth that protrude from its mouth. Some specimen are also said to be exhibit melanism, that is to say black fur. This animal while rare and difficult to find is well known to local tribes within Chad and neighboring countries. The Hadjeray tribe of southwestern Chad call it the Hadjel and confirm the unusual dentition. This animals range extends into the Central African Republic where reports emanate from the Ouanda-Djaile area where it is also called Le Tigre De Montagne or Vassako. As a general rule, these animals prefer a mountain and rocky environment, through out Central and Eastern Africa. The name Le Tigre De Montagne reflects its environment, meaning mountain tiger. If one were shall we say "brave" enough to mention to the locals that perhaps, just perhaps, they are unable to differentiate between a lion, or leopard, and Le Tigre De Montagne. They would of course respond politely, lions and leopards do not possess these teeth and are of different fur color they would explain. Each specie stays well clear of one another; and then less polite words would be offered.

Natives can differentiate between lions, leopards and these animals, and LeNoel knew it. Not wanting to lose out on a potential discovery, he decided to go hunting for the animal in the Central African Republic. Unfortunately, he never did see Le Tigre De Montagne, but on one occasion heard a very large roar coming from one of the caverns. Noel's native tracker identified the roar as a Tigre De Montagne. Maybe, maybe not, and Noel couldn't say for sure. Yet, he was unable to identify the roar, which intrigued him enough to come back the next year. This time, he brought photographs to see if the locals could match Le Tigre De Montagne with one of the animals depicted on the photographs. I surmise that the possibility was in the back of Noel's mind, but the effect was no less dramatic. They picked out the picture of Machairodus, a saber toothed cat that went extinct during the Pleistocene, rejecting in the process all major big cat species living today. LeNoel was hooked, and I understand. The idea of a living saber tooth cat is a potent narcotic.

LeNoel would never find Le Tigre de Montagne, it stayed just out of reach. A roar here and there, some tracks and a dead hippo that showed traces of two very large teeth was all Le Tigre would give him. More recent expedition have more or less obtained the same results, but in truth very few if any have ventured deep enough into Le Tigre de Montagne's territory. The animal is there of that i am certain, but it's population is most likely shrinking. Deeper into the mountains and caves we must go, especially in Chad and in the Central African republic.

Is there a secondary option however? As I briefly mentioned up above this animal seems to prefer a mountain environment, often said to live in caves. This seems consistent across central Africa, from Chad to the Central African republic to the Sudan. This makes a certain amount of sense if this animal is indeed a separate specie from African lions and leopards who prefer the open Savannah and forests respectively. Large cat species tend to not overlap in territories. One thing all big cats do share is the need for a water source, and these animals have been seen near and in even swimming in rivers.

Reports within the Sudan, are not as well known or perhaps current as the reports from Chad and the Central African republic. An article from Sudan Wildlife and Sport from 1950, mention sightings of such an animal near the border with Uganda. Once again a mountainous environment in the land of the Tribe called the Acholi.

Switching continents now; in 1966 in the famous book "The Cloud Forest" author Peter Mathiessen tells of stories he heard about a rarely seen cat in the rain forest's of Ecuador and Columbia. The animal is described as smaller than a Jaguar, stripped and equipped with two very large teeth. 1998, the Magazine Science Illustree tells of a sighting in Paraguay of a saber toothed cat, unfortunately with very little additional info.

Stories of modern day saber tooth have precedence in Paraguay as one was shot in 1975, and examined by zoologist Juan Avacar. The cat weighed 160 pounds and had twelve inch long saber teeth. Avacar mentioned the possibility that this was an example of a Smilodon, a type of saber tooth cat that became extinct 10,000 years ago. The authorities uncomfortable with Avacar's analysis renamed the corpse a mutant jaguar. The fate of the remains is unknown. In 1994, zoologist Peter Hocking obtained the skull of presumably the same specie of cat, this time from either the Ucayali or Pasco province of Peru.

For the South American sightings, another possibility presents itself, that of a sabertooth marsupial, thylacosmilus (Heuvelmans, 1955). Thylacosmilus looked just like a saber-tooth cat, striped and possessing two elongated canines. These animals were marsupials and not related to the cat family. The emergence of the teeth was a case of convergent evolution, where two unrelated specie develop identical or similar traits due to to the fact that they occupy a similar environmental niche. Thylacosmilus became extinct at the end of the pliocene, between 3 to 2 million years ago.

This theory was first mentioned by famed cryptozoologist Bernard Heuvelmans. While the geography does makes sense; if we are going to go the prehistoric survivor route, I find it more likely that an animal extinct for 10,000 years has survived than an animal extinct for a couple of million years. We know that the sabertooth cat Smilodon occupied the same ecological niche and most likely out competed thylacosmilus for the same resources. Furthermore, the reports coming out of Africa are certainly of a large cat, as thycosmilus never existed on that continent. Once again from a logic standpoint, I would have to assume that the African animals and South American animals are closely related.

This is assuming that these animals are actually a relic population of an extinct specie, smilodon or machairodus. From a biological standpoint, it is entirely possible for a large specie of cat to develop elongated canines. These cats might not be a prehistoric specie at all, but a new specie of large cats that found it advantageous to develop sabertooth like dentition. Whatever, the case may be, Africa in my opinion is the more likely candidate for the discovery of a type os Sabertooth cat. The sightings are much more specific in terms of location, behavior and physical description. In fact, I wouldn't be at all surprised if other species of undiscovered big cats are eventually uncovered in Africa. The sabertooth's aside, there are quiet a few stories of mysterious cats across Africa with a number of regional names, that may have escaped classification. But, make no mistake about it, these animals aren't going to be around forever; extinction cares little about your status.

MAMMOTH

There is perhaps no more romantic idea in cryptozoology than the survival of mammoths into the 20 th and 21 th century. School books will tell you that mammoths went extinct with the rest of the megafauna at the end of the last ice age, 12 000 years ago. That date has been somewhat adjusted in the last few years as mammoth fossils were found on the Siberian island of Wrangel dating to 3 700 years ago. The survival of mammoths anywhere in the world today pushes the cryptozoological boundary and is unlikely, and yet eyewitness accounts from Siberia may push the extension date considerably.

The Siberian Taiga is the largest forest in the world at almost 7 million square km, scarcely populated and very remote. Strange stories emerge from the Taiga from time to time. Stories that may seem fantastic from any other region in the world, but here seem almost expected. One such story dates all the way back to the end of the first world war in 1918. A Russian hunter came upon huge tracks that he could not identify. He decided to follow them, and deeper into the forest he went. For days he followed these large unusual tracks, until he arrived at a clearing where he could finally observe the animals responsible. He had seen elephants in pictures and that is what they looked like to him, even though he had not imagined them so big, he would later admit. He described two big white curved tusks and a dark body with long hair.

In 1893 an article from the Winnipeg Daily Free press switches location to Alaska. It concerns the Stickeen Indians and sightings of animals the article calls mastodons. Much like the Siberian story from above it involves a hunter that come across some large tracks which he decides to follow. This particular hunter followed the tracks for several miles until he comes to a very large animal with large tusks. Not much else is given on the animal's physiology, but does mention that native Americans were familiar with this beast. They are said to browse on herbs that grow only near rivers.

This story is followed three years later by another article, this time in the Portland Press. This also takes place in Alaska. The article mentions Col. C.F. Fowler and Governor Swineford of Alaska. Governor Swineford claims that there are mastodons on several high plateaus of the Alaskan interior. Fowler who works for the Alaskan Fur and Commercial Company also mentions stories of mastodons deep in the Alaskan interior. He was given tusks that appeared to be from a recent kill. Upon inquiring about the animal these belonged to; he received the description of a large mammoth like animal that was killed recently. Similar stories persisted into world war II where pilots have reported strange animals that look like mammoths or elephants over the Alaskan wilderness. I have also heard tales of pilot sightings over South America from the early to mid 1900's.

The proof for these animal's survival on the American continent into modern day isn't overwhelming. I do not expect a living mammoth to turn up in the next few years anywhere on the American continent. Perhaps the last remaining mammoths survived in Alaska until the early 1900's. In Siberia, perhaps longer. Where it gets interesting is, how much longer?

In 2002 the Discovery Channel aired a show about the possibility of Mammoth survival in Nepal in the present day. In terms of discovery I expected minimal result from the expedition featured. Still, I was quite exited to watch the show and curious as to why they picked an area of Nepal near the border with India and not Siberia. Apparently the expedition members had done their homework. They not only found two unusual specimens that they filmed, but also conducted subsequent DNA tests. These were not wholly mammoths, rather they appeared to be extremely large elephants with peculiar characteristics. Not all mammoths or mastodons were hairy. A similar comparison can be made with the rhinoceros. A wholly version of the rhino once existed, but today only the non hairy version is still around. In any case, the two animals involved, named Kansha and Raja by locals, had two pronounced domes on top of their heads and slopped back ends. Both of these peculiarities are known mammoth characteristics. But superficial similarities are not necessarily proof and DNA analysis would have to take place before any reasonable conclusion could be reached.

The DNA test result were even more surprising, as Kansha and Raja were not so closely related to mammoths, but rather closely related to stegodons. Stegodons were originally thought to have been ancestors to modern elephants and their cousins the mammoths, but now are regarded as a sister specie to both. Scientists explained the test results by modern asian elephants mating in a restrictive gene pool causing primitive genes to surface. Other more conservative scientists feel that it is more likely modern mutations brought about by inbreeding rather than actual atavistic traits. Either way, an important lesson for cryptozoology. While the survival into modern day of an extinct specie I maintain is absolutely possible, the expression of an ancient gene into a modern population is an equally valid possibility for certain criptids.

ON GIANT WINGS

The survival of Pterodactyls has always been a popular theme in Cryptozoology, but viewed with a little more skepticism than most, even among strange phenomenon aficionados. Yet, the Yucatan of Mexico, South America, Africa, and even Texas have offered us glimpses of what could be flying prehistoric survivors. As romantic as this notion may be, and indeed a good case could be made for the Kongamato in Africa; some of these other locations are more likely to feature undiscovered large bats and birds instead. In North America reports of gigantic flying creatures, fall within the realm of the Thunderbirds, and in South America most likely within the bat family; but once again in Africa the past has hardly stopped breathing.

KONGAMATO

The best case for a modern pterosaur relative is the Kongamato of the Jiundu swamp of Zambia. This animal's description do seem to match the physiology attributed to flying reptiles; it is described by locals as a long tailed lizard with bat like wings and a beak full of teeth. The wings are roughly 4 to 7 feet across and reddish brown. Most telling is that the Kongamato has no feathers, and is endowed with leathery wings. Reports also emanate, albeit with less frequency than in Zambia, from Angola, Zaire, Zimbabwe, Tanzania, Namibia and more abundantly from Mount Kenya where bigger specimens have been sighted.

In 1988 Roy Mackal of Mokele-Mbembe expedition fame, and partner James Cosi traveled to Namibia to investigate sightings of animals resembling the Kongamato. Similarity in description, but larger, seems to indicate a related specie in Namibia which lies southwest to Zambia. In fact, on this expedition Cosi witnessed a large black flying animal that match the Kongamato's description. Unfortunately, he was about a 1 000 feet away in his estimation, making any kind of identification problematic. Whatever this specie turns out to be, relative of the pterosaur or not, it appears to limit it's activity to eastern and southern Africa.

There two or three additional locations outside of Africa worth looking into when it comes to Pterodactyl like animal sightings. The Texan Mexico border, who has the largest amount of sightings on record. I'll address that area after the Thunderbird section, since there's some overlap and confusion in terms of what constitute a Thunderbird sighting versus something a little more prehistoric. A second area of reports is deep in the jungles of the Yucatan, on the opposite side of Mexico in relation to the Texan border. Somewhat ironic I suppose, considering that the meteor that caused the mass extinction of 65 million years ago probably hit the Yucatan The animal's description from that area is very much in-line with the Kongamato's appearance.

Another area of interest, albeit of a smaller variety of animal, is Papua New Guinea where the animal in question is called Ropen. Umboi island seems to be ground zero for reports of these animals, and sightings date back to the beginning of the 1900's and include natives and westerners alike. Living pterodactyl is the term used in cryptozoology; but in reality, the correct term should be pterosaur. Pterodactyls are just one sub order of pterosaurs. Between 200 to 65 million years ago, many types of pterosaurs thrived, coming in all sizes, with many different attributes.

What we are really talking about here are sightings of animals that resemble flying reptiles, ergo pterosaurs. The Ropen, the Kongamato, and the sightings from Texas and the Yucatan are all called pterodactyls for simplicity sake, and for lack of a better option. The pterodactyl did have a crest on the top of its heads which was very distinct, and is reported of the Kongamato and in Yucatan sightings.

One type of pterosaurs of particular interest here are the rhamphorhynchoids who predate the pterodactyls from an evolutionary standpoint and may have been a direct ancestor. They were smaller than the pterodactyls and had very long tails; both of these traits are reported as attributes of the Ropen. One unique aspect of the Ropen is that it appears to have the ability to glow, also called bioluminescence. This ability is of a very short duration, lasting only a few seconds. A couple of expedition, including one from the show Destination Truth have managed to capture this on film. Unfortunately, you cannot see what the animal looks like due to the darkness; but you can clearly see that something if flying and glowing for a few seconds. Wether this is related to daytime sightings of apparent pterosaurs in Papua New Guinea, meaning the same animal, remains to be seen. All I can safely say from having seen the films is that there's some type of flying animal that displays bioluminescence flying above the island.

Back to Africa, let's head north from the Kongamato's range into the land of the Olitiau. The Olitiau is often confused with the Kongamato, but in reality appears to be a completely different specie of animal. Located in Cameroon's Assumbo mountains, the Olitiau first gain notoriety when in 1932 Gerald Russell and Ivan Sanderson spotted this animal while on expedition. They were crossing a river when the animal flew right above their heads. Sanderson described it as black with a 12 foot wing span and a flattened monkey like face. While the wingspan is twice the size of any known bat and may lead the specie identification back to Pterosaurs, Sanderson felt that it was a new specie of bat nonetheless.

I have to concur with Sanderson. The flattened primate like face differentiates it from the Kongamato's long beak with teeth. The primate resembling face is representative of the megachiropteras which are members of the bat family. These are what are commonly called the fruit bats and flying foxes. The largest wing span attributed to any type of bat is about five and a half feet which makes the twelve feet described by Sanderson enormous for a bat, but on the small side for the Kongamato. Sanderson who had a B. A from Cambridge in zoology had travelled all over the world and certainly knew what a bat looked like. This is also further north and west than the traditional Kongamato's range; at least as far as we know from the limited data available.

Not to be outdone, western Java's Ahool appears to be a very similar animal. The wing span is comparable to the Olitiau in the eleven to twelve foot range with a head described as flat and monkey like. It is named the Ahool because of its vocalization. The body is of a dark gray fur, with large claws situated at the top of forearms. The eyes are very large and round, which is probably a nocturnal adaptation. Locals insist that it spends its days in caves only coming out at night in order to hunt fish. The behavior and physical description implies a bat, and provide a link with Cameroon's Olitiau. Only the size of the animal remains an obstacle in identifying the Olitiau and Ahool as bona fide bats, albeit giant ones.

Seram is another large Indonesian island with reports of another similar animal. It this case it is called the Orang Bati. The Orang Bati is described as four to five feet in height, a thin long tail, red skin with black fur mentioned in some instances. The face is described as simian. They are also described as humanoid which is altogether another issue, which I'll discuss in the Paracryptozoology chapter. There is less data available for the Orang Bati compared to the Ahool and Olitiau, and most of it less reliable. Still, due to it's proximity to Java, if this animal does exist, one would have to assume that it is of a related specie.

As such, a conservative hypothesis would include the Orang Bati as a member of the bat family, alongside the Ahool and the Olitiau. Again, see the Paracryptozoology chapter for a less conservative analysis of this creature and a discussion on the humanoid aspect as described by eyewitnesses. As a word of caution however, Jamaicans were once described as having tails by Europeans who saw them for the first time. The world of anthropology and zoology is full of exaggerations upon first descriptions. Furthermore, names and translation of names assigned to unknown specie do not necessarily reflect their zoological identity as the following story illustrates.

In the 1940's archeologist Byron de Prorok was exploring southern Ethiopia when locals told him about a cave near Lekempti called Devil's Cave. In typical horror movie fashion, they tell him about the Devil Birds said to live there and warn him not to go there. So naturally as any respectable explorer would do Prorok makes immediate plans to go to the cave. He procures himself a guide after much deliberation apparently; meaning, when enough money was offered.

What he found at the cave were bats, but with unusual properties as was explained to him by local goat herders. These bats lived on animal and human blood, attacking at night. The goat herders showed Prorok puncture wounds on their bodies suffered during those attacks. Some of the herders, they said, became so week from continual loss of blood that they died. They even took Prorok to their village to show him a dying man with blood soaked clothes, as a results of attacks from the Devil Birds. There were no doubt as to the identity of these animals for Prorok. They were clearly from the bat family, but vampire bats do not exist in Africa. There are three specie of vampire bats in the world today, and all three are known from the New World. If this story is accurate, it would indicate a new specie of vampire bat in Africa, and a very aggressive one. So, maybe the bat family has more than one surprise waiting for us in the old world.

THUNDERBIRDS

Not a subject you hear much about in mainstream media, but in October 2002 newspapers and news programs here in the United States were talking about Thunderbirds. Villagers in Togiak and Manokotak, Alaska, claimed to have seen a bird whose wingspan was at least 14 feet across. At least that was the estimate given by pilot john Bouker who along with several passengers saw the bird soar near his Cessna 207 as he was approaching Manokotak.   The media interest was cut short unfortunately, as a 7.9 earthquake hit Alaska that November. Understandably, that event took precedence with the media. I remember that time quite well; living in Southern California, you tend to pay attention to earthquake news from anywhere in the world; both with a sense of concern for the people affected and a selfish sigh of relief that it wasn't your turn.

Traditionally, Thunderbirds have been predominantly a mid-western and Eastern United States phenomenon; concentrating on the plains of the mid-west, the Ozarks in Arkansas, Appalachia and the Black Forest of Pennsylvania.   Thunderbirds are described as resembling condors, with black feathers, except around the neck area where the feathers are white. The closest physiological match with a living bird is with the Andean condor whose feather color pattern matches the Thunderbird.   The Andean condor resides in the Andes of south America usually between 7 000 and 16 000 feet in altitude. Having seen one myself at the Los Angeles zoo, they are very large and imposing with the largest wingspan of any bird of prey at up to 12 feet in some instances.

The Thunderbirds wingspan has been described as anywhere from 14 feet to a colossal 20 feet.   The largest flying bird in North America is the California condor. Smaller than its Andean counterpart, with a maximum wingspan of 10 feet across. The California condor does not have white feathers around its neck and is incapable of grasping anything heavy with its feet. The later is why the Condor is not a hunter but a carrion eater, usually feeding on already dead animals.

Much of Cryptozoology is based on the supposition of survival of officially extinct species. From an theoretical standpoint the Thunderbird is no exception, and the closest match in the fossil record is a gigantic bird called the teratorn. Teratorns went extinct around 8 000 years ago, and fossils have been found from California to Florida. The North American variety had a wingspan of up to 17 feet, while in South America, teratorn's wingspan approached 25 feet which is the largest recorded for a bird specie.

I've seen fossils of these creatures which are quite imposing. All that said, birds flying above in the sky with no frame of reference are notoriously difficult to estimate in size. Fortunately we have a number of up close sightings of thunderbirds including on the ground. We also, have several sightings of these animals flying low over highways, thus using the width of the highway for size comparison. 8 000 years is a blink of an eye in evolution. So if the teratorn did survive we would not expect drastic changes in its anatomy.

The Ozarks of Arkansas and the Black Forest of Pennsylvania supply a consistent stream of Thunderbird sightings, but in the 1970's Big Bird was king. By Big Bird, I don't mean the Sessame Street Big Bird character, of questionable sexuality, if you ask me. Rather, it was the name given to the animals responsible for Thunderbird sightings at the Texan Mexican border of that decade. The name stuck and is still used today, as sightings have continued, but with much less frequency. I received a couple of sightings myself by telephone in early 2001.

For whatever reason, everyone was seeing Thunderbirds in those days, including a number of law enforcement officials. The problem is that some of the reports were clearly of Thunderbirds, meaning giant birds with huge wingspan, while others described featherless animals resembling pterodactyls. This amalgamation of reports is a pattern that extends to the present day. In all other locations mentioned in this chapter, there are clear specie delineations in reports. Texas is different, but you already knew that.

I get uncomfortable when two mysteries overlap in one location. It reduces that location's credibility; but data is data, and so little is known about these animals. Mexico certainly has plenty of wilderness and mountain ranges to hide a pterodactyl like specie. I assume that sightings across the border occurs when these animals, for whatever reason, venture away from their usual habitat. The Thunderbird on the other hand isn't reported from Mexico, and perhaps only crosses Texas on it's migratory voyage. Personally, I'm more astounded by the fact that neither of these specie have ever been shot, or held for ransom, while vacationing in Texas or crossing the border. I mean, this is Texas and Mexico.

5

LORDS OF THE DEEP
THE GREAT SEA SERPENTS

CADDY

I like Vancouver. The over-abundance of Hockey shows on television let's you know that you've crossed the border, but it's proximity to the United States forces it to retain a certain familiarity. Vancouver lies next to the Pacific ocean, and here are sea monsters. This was the reason I found myself on a boat staring at the ocean, feeling a tinge of excitement at every disturbance in the water; but they were all just that, minor disturbances created by waves, currents and known ocean life.

The Manhousats called it Hiyitl'ki, the Comox called it Numkse lee Kwala, the Sechelts called it T'chain-ko, and modern British Columbians calls it Caddy. The first recorded eyewitness accounts of a strange animal in the waters of British Columbia originate with the early settlers. However, Native American petroglyphs of creatures resembling Caddy predate the settlers. The public first started taking notice of strange animals in these waters in the 1930's, around the same time as Scotland noticed something strange in one of their Lochs. Sightings near Vancouver have a very specific distribution; which follows the coast of British Columbia, with an influx in the Strait of Georgia and the Juan de Fuca strait off Vancouver Island.

The animal is described as between 20 to 40 feet long, a serpentine body with extraordinary flexibility in the vertical plane. A long neck and a head that resembles a horse or camel. Caddy also has a pair of both anterior and posterior flippers, and a tail that splits, like a seal. Part of this description is based on photographs of a potential specimen found in 1937. The remains which include a complete skeleton was found inside a whale.

A mane is at times described, as are whiskers, ears and fleshy horns; with the later perhaps some kind of breathing apparatus. Eyewitnesses have also described a whooshing sound coming from the animal, as well as steam ejected from the nostrils. This points towards an air breather, perhaps related to whales or seals. Primitive whales such as Zeuglodons were serpentine in form, indicating that a sea mammal can resemble primitive ocean reptiles; a case of convergent evolution. The facial structure however, as well as the possible mane, does not correspond to what we know of whales. Caddy has been heard yelling and bellowing loudly which may point towards a relationship with the seal family instead. Sighting of these animals extend from Alaska to the north and California to the south. The majority of modern sightings occur near Vancouver with northern California a distant second. To be fair, we would not expect many reports from above British Columbia through Alaska, due to a smaller human population. Occasional reports emerge from central California to the waters between Los Angeles and Catalina, but are very few in numbers and appear to have diminished in time.

CHESSIE

Chessie is the name given to sea serpent reports near Chesapeake Bay, Maryland. Very similar in reported appearance to sightings from the European side of the Atlantic, possibly indicating the same specie, sub-specie, or at the very least a relative. The mammal hypothesis is equally valid here as well, and while the genetic relationship with Caddy remains to be seen, enough similarities exist to suggest a close affinity. From a morphological standpoint sightings on the east coast pretty much follow the classic sea serpent elongated form; with some reports indicating a physiological similarity to Nessie of Loch Ness, where the animal is thicker, silent, and does not appear to possess a split tail. Wether these differences are due to actual physical attributes or due to eyewitness interpretation is unknown at this point.

Chessie as a long historical presence in these waters. In fact, sea serpent reports up and down the East Coast were common in the 1800's and early 1900's, especially in New England, with a slight resurgence in the 1970's and 1980's. That later time period aside, this specie does appear to be in decline, and has possibly moved away into deeper waters to avoid noise and pollution. Historical and modern sightings appear to be concentrated in Maryland and up and down the coast of New England.

MORGAWR

As I mentioned with sightings from Maryland and New England, the animals reported from the European side of the Atlantic vary from the traditional sea serpent form to resembling creatures described in Loch Ness and in other Lochs and lakes of the British Isles. One of the more publicized location around the UK for sea serpents sightings is Falmouth Bay in Cornwall. Called Morgawr by locals, sightings date back to the 1800's. A specimen was supposedly captured by fishermen in 1876 as well (Woodley, 2008). Morgawr made international news in 1976 due to an anonymous photograph published in the local paper. Unfortunately, the photograph is now believed to be a hoax. Sightings sporadically continue at about the same rate as across the Atlantic, but have also diminished at the same rate as in North America. I have no doubt that these animals are genetically related on both side of the Atlantic. The question is wether these animals are disappearing, or have just diminished in numbers and retreated into deeper waters and away from shipping lanes? Further questions surround the relationship between sea serpents off the coast of the British Isles and Nessie; as well as between North American sea serpents and lake monsters such as champ in Vermont, for example. This is important because, any relationship points to a specie that is equally comfortable in sea water as it is in lake water.

SOE ORM

The area of the world with the longest history and mythology of sea monsters are the waters around Norway, Sweden and Iceland. These animals were first mentioned in a historical context by Olaus Magnus in the 1500's where they were called Soe Orm. Modern reports in these waters are of the classical sea serpent form. In fact, this type of sea monster originated in Scandinavian tales. So did the giant squid incidentally, when it was known as the Kraken.

This area's proximity to the British Isles would suggest a close relationship with those animals, with perhaps larger specimens in Scandinavian waters. Sightings have unfortunately diminished here as well, although there's a lot of water and very little population in this part of the world. It is feasible that this specie has found a refuge in northern waters away from human populations. Where sighting have not diminished, and actually increased are in lakes of the region, which I'll address a little later.

MODERN REPORTS FROM ASIA AND AFRICA

Within the last ten years or so, sea monster reports have shifted from being mostly reported in the United States and Europe to various locations in Africa, and specifically in South East Asia. Most of these sightings do not reach the European or American press, partly due to a language barrier. The fact is, the waters around Africa and south east Asia have a rich history of sea monster sightings. These areas, including sightings off the coast of Africa, also have a piracy problem which has certainly limited the amount of research conducted in those areas. Sea monster research is usually more productive without Kalashnikovs up your ass.

SEA SERPENT IDENTIFICATION

From sea monsters such as Caddy to Lake monsters such as Nessie; theories to their identities is fiercely debated. Some of the more popular theories range from surviving plesiosaurs to zeuglodons, with various relatives of these two thrown in for variety sake. The plesiosaur identity is intriguing for some of the Australian sightings as will see in little while, but overall problematic. From the way these animals swim, vocalize, and from the physical description which possibly includes fur, points to a mammalian identity. I know a lot of emphasis has been placed on primitive whales such as Zeuglodons to identify modern sea and lake monster, but the truth is that these animals may just as well be a more modern specie with very unique traits. Without a tissue sample and DNA test, we're just making educated guesses.

Lake monsters have to survive and remain undiscovered in a finite environment. A difficult task, especially if the animal in question is an air breather. The ocean on the other hand, could easily conceal a mystery mammal, reptile or fish, primitive or otherwise. The giant squid, megamouth shark and the frilled shark, who is a living fossil dating back over 80 million years, are recent addition to official zoology. These animals once roamed the same cryptozoological waters that "sea monster" currently swim in.

I've always felt that the best hypothetical culprit for sea serpent report would be a long necked pinniped (seal family), and this is where Acrophoca longirostris comes in. Acrophoca, whose fossils were discovered in Chile and Peru, date from the Miocene through the Pliocene. Acrophoca longirostris looked like the seal version of a plesiosaur, elongated body with a long neck. The neck not quite as long as in plesiosaur but roughly accounting for 21 % of the animals length. These animals were related to elephant seals and Antarctic seals.

The fossils found were in the five feet in length size range, too small for the majority of sea serpent reports; but it does open up the possibility of undiscovered relatives of this specie that could account for modern sea serpent reports. Too long has cryptozoology rested on the primitive whale versus the primitive reptile debate to explain sea monsters. While I do not necessarily refute these two hypotheses, we should not rule out other options, and they are many.

THE SHARKS

JACQUES COUSTEAU

There is the Jacques Cousteau that everyone knows; the affable frenchman that introduced so many to the sea. Then, there is another side that we don't hear very much about, a man well aware of the business side of things, a less gentler side. I personally have no desire to reconcile both sides, because the part of Cousteau that interest me is the secret side. The side that Cousteau must have known, could never publicly co-exist with the other two. What are the things that he has seen that don't fit in so nicely with what we think we know about the ocean?

Perhaps Cousteau has never seen any unusual animals out there, or perhaps in those days, you didn't speak of strange things if you wanted to keep making documentaries. In my research I haven't come across much that indicate that Cousteau has seen anything out of the biological ordinary; except for one story. One story that just won't go away, one story I keep coming across.

Cousteau was in the golf of Tadjoura, of the coast of Djibouti filming sharks. In order to obtain footage, a shark cage was lowered in the water containing the carcass of a camel. The idea was to excite the sharks and film their behavior. What happened next was unexpected. The cage was mauled and destroyed by, something. The entire affair was filmed, but never showed publicly. Cousteau who saw the animal firsthand refused to release the film, and refused to talk about it. "The world is not ready for this" was a quote attributed to Cousteau. A later slightly more pragmatic reason for not showing the film, was that it was of poor quality; and Jacques Cousteau felt it could damage his reputation.

Before this story gets assign to the urban legend category, it does have a source. In fact the story emerged from two independent sources, and one of them the Djibouti military. The other source was French writer Jean Jacques Barloy, who talked about the event in a documentary on France-inter that aired in October of 1987. According to Barloy, Cousteau did indeed film a mysterious animal, but the film was also of poor quality. Furthermore, the film and subsequent written report by Cousteau was in a safety box somewhere. As for the area in question, unfortunately, the area is off limit to diving

MEGALODON

The preceding story has led to a deluge of speculation that range from prehistoric creatures to aliens and other weird stuff in between, but the most persistent rumor in regards to the Cousteau film was that a giant shark was responsible, and more specifically Megalodon. There is of course no real basis that I'm aware of for the Megalodon hypothesis, not that it ever stopped the internet. Whatever the case may be, it gives us a nice segue into a discussion on Megalodon.

Megalodon resembled modern great white sharks, only much bigger, larger, exceeding length of 50 feet, perhaps as long as 80 feet, and weighing 49 tons. Due to the fact that sharks are mostly cartilage, we have no fossilized body of this animal, and size has been estimated by fossilized teeth. We have plenty of those. Megalodon officially became extinct at the end of the Pliocene, 1.5 million years ago.

In 1928 author Zane Grey was deep fishing near Rangiroa Island in the South Pacific. Accompanied by his son and a crew from New Zealand, they spotted a shark they estimated to be between 35 and 40 feet long. The shark was yellow and green with a few random white dots or markings. It had a very large pectoral fin and a square head.

The preceding account can usually be found in cryptozoological literature discussing the survival of Megalodon into modern times. There is absolutely no doubt that there are still undiscovered species of sharks in the worlds oceans, most of them probably deep water sharks, but there is no reason at this point to necessarily point to Megalodon for the preceding sighting. On a more conservative side, the description does bring to mind the whale shark which can attain 40 feet in length. Grey acknowledges the issue and has stated that he is familiar with the whale shark, and this wasn't it.

Grey and son had another sighting off the same island, this time in 1945. Grey initially assumed the large mass to be a whale, but soon realized that he was looking at the same type of animal he spied seven years earlier. This specimen was bigger; at an estimated 40 to 50 feet in length.

There are several stories of giant sharks reaching close to 100 feet in the South pacific. The animal is referred to as "The Lord of the Deep". Many cryptozoologist equate the Lord of the Deep with Megalodon. While enticing, this is predominately based on a sighting from 1918 which depicts a very large ghost white shark. While the romantic in me almost necessitates the survival of Megalodon, I must once again bring up the fact that another specie of giant shark is an equally valid hypothesis at this point. Sharks do not fossilized very well, and thus a number of giant extinct specie could have easily escaped our attention. Furthermore, there are no biological reason why giant sharks cannot exist today. The oceans of the world are certainly big enough to hide in, and there's plenty of food. As far as Megalodon is concerned, sharks being rather primitive species, relatively unchanged in millions of years, it's survival into modern times deserves at the very least our attention. In essence, sharks are living fossils, and the survival of Megalodon, or a relative, would fit within that model.

Taking into account a certain amount of exaggeration, the possibility exists that some of these reports are of the typical great white, exceeding their known maximum size. Officially, great whites may attain a length of 20 feet at most. However, fishermen is certain locations such as South Africa speak of great whites that they have estimated at 30 feet, with a few tales of 40 footers. For your metric system lovers, thats 9 to 12 meters.

Most great white sharks that are studied and measured by science are specimens that come close to shore in order to feed on seal colonies. It is also known that the bigger specimens tend to feed further out to sea. If this pattern holds true, larger great whites approaching 30 feet would most likely feed far from shore in deep waters, on large squids, octopi and whales. It must be noted that sharks are a very primitive order, and that seals are fairly recent in evolutionary sense, thus a relatively new food source for sharks. Continuing that train of thought, more primitive sharks may prefer a more traditional diet so to speak, further out to sea and away from human eyes.

One exception to an unusual large shark close to shore, is South Africa's False Bay great white named the submarine. Sightings of this animal date back to the 1970's and is thought to be between 19 and 30 feet in length, depending on whom you talk to. That's over 40 years you say, a long time for a single specimen to be alive and thriving. Well, welcome to the weird world of sharks and a concept called negligible senescence. Negligible senescence is when an organism does not exhibit signs of aging, at least as far as can be measured. Sharks do not age, they are theoretically immortal, and keep growing until death. Nature keeps this in check by other means of death such as attack by other sharks, and by the inability to hunt due to the accumulation of injuries. So, from a biological standpoint there are no laws prohibiting 40 foot great whites or much bigger sharks, Megalodon or close relative included.

Sceptic bring up the fact that if Megalodon or another type of giant shark was alive we would see signs of attack, on whales for example. This is true, we would expect to see more signs of its presence, but then again, the ocean is a big place. The other part of that argument argues that there isn't enough of a food source to support such a large specie. This is false, and an assumption based on the 5 percent of the ocean that we have explored. Could a creature the size of Megalodon stay undetected in that 5 percent of the ocean that we have explored? Would we see the effect of such a large scale predator on the seal population, for example? Certainly, but as I've pointed out, we are not dealing with the 5 percent of the ocean that we have explored or seen from the air. We are talking about an animal that spends almost all of his time in that other 95 percent. The occasional sighting of the giant shark may just be rare occasions when one of these animals ventures, for whatever reason, into that catalogued 5 percent.

All that been said, there is a definite geographical boundary to these sightings, the southern hemisphere. So we have a pattern of where these animals might be, and my fins are always ready to go. The other 95 percent of the ocean awaits. We just need a really big cage, and a bigger boat.

MONSTERS OF THE LAKE

NESSIE

The Loch Ness monster is by far the most recognizable cryptozoological animal worldwide. Countless eyewitness accounts, pictures, films, sonar readings, and not to mention hoaxes to it's credit, Nessie is a superstar. Giant slug, eel, oarfish, log, sturgeon, plesiosaur, zeuglodon, full time hoax, have all been put forward as the real Nessie. So far, it seems not a single theory account for all the facts. What can be said with certainty is that people are seeing something and equipment is detecting something. Furthering the case for its existence, or inhibiting it, depending on how you look at it, unidentified lake creatures is by no means restricted to Loch Ness. Similar creatures have been reported in other parts of Scotland and in Ireland, Australia, Canada, South America, the United States, Sweden, Norway, China, Siberia, Turkey, Japan, Trinidad, and New Guinea. Some have and will turn out to be hoaxes and misidentification, yet among the ones deemed more probable a pattern begins to emerge. The environments and lakes are very similar, as well as certain physical aspects of the animals in question.

If Nessie, as the Loch Ness monster is known by aficionados, is a bona fide new specie or primitive survivor, it will at some point be officially discovered by science. Even then, the work will only be beginning as members of that specie from other locations around the world will also have to be validated in order to establish a geographical distribution for these animals. The question for now is how real is Nessie, and can these lochs and lakes support a breeding population of large predators?

During the last ice age much of Scotland was covered with ice. Around 10,000 years ago, when the ice melted, the area where today numerous lochs lie, including Loch Ness, was part of the ocean. Subsequently, many of the lochs which were filled with salt water became a home for sea life. Similar conditions existed in Scandinavia, Siberia and North America where other Nessie like animals are reported.

In time, the lochs became of the fresh water variety and marine life had to adapt to a fresh water environment or die. This is not an uncommon phenomenon as a number of species alive today exist in both fresh and salt water. Sharks and dolphins are prime examples of this phenomenon.

As expected, many species could not adjust to the changes in the lochs and died, while others adapted and evolved, physiologically and behaviorally. So the question is, what kind of animal are we dealing with? As you would expect there are numerous theories out there, some valid and some completely absurd. The animal would have had to be an ocean specie as we just discussed, one that could adjust and ultimately thrive in such an environment.

One of the more plausible theories, as it is with sea serpents, is that Nessie is a mammal. A couple different theories then present themselves, one is that Nessie is related to the whale family. As we briefly discussed in the sea serpent section, Zeuglodons were primitive whales who officially died out 25 million years ago. They were extremely long and serpentine, very different from modern whales. They had small heads, two fins in the front and two little vestigial hind limbs. The longest of the zeuglodons were 60 feet in length. These animals swam by vertical undulation, meaning an up and down motion as opposed to side to side for reptiles. This could explain the humps that are so frequently associated with Nessie as an expression of that up and down swimming pattern. Aside from the humps however, Nessie's locomotion pattern seems much more reminiscence of penguins and plesiosaurs, at least based on eyewitness reports and sonar readings. Here lies the problem with any attempt at zoological identification for Nessie; not all the data point to a clear and consistent identity.

Another problem with the zeuglodon identity is the long neck that Nessie appears to exhibit. The zeuglodons backbones were very flexible which is needed for a vertical undulating locomotion, and the neck vertebrae while unfused was still very short. Zeuglodons were able to move their heads side to side, but weren't able to stick their necks out the water. A trait attributed to Nessie, but in my opinion overstated. Looking back at the majority of reports, pictures and films; very few point to the traditional image of Nessie with the long neck sticking out of the water. But those descriptions due exist, especially in sightings of the animal on land near the water's edge. There's very few of those, but they do exist, and if accurate point to an animal that is an air breather and able to at the very least waddle on land, at least for a short period of time. All that said, million years of evolution can change a specie dramatically, and in that time perhaps it became advantageous for zeuglodons, or a close relative not yet known from the fossil record to inherit a longer neck.

The plesiosaur theory is seductive, but not a perfect match either. Plesiosaurs were aquatic reptiles whose last remaining specie died out at the end of the Cretaceous. Plesiosaur fossils have been found at Loch Ness, incidentally. There were basically two types of plesiosaurs, short necked and long necked. The long necked version has been used as the model for Nessie in almost all depiction's, with the short necked version never really discussed. That could be a mistake in terms of what I just stated about the actual majority of reports pertaining to Nessie's morphology. Again within the paradigm of possible pre-cretaceous reptilian survivors for Nessie, other reptilian species can just as well be considered as potential candidates.

Parts of an elasmosaur's, a long neck plesiosaur, fossilized vertebra was found in California, alongside some invertebrate fossils dating from just pass the Cretaceous. In other words, past the religiously accepted extinction date of 65 million years ago. Usually fossils, found next to one another Indicate the same time period, but do to the nature of this find the scientist went the cautious way and declared the find inconclusive. This is not the only case where we have seen this problem. A few dinosaur bones have also been found in post Cretaceous strata but again officially remain inconclusive.

Numerous traits are shared by the Loch Ness monster and the plesiosaurs. The "long neck", small head, body shape (minus the humps), fins and tail are traits descriptive to both. The tail is not often reported by eyewitness reports of Nessie, but reports do exist. The humps offer a problem as plesiosaurs did not exhibit such an adaptation; but with 65 million years of evolution, who knows. The humps may serve some evolutionary advantage; perhaps as Dr Karl Shuker has proposed, they are air sacks (Shuker 1995)

The air sack theory is an ingenious one because it would unable the animal to remain underwater for much longer periods of time. Which could be one factor contributing to the fact that Nessie does not appear to spend a whole lot time at the surface, or we would assume more sightings by the hundreds of tourist, with their I survived Loch Ness T-shirts.

The physiology of the animal brings up the next point, swimming pattern. The plesiosaurs used underwater flying much like turtles and penguins do today. This seems consistent with report of Nessie underwater. It is an extremely fast way to move about. Sonar readings in Loch Ness suggest a large animal moving very fast while chasing schools of fish. This is where the famous flipper picture of Nessie comes in. Dr Robert Rhine in 1972 had set up sonar and underwater cameras with the hope of capturing Nessie on film. At one point sonar picked up a 20 to 30 foot object moving rapidly under the boat, and the under water cameras took a picture of one of the flippers of the animal. Many still adhere to the idea that the picture shows an inanimate object, but different frames show different orientation of the flipper, indicating movement. It has a rhomboid shape which is a characteristic of plesiosaurs, and not characteristic of any known aquatic mammals or birds. Again the shape suggests an under water flying type of locomotion. Whether the picture is accurate or distorted due to enhancements may come into play. I will admit that much of the analysis, mind included, was conducted on the enhanced photograph.

Many argue that a cold blooded reptile could not survive in the cold waters of Loch Ness and that plesiosaurs were strictly marine animals to begin with. Marine animals like sharks and dolphins can adjust to fresh water; why not a reptile? A handful of plesiosaur fossils have been recovered where once there had been fresh water rivers. As for the cold blooded problem there is a phenomenon known as gigantothermy. This is a mechanism where cold blooded creatures above 2000 pounds lose body heat at an extremely low rate, thus enabling them to function like warm blooded animals.

There are some major problems with the plesiosaur hypothesis, aside from the ones already mentioned such as the humps. One is that plesiosaurs were aggressive predators, theoretically dangerous to man. Yet for the number of lakes worldwide harboring Nessie like animals, there have been very few attacks, a few accidental bumps, and a handful of unconfirmed fatal encounters. Being air breathers, you would assume that plesiosaurs wouldn't be so elusive. The reality is that, yes it is a stretch for any large animal to remain undiscovered in a lake, but we are still left with a plethora of sightings, a historical presence, and films of photographs of something large in Loch Ness and in other lakes.

The perfect identification for Nessie would be a warm blooded animal such as a mammal that resembles a plesiosaur, a case of convergent evolution. A theory that becomes more likely if you consider the sightings of Nessie on land. Unfortunately, we have no such animal in the fossil record, but we still have to consider the possibility of an unknown pinniped (seal family), as we have discussed in the sea serpent section. Bernard Heuvelmans actually felt strongly on the existence of such an animal responsible for some sea monster sightings, an argument equally valid for Lake Monsters.

I for one favor the convergent evolution model. The seas were once teeming with reptiles now extinct, and nature abhors a vacuum. As we have seen the prehistoric reptiles form and locomotion was extremely efficient. There is no biological barrier to a mammal specie taking over that spot, a specie that came in from the sea and populated several lakes around the world. I propose that it is no coincidence that animals resembling lake monsters are described from several ocean locations. Specifically, in locations, such as around Britain and the Scandinavian countries, where there are many reports of Lake monsters. The prehistoric reptiles were many and varied. Such is not the case with our hypothetical mammal plesiosaur, but perhaps some genetic diversity is expected. This could account for some sea serpents, such as Caddy in Canada and some of the North American east coast sightings. This model would propose then, a larger more elongated form in the ocean.

One last interesting aspect of Nessie's description are the two soft looking horns on top of the animal's head, that have been mentioned by several eyewitnesses. These could be a breathing apparatus that enables the animal to breath while remaining under water. The purpose being just like a skin diver whose snorkel enables him to watch the fish without worrying about lifting the head out of the water in order to breath; which would cause him to loose sight of the fish. Loch Ness is extremely dark with almost zero visibility. With this breathing apparatus on top of the head, the animal would be able to stay hidden from view, which explains all the pictures of wakes in Loch Ness suggesting a large animal just below the surface. It would also enable the animal breath while keeping tract of the lunch he is pursuing. These fleshy horns have also been reported in some sea monster sightings, in Mokele-mbembe, and in the Malaysian Ular Tedong.

LAKE MONSTERS IN SCOTLAND AND WALES

Go to Loch Morar, Lochy, Lomond, Oich or Lake Bala in Wales, I always answer the hypothetical question of where does Nessie research go next? The Scottish Lochs in the highlands have a long history of lake monsters. It would actually be much stranger if Loch Ness was the only Loch in the region with a lake monster tradition. It makes perfect sense that a specie inhabiting the ocean in this area during the ice age would be trapped in numerous Lochs, not just Loch Ness, when the Lochs became separated from the sea.

With this is mind, the second most famous lake monster in Scotland is Morag of Loch Morar. A very distant second I might add, but sightings in Loch Morar suggest an animal related to Nessie. There are also accounts of the animal at the water's edge and on shore, as there is at Loch Ness. Eyewitnesses describe the animal as having humps when swimming, about 30 feet long with flippers, small head, wide mouth, slit like eyes and a tail. The head has been reported as snake like. One eyewitness who saw the animal in clear shallow water said that it had four legs with three digits on the front legs. He was unable to clearly make out the back limbs. Other witnesses describe flippers which makes more sense for any aquatic animal.

Loch Oich is connected to Loch Ness by the river Oich, which makes it a prime candidate for the expansion of that specie. Loch Oich is also known for a strange story that locals tell. This story supposedly took place sometime in the late 1800's or early 1900's. Children were playing by the Garry river which leads directly into the Loch, when they observed on the shore a creature they described as a deformed pony. This led to the decision to see if this creature could be ridden like a pony. They approached it and the creature did not move. One of the children climbed on its back to ride this pony, when the creature suddenly plunged into the river with the child still on it's back. The child was never found.

A story whose authenticity by now cannot be ascertained, sometimes tales are just tales; but If true, the behavior of the animal is peculiar. It is definitely unlike an aggressive predator. More modern report are in line with what we known about Nessie and Morag, except that occasionally the animal is reported as having fur and a mane, a trait usually associated with sea monsters such as Caddy. A mane and fur would indicate a mammal, perhaps Heuvelmans long necked seal? In any case, the animal probably migrates from Loch Ness into Loch Oich and even further to Loch Lochy when again the description of the creature matches Loch Ness. Every fall, Salmon swim up from the sea into all three of these Lochs, which should provide research potential as any large predator in these Lochs would be active in that time period in order to feed.

On the coast, facing Ireland lies Wales, who also has an unknown creature that goes by the name of Teggie. Teggie inhabits lake Bala and seems to be of the Loch Ness variety. There isn't a whole lot of information on Teggie, due to very little research on the subject. All that's been stated in relation to the Scottish Lochs applies here as well. This is a location I would love to visit, the lake is deep but much clearer than Loch Ness, and in need of further research.

SCANDINAVIAN LAKE MONSTERS

As we have seen, the cold waters of the Norwegian sea, the North Sea and the Baltic sea are prime sea monster territory. This usually overshadows the fact that Sweden, Norway and Iceland have a few internal monsters as well. One of the more popular cryptid is the Lake Seljord animal in Norway. From a biological standpoint, this lake isn't one of the better candidates for harboring a large unknown Nessie type of animal, it isn't particularly deep and doesn't appear to support a substantial enough food source. Yet, Selma, has the creature is called, has a good track record when in comes to sightings and has some impressive video evidence to her credit.

This dichotomy is very much an issue when it comes to Lake Monsters in general. Organisms of the size reported for Selma and friends need a large and consistent food source for survival, as well as a certain population size in order to breed. This is by far the number one argument used by skeptics, and by people that piss me off by arguing that all sea serpents are oarfish. The oarfish thing is unrelated to my first point, but I just thought that I would mention it anyway. I was involved in a screaming match that almost turned to blows, while in college, over a friends equating Nessie with an oarfish.

Parthenogenesis as you recall is a biological process where females of a specie can reproduce without the need of a male. This is not as uncommon as you may think. This has been observed in certain reptiles, amphibians, and fish. Could this be an adaptive trait common to Lake Monsters? This certainly could be a factor in maintaining a small population pool, in order to maximize a reduced food source and a limited sized habitat; something to consider, for further study.

Even more impressive from a video standpoint is the Lake Storsjon animal from Sweden, where the Swedes use the PR friendly name Storsjoodjuret for their monster. The name could explain the Storsjoodjuret lack of media coverage, since no one outside of Sweden can pronounce it. In cryptozoological circles however, this is a very well known cryptid with a plethora of reported sightings.

A fairly recent video, shot underwater, shows a very thin elongated animal swimming with a noticeable head, very different from the traditional lake monster. Perhaps the video is of a juvenile? Lake Storsjon is similar to Loch Ness in that it was formed post ice age. Sightings of a large animal in the lake date back to at least the 1600's (Costello, 1974).

Iceland is famous for the culinary delicacy, and I use the term loosely, fermented shark, an excellent Handball team, elves and the Lagarfljot Worm. There's a trivia question in there somewhere. What does Handball, fermented shark, elves and the Lagarfljot Worm have in common? It's like a demented version of the riddle of the Sphinx. Personally, I've been fascinated by the Lagarfljot Worm for years. From a purely scenic standpoint, this is a perfect lake for a lake monster, dark, remote and very desolate. This is definitely lake monster, Icelandic style.

The Worm, as locals call it, is closer in description to the elongated form of the classic sea serpent, and also similar to the video taken in Lake Storsjon. The lake itself is about 25 miles long and 367 feet deep (Mcqueeney, 2012). A recent video of the Worm made worldwide headlines, but was ultimately declared an inanimate object. This had the unfortunate side effect, of everyone declaring the whole affair of the Icelandic Worm a hoax. That limited viewpoint fails to take into account the long history of sightings of the Worm dating back to the

1300's, which brings up the fact that Scandinavian waters in general show great promise in Lake Monster research.

The world has focused on Loch Ness exclusively, with so far, little scientific proof. Do not misunderstand me, research in Loch Ness is worthwhile, and there is a mystery there. The point I'm making is that data is available elsewhere, and that this specie, whatever it may be, extends outside of Scotland. We may have to discover Nessie elsewhere, before we find Nessie back in Scotland. Scandinavia is at the top of the list of potential destinations, but there are others.

AMERICAN LAKE MONSTERS

There are a few big lakes in the US with supposed monsters of their own, including the Great Lakes. The former lakes have various degree of reliability in terms of sightings and evidence, and in truth haven't been studied and investigated all that seriously. The following lake has, with a reputation rivaling Loch Ness.

Lake Champlain is 109 miles long, 11 miles wide in some parts and covering 440 square miles. It extends from Vermont and New York to the tip of Quebec, and can be as deep as 400 feet. Recorded sightings of Champ date back to the 1800's with early settlers. Appearance and behavior mirrors Nessie, at least 20 feet long, dark brownish in color, long neck, short head and the mysterious humps.

The Lake Monster scene in the United States is chaotic, too many lakes with too many stories. The truth is that many of these locations have seen the tourist money brought in at Loch Ness, and wanted in. Many of these lakes are far too small with too little of a food source to support a large breeding population of large aquatic animals. Some of these lakes that claim their version of Nessie, are actually man made lakes, but tourist are a gullible specie.

Lake Champlain is the real deal however. The evidence is just as compelling as anywhere else in the world. Others, such Lake

Iliamna in Alaska for example, where there is a long history of sightings, are clearly of very large fish. Unusually large Sturgeons, Catfish, and even sharks may be to blame for some of the sightings in several of these lakes.

Otherwise, a good case can be made for Tessie, the lake monster from Lake Tahoe. Lake Tahoe sits between California and Nevada, and is a great skiing destination. The descriptions fit the traditional Lake Monster model, and sightings have been occurring for hundreds of years. Lake Tahoe was formed during the last ice age, is very large and deep at over 1500 feet.

Otherwise, some of the best evidence outside of champ is in Lake Memphremagog which also stretches from Vermont to Quebec.

CANADIAN LAKE MONSTERS

In 1974 Mrs. Clark was leisurely swimming in Okanagan lake when she was bumped by a large animal. Scared, she swam as fast as she could to get back into her raft, that was only a few feet away. It was only then that she managed to get a good look at whatever it was that bumped her. What she saw was a hump that was about 8 feet long, and 4 feet out of the water. About 10 feet behind the hump was a tail, forked and horizontal like a whale. The creature was swimming with an up and down swimming pattern which reminded Mrs. Clark of a whale, a very skinny snake like whale.

Okanagan Lake is in British Columbia, and their creature is called Ogopogo, originally called Naitakas by native Americans. Lake Okanagan is 79 miles long, 2 miles wide and up to 800 feet deep, certainly large and deep enough to support an unknown specie. Based on hundreds of recorded sightings, several photographs and films, Ogopogo is described as up to 40 feet in length with dark green brown or black skin. Ogopogo is one of the larger reported Lake Monster, and very much fits in with the more elongated form that we discussed earlier.

Canada has over a thousand lakes, with only a few of the bigger ones with Lake Monster tradition. These lakes were formed at the end of the last ice age after the waters retreated. Which, would indicate that certain animals were trapped, and in time adjusted to life in a lake, and perhaps evolved.

SOUTH AMERICAN LAKE MONSTERS

A world away is Patagonia, South America, one of these locations that comes up repeatedly in my research into these phenomena. Of particular interest for this chapter is this whole affair with the Patagonian plesiosaur. The animals that are referred as Patagonian plesiosaurs are actually of several separate animals in South America, that may or may not be related. The Patagonian plesiosaur affair also includes sightings in rivers and lagoons of Venezuela, which for the geographically deficient is nowhere near Patagonia. Oh, what a tangled wave we cryptozoologist weave.

The first resides in a lake near an excellent skiing resort, Bariloche, Argentina. The lake in question Nahuel Huapi, has a surface of over 200 sq. miles and is about 1 500 feet deep. There are historical native legends of a large and strange animal in the lake, and modern sightings predate Loch Ness. Sightings, films and photographs are to some extent identical to Nessie and company, but with some emphasis on the elongated neck and reptilian head. The later is where Nahuelito crosses over into the plesiosaur paradigm. At least, that is half the reason, for the other half we have to go back to the early days of the 1920's.

In 1922, Dr Clementi Onelli was the director of the Buenos Aires Zoo, and living plesiosaurs were probably the last thing on his mind. That was until he received a letter from an American by the name of Martin Sheffield, who described a longed necked reptilian animal he saw in a Patagonian lake near Esquel. Onelli was immediately enthralled, after all, this was only ten years after Arthur Conan Doyles Lost World was published, and what could be more glorious then to be a real life Professor Challenger. It must said though, that most people's romantic notions of exploration fades quickly after two days in the jungle.

An earlier report form 1897 of a similar creature, this time from White Lake, also in Patagonia, further reinforced the idea of the Patagonian Plesiosaur in Onelli's mind. As a result, an expedition was launched and the term Patagonian plesiosaur was birthed. Onelli did indeed reach the lake near Esquel, but winter was setting in and the expedition had to turn back earlier than planned. They never saw the animal.

Nothing more was heard of the Patagonian Plesiosaur until 1955, and this is where Venezuela comes in. Explorer Alexander Laime was looking for diamonds at the Venezuelan mountain called Auyan-tepui. Upon over looking a river, Laime saw three odd looking animals lying on a rocky ledge. They were relatively small at three feet in length, long neck, small reptilian head and two pairs of flippers. They looked like seals with the heads of reptiles, was the way Laime would later describe them.

They were automatically linked with the Patagonian Plesiosaur, partly due to their South American connection. The long necked seal model once again come to mind, due to the fact that the animals were engaged in a very seal like occupation, sunbathing. That said, cold blooded species, such as reptiles, must also warm up in the sun. Yet again, we are lodged between the mammal and reptile hypothesis.

Another sighting at Auyan-tepui occurred in 1990, this time by a biologist named Fabian Michelangeli (Shuker, 1995.). Michelangeli briefly saw the animal go from another rocky ledge into the water. His description matched Laime's. Sightings of an animal called the Lagoon Serpent also surfaced in the mid and late 1990's, this time by explorer Marc E. W Miller. Miller saw the animal himself near the Ventuari river deep in the jungles of Venezuela.

HOLADEIRA

There are certain images in life that for one reason or another may dissipate, but never quite disappear. Such an image was this picture I saw in an issue of Fortean Times some time in the 1990's. It was taken on the Amazon, and shows the back of creature just out of the water. Everything about it says dolphin, except for the back of the creature which is serrated looking like a saw. At the time there's was very little information on this animal. Yet this picture stood out, because it was certainly a real animal.

I went on to other things, most of them in this book. The Amazon basin isn't quite the cryptozoological gold mine one would expect. There are certainly surprises there, for sure, but not to the extant offered by the Congo basin, or staying on the same continent, Patagonia or the Mato Grosso. Still. when researching tales of the Giant Anaconda in the Amazon basin, I came across the term Holadeira, the saw toothed dolphin of the amazon. Truly, one of cryptozoology's forgotten child; but immediately my brain remembered the picture.

The Holadeira is often confused with the Brazilian term Encantado. Encantado in mythology is an Amazon river dolphin that has the ability to shapeshift into a young man in order to seduce young Brazilian girls. This is usually accomplished at a dance. Dancing with an Encantado if okay, but letting him take you home isn't a particular good idea. The sociological subtext is obvious.

The link with the Holadeira is based on the association with the river dolphin, the pink dolphin of the Amazon. These animals have adapted to function in fresh water, can reach up to 8 feet in length and are immediately recognizable by their pink coloration. They have also developed a very unique adaptation for dolphins, an adaptation that is of a particular interest for this chapter. They can turn their head 90 degrees due to their unfused neck vertebrae. They also have elongated beaks, as compared to salt water dolphins. A few more million years of evolution, and perhaps we may have a long necked dolphin.

One trait that is not associated with the river dolphin is a serrated back, yet one swims among them. Another picture would surface of this animal, and fleeting fame. The later because the Holadeira would be photographed by Jeremy Wade, famed fisherman and star of the show River Monster for Animal Planet. The premise of the show is Wade traveling the world in search of the biggest and most dangerous of fish. The title is somewhat misleading as it is not a cryptozoology show per say, as the fish in question are known species such as the catfish, or sturgeon. It's a good show. As it relate to our topic, Wade came upon the Holadeira quite by accident, and identified it as a dolphin.

Case closed you say. Not so fast L'estrade; yes the Holadeira is certainly a dolphin, but some questions remain. Was it a genetic aberration, and thus only one specimen? It wasn't the result of an injury, since the "saws" are evenly spaced and very well formed. Was the photograph in Fortean times the same animal photographed by Jeremy Wade years later? If it wasn't, do we have a new type of dolphin in the Amazon river system?

SIBERIA

Lake Labynkyr is one of the most remote locations on the planet, deep into Siberian territory. Rumors of strange animals in Siberian waters have echoed for centuries. Recently though, Labynkyr has received a considerable amount of interest from Russian scientists and subsequently a certain level of crypto-zoological notoriety. In a Siberian Times article, Dr Lyudmila Emeliyanova of Moscow State University claimed that they have captured "seriously big underwater objects" on sonar. She went on to discuss how after several days on the lake her sonar reading picked up an object that was bigger than any known fish in the lake. It was definitely a singular object and alive, Emeliyanova also stated. A prior scientific expedition also recorded sonar readings of a large animal of about 21 feet.

Based on sonar evidence, the animal appears to be between 20 and 33 feet in length.

Natives of the area call the monster "The Devil", and has a rich oral tradition dating back some centuries. More recently, several fishermen had a rather unusual day on the water when their 30 foot boat was hit from underneath by, something. They never got a glimpse of that something, but it was powerful enough to lift the bow of the boat slightly out of the water. Unlike Loch Ness and North American lake monsters, these animals do not seem to break the water's surface very often, resulting in a limited visual history. As a result, we don't know if the Lake Labynkyr really fits within the Loch Ness model. This effect, certainly enhanced by it's more remote location and lack of research.

In 1953, Soviet geologist Viktor Tverdokhlebov reported a strange creature in Lake Vorota to Soviet officials. Tverdokhlebov and nine other geologists were on expedition for the East Siberian Branch of the Soviet Academy of Sciences. As remote as the area is today, in 1953 this was essentially the edge of the world. Lake Vorota is is a mere 12 miles from Labynkyr, which would indicate to me that we may be dealing with the same type of animal in both of these Siberian lakes.

The story goes that Tverdokhlebov stopped off at Labynkyr first, where he heard all the stories about the "Devil" in the lake. What he initially thought of the stories, if anything at all, is unknown. Lake monsters were probably not a high priority for the Soviet Academy of Science's scientists in 1953, and Vorota was still 12 miles away on horseback.

Once arrived at Vorota's waters, everything changes, Tverdokhlebov sees a creature he cannot identify. He described the animal at 30 to 40 feet in length with a 6 foot wide head, and with what appeared to be a dorsal fin. Another sighting from the 1960's from another group of geologists described the animal as gray, again with a dorsal fin. The fin is obviously the focus here, differentiating the Vorota beast from traditional lake monsters.

A dorsal fin, would eliminate the classic sea serpent and

plesiosaur theory right off the bat. Sturgeons, fresh water sharks and whales, primitive and otherwise immediately become possibilities. A more farfetched but tantalizing possibility are the ichtyosaurs, or modern descendants. Ichtyosaurs were marine reptiles resembling dolphins that became extinct about 90 million years ago. A perfect example of convergent evolution; if you or I were to see one swimming today, we would think dolphin. These reptiles had an elongated snout and a dorsal fin as well.

This area of Siberia contains a great number lakes and rivers and with a limited human presence, especially in the winter time. This area could support an unknown specie without great difficulty. What is interesting here is that the animals reported in both Labynkyr and Vorota are very similar to the animals reported from lake Iiamna. Lake Iiamna is in southwestern Alaska; not all that far away.

HAWKESBURY RIVER

Lastly, bringing us full circle and back to the sea is the Hawkesbury River monster, north of Sydney, Australia. Tradition of a strange animal named Mirreeulla by local aborigines date back thousands of years, and is featured in ancient cave art alongside the river. Europeans that made their way to Australia were having their own sightings as well, sightings that have continued to the present day.

The cave art combined with physical descriptions of the animal brings to mind the Patagonian plesiosaurs. The morphological similarities are inescapable. The Hawkesbury animal is larger, with two sets of flippers, a long tail, long neck and a reptilian head. Perhaps this a specie native to the southern hemisphere. Wether a relationship exist with the northern hemisphere version is unknown, but I would expect so.

Sightings far up the river have diminished through out the centuries, perhaps indicating either a reduction in numbers or an aversion to the increased human population. The added pollution which is today inevitable in all rivers, may be a contributing factor as well.

The majority of sightings within the last 50 years have focused on Broken Bay, at the confluence of the river. Broken Bay is an inlet of the Tasman sea, where a number of offshore sightings have been catalogued as well. This is clearly an ocean animals that frequents the Bay and occasionally ventures up the river. Aboriginal traditions are that the animal ventures up the river to deposit its eggs.

Behaviorally, this is a very aggressive animal, as it has been known to snatch sheep that venture to close to the water's edge. That are several unconfirmed reports of people been snatched from the side of boats, and justified or not, the animal has been blamed for several disappearances on the river. Boats have at times been hit from below with such force as to slightly lift upwards. Witnesses to these events have described a long necked animal swimming away.

These animals have also the ability to briefly come on land. We have seen this ability across several of these crea- tures, including the Patagonian plesiosaur. To my knowledge however, only Loch Ness has reports of these animals venturing further than the water's edge, and actually crossing the road. These reports involve smaller specimens, thus more nimble. Perhaps only juveniles have the ability to come on land, while adults with their bulk are unable to do so.

6

THE BEAST
PART I

Jean-Pierre Pourcher can barely hold his gun, he is so afraid. He waits at the window in the stable ready to shoot. Out there in the snow something is stirring, coming, it is so close now. Finally, the Beast is seen, because that's what it is, a beast. An animal the like Jean-Pierre and the other inhabitants of Gevaudan had ever seen. His hands still trembling he makes the sign of the cross and he shoots. The Beast falls, but gets back up immediately, shakes itself off and looks around, undaunted. So, Jean-Pierre shoots again, the Beast falls for a second time, yells and gets back up yet again, apparently unharmed. What kind of creature can this be, Jean-Pierre thinks? What kind of creature is so large, so cruel and so invulnerable?

Those were the questions asked by the people of Gevaudan between 1764 and 1767. Officially there were 230 attacks, 121 of them resulting in death (Louis, 1992). There were probably more. Gevaudan lies in central France and in the 1700's a scarcely populated area, with dense mountainous forests. The winter is cold, life is hard and the majority of the population, scattered in small villages cannot read or write. By necessity the people of Gevaudan are very knowledgeable about the local wildlife, especially the wolves; and they have always maintained that the Beast is not a wolf.

The attacks began in June of 1764, mostly directed at children and women who were out tending to the sheep and cattle. The attacks were brutal and the Beast showed tremendous strength; heads, arms, legs were ripped off and the bodies were often found half devoured. Over the course of that summer, panic and a sense of helplessness would take hold of the people of Gevaudan as organized hunts for the Beast became exercises in futility. By September of that year captain Duhamel and the Dragons (French soldiers) join the locals in the hunt, inspiring cautious hope. In February of 1765 Duhamel organizes a hunt made up of 40,000 people. It fails; it is as if the Beast knows how to avoid the Dragons. By March, Duhamel and the Dragons have still not killed the Beast and talk of werewolves and the Devil begin to surface.

Enter Martin Denneval, a man whom is said to have killed 1200 wolves. Some are hopeful that this man can finally bring deliverance, many are not. They keep repeating, the Beast is not a wolf. By April, Denneval is not so sure either, as the body of Gabrielle Pelissier is found mutilated with her head severed. Strange thing though, her clothes have been put back on, and her head back on her neck. By June of 1765 Denneval is frustrated and King Louis XV is not pleased. The news of the killings have spread across Europe, and the King does not want to be laughed at, just because he cannot kill a simple wolf.

As a definitive measure the King sends Antoine de Beauterne, his own personal «lieutenant of the hunt.» Beauterne meets up with Denneval on Saturday, June 22. The prior two days have been busy ones for the Beast; six attacks, four deaths. Curiously, after that, coinciding with the arrival of Beauterne, the Beast lies quiet until July 4 where it kills again. On August 11 the Beast attacks Marie Jeanne Valet who stabs it in the chest. It is wounded now and some think the beast dead, but Beauterne is skeptical. He is right, in September it kills again.

On September 20 the people of Gevaudan have cause to smile, rumors have it that Beauterne has killed this unholy Beast. However, doubts set in when it is found that the animal was killed in a forest 22 kilometers away, an area where the Beast had never been seen. Beauterne has indeed killed an unusually large wolf, but the autopsy found no human remains in the wolf's stomach, and the Beast had been busy of late. Marie Jeanne Valet and other eyewitnesses are brought in. The wolf has a scar on its shoulder. Everyone agreed that this is where Marie Jeanne had stabbed the Beast even though she had said that she stabbed it in the chest. Quickly, the wolf is shipped out of Gevaudan and on its way to Versailles. Beauterne continues to hunt wolves in the region, just in case, and leaves the Gevaudan on the third of November. But the killings start again in December. The king is now disinterested, to him, politically, the Beast is dead. From December 1765 to May 1767 the Beast continues its rampage.

Rumors of lycanthropy associated with a Antoine Chastel surfaces and the people are beginning to wonder whether there isn't more to this story than just this Beast. After all, some of the bodies were found naked, or with the head cleanly cut off. I cannot imagine that the Beast took the time to undress its victim before tearing them apart. A hairy dirty man had been seen in the woods often near where the Beast was active. The man is identified as Antoine Chastel, a mean man it is said, everyone is afraid off. Some think him a sorcerer. He wasn't, but he was a trainer of dogs, large reddish dogs that were said to be much meaner than wolves.

On the 16 of May 1767 Marie Denty, a twelve year old girl, is killed by the Beast. Jean Chastel, Antoine's father, had befriended this girl and her death upsets him deeply. On Friday the 19 of June he loads his gun with silver bullets and sets out to kill the Beast. On a break while reading a religious text he sees the Beast approaching. Uncharacteristically, the Beast calmly sits down and looks up at him. Calmer still, Jean Chastel takes off his glasses, puts them and the book away, raises his gun and in one shot kills the Beast.

Jean Chastel is not hailed as a hero in Gevaudan. Yes, the people are glad the Beast is dead, but they suspect the Chastels. Why is it that for years the best hunters in France had been unable to kill the Beast and Jean Chastel in one shot kills it; and the Beast waited patiently for it? Too many times had Antoine Chastel been seen near places where the Beast had killed. Something is not right here, the people think.

When the killings began Antoine Chastel was around twenty years of age. He lived alone in the forest with his dogs. He had run away from home at an early age and found himself living among the Huguenots, whom are Protestants, often at odds with the Catholics of Gevaudan. The turning point in his life was the time he spent as a prisoner in North Africa where he became a wild animal trainer. That is, until a mysterious unidentified man brought Antoine back to Gevaudan in 1763; but by then he was a different man. 9;

On January 28, 1765 a man on horseback encounters the Beast near a small village. The Beast remains calm simply looking up at the man. The man decides to try to conduct the Beast to the nearby village where he could obtain help in capturing it. Strangely, the Beast seemingly docile lets itself be guided all the way to the village. Once at the village things change, it attacks a child and escapes.

In 1766 another bizarre story emerges. The Beast attacks two young men whom are tending cattle. These two, being rather robust, manage to fight it off. The next few days it keeps coming back and play fighting with out trying to injure the two young men as if it was a game. One of the two boys Pierre Blanc, affirmed that the it had buttons on its under belly. Could this explain how the Beast had been shot on numerous occasions, but remained unhurt? Often in the history of warfare dogs were used to attack the enemy. In order to protect the animals, their trainers would dress them with a cuirass that usually covered the sides and was attached underneath the belly of the animal. This could explain why the Beast seemed impervious to shots and pitchforks. But then, someone must have put it there.

In May of 1767 a man by the name of Pailleyre wakes up at what he thinks is dawn; it is actually the middle of the night. He notices outside that a tall hairy man is bathing in the stream across from his house. This man upon noticing that he is being watched, jumps out of the stream and the next thing Pailleyre sees is the Beast running towards him. Luckily Pailleyre was able to run back inside and lock his door before he became a midnight snack. Pailleyre assumed that the man was a were-wolf, that the man became the Beast. He was asked if he recognized this man. He said yes, it was Antoine Chastel.

Antoine Chastel already had a reputation for sorcery and was hated and feared, so it is possible that Pailleyre said that he saw him because in his mind Chastel was the most likely candidate. Still, Antoine Chastel was known to frequents the forest, was a hairy man, was seen near the Beast and was a trainer of wild animals in Africa. As we have seen, the Beast at times acted as a trained animal and may have worn a cuirass, which it obviously didn't put on by itself. It had been known to attack up to five people in one day, a little much if motivated solely by hunger. And why was it so passive in front of Jean Chastel? Could it be that the Beast recognized him? Furthermore, it always seemed that the Beast was able to avoid hunters, even 40,000 of them. A fact much more easily accomplished with aid, and a hidden shelter. And what about the naked bodies and the cleanly cut heads of some of the victims? Someone was working along side the Beast. As we have seen the evidence points towards Antoine Chastel, but was he alone, or was he guided by that mysterious man whom brought him back from Africa just a year before the killings began? If not Chastel, then who served the beast?

Historians generally feel that the Beast of Gevaudan represents numerous large wolves with exaggerated dimensions due to local fear and superstition. That's great, but, it becomes somewhat obvious from the preceding evidence that the Beast was not only trained to kill, but was also accompanied by an all too human ally. Survivors of the attacks and other eyewitnesses were adamant about the fact that this animal was not a wolf. Wolves were abundant in France in the 1700's and people were accustomed to seeing them. Wolves very rarely attack men and were never this hard to kill. The latter exemplified by the fact that wolves have almost been hunted to extinction in Western Europe. The red hair of the creature also argues against the wolf hypothesis. Red hair is not typically associated with European wolves. We could deduce that the Beast was simply one of

Antoine Chastel's unidentified large red dogs. But the size of the Beast as determined by both eyewitnesses and footprints suggests an enormous animal, much bigger than a German shepherd for example. Yet the Beast's long muzzle and hairy tail are traits belonging to either wolves or middle sized dogs, such as the German shepherd. Dogs whose sizes are comparable to the beast tend to have short or medium sized muzzles and thin tails (Louis, 92). Reports mention that the Beast growled, maybe howled but never barked. While dogs can be trained not to bark, it would be unusual in all witnessed killings and attacks that a dog wouldn't even bark once.

The Beast is described as hairy, which includes the tail and feet. Large in front and thinner towards the back with a large jaw. The ears were straight like a wolf but shorter. The hair was mostly red with white on the underbelly and a black stripe on its back; perhaps due to the cuirass. The claws were non retractable thus eliminating any wild cat from consideration.

A popular theory is that the Beast was a hyena. Hyenas do reach this size, and certainly have the bite power attributed to the beast. One of the problem with the Hyena hypothesis is vocalization. The Beast was very quiet, as a trained animal can be. Hyenas have a very distinct and loud vocalization which has never been reported in any of the attacks. Otherwise, the hyena makes a relatively good suspect; it doesn't bark, it is larger in the front and thinner in the back and it has an extremely strong jaw. Chastel may have been familiar with training hyenas from his stint in Africa. A stuffed striped hyena was kept at the National Museum of Natural History in Paris between 1766 and 1819 which has led some researcher to believe that this may have been the Beast (Coleman, Clark, 1999). Unfortunately, the actual Beast wasn't shot until 1767, and never made it to Paris, having been buried on the way. Both the hyena and Chastel's red dogs make decent candidates, but not perfect ones. We do not know what specie of dogs Chastel had. The only descriptions we have is that they were large and red.

The Beast seems to represent an amalgam of wolf and dog

traits, leading to the possibility that it was a hybrid between the two. We know that such a coupling is a biological possibility. Chastel had the skills to train such an animal, and as we have already seen, wolves weren't hard to procure in France at that time. The forest was teeming with them.

The Beast had a long muzzle and did not bark perhaps because it was part wolf and wagged its tail in excitement and was trainable perhaps because it was part dog. In terms of what we know about the behavior and morphology of the Beast, the wolf-dog hybrid hypothesis may be the best match.

OTHER BEASTS IN FRANCE?

The Beast of Gevaudan is thought off as a historical footnote, an isolated incident; best left in the days where people still believed in werewolves in the forest. A valid position I myself held until just a few years ago when I started digging. To be clear, the tale of the Beast of Gevaudan as it was, is a finished story, the killing stopped and the Beast presumably dead.

While there is very little doubt in my mind that a human killer orchestrated the carnage carried on by the Beast in Gevaudan; sightings and killings perpetrated by "similar"animals, at a much smaller scale, did not end or even began in Gevaudan in the 18 th century. From 1633 to 1634, there was La bête D'Evreux, in 1783, la Bête de Brive and even as late as 1946 to 1951 with La Bête du Cazailler.

1731, in the Trucy woods near the city of Auxerre a twelve year old boy is attacked by an animal resembling a wolf. The child's mother manages to free the boy from the beast; the beast runs away, but the boy dies in the arms of his mother. These attacks would continue until 1734, when the beast goes silent. Named the Beast de L'Auxerrois, it killed 28 people, 9 of them children (Cazottes, 204). It was described as resembling a wolf, but not a wolf. A description we know so well by now. As with Gevaudan, this beast showed tremendous strength. A child was attacked in broad daylight in a village. He, the child was in the arms of his babysitter when the beast grabbed him. The child's sitter was left with a foot, as the beats carried the rest of the child away.

A strange footnote to this story occurred eighty years later in 1817 in these same woods. Two children were devoured, and numerous individuals were attacked by an animal described as a very large dog with straight ears. The attacks only lasted a few months before it all stopped. That animal was also never heard from again.

In 1796 in the region of Chateauneuf- Brinon, a wolf said to have been of "extraordinary size" kills ten people. This time, the beast is killed, but taking twenty five shots to take it down. In 1799, another beast appears, this time not far from Gevaudan in Veyreau in the forest of le Causse Noir. La Bete de Veyreau the people call it, attacks mainly children.

Ten years later, also fairly close to Gevaudan appears La Bete des Cevennes. While a case can be made that some of the Beast's described above are simply dogs or wolves, this animal is uncomfortably close to the Beast of Gevaudan. It is described as resembling a wolf, the size of a donkey, black with some red and white on its underbelly. It also possessed prominent ears, a long muzzle and a long furry tail. The number of people killed by this beast is unknown; only twenty people are listed as officially killed by the beast. In 1817, the killings stopped, and the beast never seen again. Another curious aspect of the Beast of Cevennes is that six of its victims were found decapitated.

More recently, in 1966 a strange animal is seen in the department of the Var. It was described as huge, with a long muzzle, short and pointed ears, long tail and fur ranging from reddish to black. Some sightings at very close range described the animal as like a wolf, dog or fox. This time however, the animal threatened by crawling on the ground, as one witness described it; but no one was attacked.

The latest beast compared to Gevaudan was La Bete des

Vosges which between 1977 and 1988 became responsible for the death of over 300 animals.

Between the towns of Epinal and Bresse, numerous sheep, chickens were slaughtered during that nine year period; and even horses were attacked. However, to my knowledge no human was ever attacked. Initially, the Beast of Gevaudan was very far from anyones mind as it was assumed this beast was most likely wild dogs or perhaps an escaped big cat. Nearly 30 hunts were organized involving hunters, the police and the military; all with no results. It was only then that Gevaudan was brought up, as this beast seemed also adept at avoiding men.

Most likely, all these beasts are a combination of wolves, dogs, wild cats perhaps, and possibly copycat killings. Certainly, the woods in France are unlikely to hide a new specie of uncataloged canine. Furthermore, what differentiates these other beasts from Gevaudan is the apparent lack of human help, which was certainly a factor in Gevaudan. The sole exception may lie with La Bete des Cevennes where some of the victims were found decapitated. Its proximity to Gevaudan both geographically and in time may indicate a copycat killer was involved.

THE BEAST
PART II

SHUNKA WARAK'IN

Shunka Warak'in is a North American mystery animal that from a morphological standpoint looks like a mix between a wolf and a hyena. The name Shunka Warak'in means carrying off dogs in the Ioway tribe language. Recorded sightings of this animal dates back to the 1880's when the Hunchins family were settling down in Montana.

The younger Hunchins, a zoologist, was one of the early witnesses of the strange animal. Having seen it on several occasions, he became intrigued since he couldn't match it to known local animals. He described it as resembling a hyena, with high shoulders and a downward sloping back. At some point, a specimen was shot and donated to a grocery store/museum in Henry Lake Idaho. It was mounted and photographed. The owner of the store/museum called it ringdocus. Still officially unidentified; sightings have diminished pointing to a possible decrease in population. It's range includes Idaho, Montana, Illinois, Iowa, Nebraska and Alberta Canada.

WAHEELA

The Arctic wastes of Canada's Northwest Territories and Northern Alaska are home to a mysterious giant white «wolf» called Waheela. The creature is described as about 3 to 4 feet in height at the shoulders, wide head, and a shaggy white pelt. Much like Jean-Pierre Pourcher in Gevaudan, a hunter once spotted one of these animals in the Nahanni valley of the Northwest Territories, the hunter raised his shotgun and shot the animal on its left flank. The animal apparently unharmed looked at him and calmly walked back into the forest. The hunter who by obvious necessity was familiar with wolves, was sure it wasn't a wolf. The tail was thicker, the ears smaller, and despite its height the legs shorter. According to natives and inhabitants of the Northwest Territories the Waheela, unlike the wolf, is not a pack animal, it hunts alone. The Nahanni valley is a beautiful place to visit, but it has a reputation, and it has another name. Called the Headless Valley, due to the number of human disappearances in the area, and due to a number of travelers and animals found dead with their heads apparently bitten off. The name was coined after the McLoed brothers were found with their heads missing in 1908. Mounties have expressed concern over these deaths, since wolves and bears aren't known for biting off heads.

A few hundred years ago stories of the Waheela went as far south as Michigan, but now appears to be restricted to the Canadian far North, and into Alaska. There is a minimal amount of literature on the Waheela and most assume the animal to be a just a wolf. A possibility I have to acknowledge, but the wolf is a pack animal and the Waheela a solitary hunter. In fact I am unaware of any sighting of two or more Waheelas together. A new specie perhaps, or an older one?

Several Cryptozoologists feel that we may be dealing with a relic population of bear-dogs, a specie that went extinct in North America 3 to 4 million years ago. They were actually not related to either bears or dogs, but formed their own family, the amphicyonids. They were large thick animals, with short limbs, bear like feet, and wolf like heads. It's a fairly elegant theory; but the North American landscape has been through numerous changes in the last two million years. The chances that a specie survived relatively unchanged for the last 4 or 3 million years in an environment such as North America is remote.

Bear-dogs were also thought to have been plantigrade rather than digitigrade. All members of the dog family are digitigrade which means that part of the foot bone is off the ground. Humans and bears for example are plantigrade with the entire foot on the ground when walking. This difference would show up in tracks left behind by the Waheela. To my present knowledge, Waheela tracks appear to be similar to dogs and wolves, thus possibly dissimilar to bear-dogs.

Another theory set within the prehistoric survivor paradigm is the survival of dire wolves. Were dealing with a much smaller time frame in this case, 12,000 years, which makes this theory a little more attractive. The dire wolf like the Waheela had a thick body with short legs. The dire wolf also had much stronger dentition as compared to modern wolves. The later, a necessary adaptation due to the dire wolf's prey; which consisted of ice age megafauna, much larger animals compared to today. Furthermore, these teeth were very large, with a bite strength considerably stronger than modern wolves. Can the later explain the severed heads? Perhaps, but this does not preclude the possibility that the Waheela is another type of unidentified canid with a very powerful jaw. The dire wolf was also a social pack animal. All that can safely be said about the Waheela is that it is in all likelihood from the canid family, and quite possibly related to the wolf in some manner.

THE BRAY ROAD BEAST

Elkhorn and Delavan, Wisconsin, are two small towns where not much ever happens. Bray Road, near both communities, is where the Bray Road Beast first gained national notoriety in the early 1990's. This potent dichotomy was a perfect storm for the creation of the next cryptozoological star, the Bray Road Beast. In truth, this was not a new phenomenon, sightings had been going on for decades. But, the timing was right, the internet was about to explode; and much like the Chupacabra in very different Puerto Rico, the Beast of Bray Road was about to go mainstream.

Doristine Gibson ran over the animal in her car and stopped about 50 feet from it. Angry, the creature charged and jumped on the trunk as Gibson sped away. She described the animal as wolf like, covered with brown hair and as having a huge chest. Lorianne Endrizzi saw the creature from only 6 feet away while driving to her mother around 1 A.M. She described the animal as having a long snout like a wolf, grayish brown fur, very wide chest, pointed ears and large fangs. She felt the animal to be somewhat human looking, with paws that looked like hands and back legs that were crouched as if the creature was kneeling. She observed it for about 40 seconds (Godfrey, 2012). Scott Bray is another witness who saw the creature up close, in his cow pasture. He approached it thinking that it was a strange looking dog. He described it as taller than a German Shepherd, with pointed ears, large head, dog like legs, long hairy tail, gray and black fur and a strong chest. These were some of the first stories to make headlines, but it was about to get weirder.

Some of the reports, both modern and dating back to the 1940's described a creature standing upright and able to walk bipedaly, which I'll address in the Paracryptozoology chapter. In a more realistic biological paradigm, eyewitnesses have had a hard time equating the animal with a dog or wolf, saying that it only vaguely resembled either. The creature may be too big to be a dog, and one would think that a dog would be recognizable. The only North American wolf that approaches the Bray Road Beast in size is the gray wolf; and honestly it's really not that close. Furthermore, the gray wolf is not known to frequent Wisconsin, has a narrow chest, and certainly cannot walk on its hind legs.

The publicity I suppose gave people the courage to come forward with their sightings. Sightings out of Kentucky and Michigan emerged, late night drivers, Department of Natural Resources employees, hunters and even law enforcement officers came forward with their stories. I had a hard time initially.

Even in my world this seemed farfetched, bipedal primate in the Pacific northwest, I could make a very convincing biological argument for its existence; werewolves look alike, not so much. But in this field, you cannot chose where the evidence leads; and a great majority of these sightings were of exceptional quality by reputable individuals. So, what to do? How do you eliminate the impossible, and how to you reconcile with the fact that whatever remains, however unlikely is the truth?

AL SALAAWA

Some ten years later another Beast was reported, this time in Egypt; perhaps bringing us full circle from Gevaudan and Antoine Chastel. According to the Cairo Times the Beast called Al Salaawa has attacked numerous people, especially children and killed 400 dogs. This animal is described as bigger than a dog, beige fur, a wolf like tail and a long muzzle with fangs. Al Salaawa has been active since 1996. One of the animals has been killed and described as hyena like but smaller. The size thing is contradictory, but it may be that the dead animal was an immature specimen or perhaps just an hyena or wild dog such as a jackal. Things have been quiet of late on the Al Salaawa front, but quite honestly Egypt has been rather busy with other matters of late.

THE BEAST
PART III

THE BEAST OF EXMOOR

Exmoor, Dartmoor and Bodmin Moor are small communities in Southwestern England, mostly known for foggy moors, deep forests and sheep. Exmoor has half a million sheep alone. The type of environment that can provide cover and a food source for a large predator. This isn't Africa, yet wildlife, especially sheep are been slaughtered by something large and aggressive. These moors are the home of the Hound of the Baskerville, but it doesn't take Holmes to solve this puzzle, Watson will do. The signs point to the obvious, puncture wound near the neck and claw marks across the body. Foxes are too small and badgers are too slow. Wild dogs bite the legs to take a prey down, and the teeth marks on the victims here are indicative of large cats. Not native wild cat large, but panther, puma large. Tracks and eyewitness description seem to confirm the large cat hypothesis. Once upon a time Britain was home to cave lions, leopards, cheetahs and up to the eighteenth century wolves. Today, the Scottish wild cat, which is no bigger than a domestic cat, is as wild as Great Britain supposedly gets.

Our story really began in the spring of 1810 when a mysterious predator began to leave stripped carcasses of sheep for locals to find among the fog in the morning. Night vigils by the farmers failed to produce a culprit. Superstition aside, not always easy in the early 1900's, most assumed the animal responsible was a dog of some kind; hence the original name of the beast, The Girt Dog of Enverdale. The dog identity began to be challenged when one morning a shepherd saw a strange animal among his flock. He was unable to offer up a definite identity, only saying that it was very large with gray stripes and resembling a lion. As time went on and sightings accumulated the animal metamorphosized from a dog to a large cat, and there it stayed.

Where the Picts once hid, now these cats do. In and out of folklore, these animals have persisted, especially in the south-west of England. Whatever mythological status these animals once had; it all that changed in the 1960's. There were no mistaken their zoological identity this time, they were large cats loose in Surrey. Now referred to as the Surrey Puma, the animal was described as the size of a Great Dane and either black or tan colored.

West of Surrey, in Exmoor, sightings and killings go back to the 1970's and center around Devonshire. The term, Beast of Exmoor was coined in 1983 when Eric Ley of Devonshire lost around 100 sheep to an unknown predator. Their throats were all ripped out. Then and now these animals have been described as about 8 feet in length with a broad head and small ears. They have been reported black more often than not, but sometimes tan or even gray.

Heading southeast from Exmoor you'll find Dartmoor and southwest from there Bodmin Moor. The later two seem to have a higher concentration of big cat sightings after the 1980's, compared to Exmoor. Perhaps due to all the attention in Exmoor throughout out the 1980's, some of the animals have retreated south. In any case, the physiological description is the same as in Exmoor, big, black, sometimes tan. There is no doubt that these animals are breeding and possibly increasing in numbers and increasing their range. While true that the south of England remains big cat central, today sightings occur through out the British isle.

Back in 1976, Britain passes the Wild Animal Act, which stated that any individual keeping wild cats, a popular pass time in the 1970's, had to purchase an expensive license and be able to meet certain zoological requirements. As a result, many people turned the cats loose in the wild. Are we seeing the results today of the Wild Animal Act? Have large cats reproduced and interbred in the wild, creating a hybrid specie in the process?

Another fact to consider is that Roman soldiers brought back many exotic species from their travels, including leopards from Africa. Could some of these animals released into the English woods have survived as a small breeding population. A breeding population that was suddenly increased in 1976 when the Wild Animal Act was passed?

As a result, what may be happening in Britain today is something called the bottleneck effect. In evolutionary biology, the bottleneck effect happens when a small number of a specie become isolated, creating a small gene pool. Forced to mate within this reduced gene pool, certain mutations are inevitable. Usually, mutations are negative to an organism, resulting in an inability to survive. However, on rare occasions the mutation can be beneficial and give rise to either new traits for a particular specie, or in time a new specie altogether.

The reason I bring this up, is because of a small percentage of sightings that mention a grey coat, or a spot of grey or white on the animal's throat or belly. Undoubtedly, some of these are domestic cats. People aren't always great at estimating size for animals in the wild. But, misidentification aside, this color pattern does not occur naturally in known big cats. If these turn out to be true, then it may support the idea that a bottleneck effect has occurred; giving rise to a new type of big cat, and in essence reclaiming a territory large cats once owned.

BLACK PANTHER

There is officially only one specie of big cat in the United States, which is the mountain lion. The mountain lion's range includes the west coast as far east as New Mexico and Texas, as far north as the Dakota's, with a small population in Florida. Depending on where your from, the mountain lion is also known as a panther, puma or cougar. There are officially no mountain lion population in the mid west or in the eastern United States. Yet, people keep seeing them in places such as Kansas, Louisiana, North and South Carolina and New York state, among others. There's a twist though, a great percentage of sightings are of a jet black animal, the Black Panther.

I've received through out the years a number of sightings and photographs of Black Panthers that turned out to be melanistic Bobcats. These make up about 30 % of reports that I've received personally. Bobcats are easily identified by certain physical characteristics as the tail and ears, which are different from mountain lions, but also by the size of the animal. Bobcats have very short tails and pointed ears. Adult Bobcats are true wild cats, belonging to the lynx family, but weight between 20 and 40 pounds, at the very most 50 pounds. A far cry from mountain lions who weight up to 250 pounds. Jaguars will also at times cross the border into North America, usually in Arizona; but do not constitute a breeding population, and melanistic specimens line in the jungles of South America. Taking all that into consideration, we're still left with a mystery; a large black cat with a long tail.

"Suspicious Animal Sighting" is what the sign said, in Tallman Mountain State Park, New York, as a response to a series of Black Panther sightings in 2009. Due to the amount of sightings and press this area had received that year, not to mention a Monsterquest episode, local police and various state agencies took the sightings seriously.

One of the more dramatic sightings involved Dorian Tunell and his son. They were out in the woods riding bicycles, when a large cat appeared on the trail ahead, about 25 yards away. "It was a large black panther or leopard" were the words used by Tunell.

As a response to public scrutiny, the Department of Environmental Conservation (DEC) spokeswoman Wendy Rosenbach mentioned that the DEC receives about two sightings a year of mountain lions. She went on to assume that bobcats or large dogs are responsible for these sightings. She made no mention of the DEC's official position on Black Panthers. The animals themselves have been described as slightly larger than a labrador, or German shepherd, sleek, feline in appearance with a long curved tail.

Norther California is a known mountain lion habitat, but in East Bay Hills, Castro Valley, you can add Black Panthers to the mix. Here is a report I investigated and wrote up, also in 2009.

"Lynn Reed and his wife were exiting the 580 freeway in East Bay Hills, when they spotted a large black cat, approximately the size of a mountain lion, last July 30 th at around 6:30 in the evening. Curious, the couple found a way to pull over and preceded to observe the animal for approximately 10 minutes. Lynn, a fisherman and hunter, felt that the animal appeared to be hunting. He described the cat as resembling a mountain lion, about five feet long, completely black with no markings of any kind. This is Lynn Reed's second sighting. The first took place 14 years ago in Cull Canyon, not far from East Bay Hills.

The area is a mountain lion habitat, as is many areas of California, but a large black cat is problematic for wildlife experts. There are no known specimens of melanistic mountain lions in existence and the Jaguar is not known to live this far North. The Jaguars range north of the Mexican border is a hotly debated topic. Regular spotted jaguars have been photographed in recent years in Arizona but traditionally melanistic jaguars are not typically found outside of a jungle habitat.

States that have no official mountain lion populations, are stuck in a conundrum when it comes to both Black Panther and regular mountain lion sightings. These states want to maintain the party line, but have a hard time ignoring signs of the animals, such as livestock killings. Not to mention the plethora of photographs and videos that exist, and even a few mountain lion carcasses that have been found.

Alan Peoples, chief of the wildlife division for the Oklahoma Department of Wildlife Conservation stated the following; "we know we got them, but we don't know how many". The department receives about three or four reports a month which is, in my opinion, considerable. Spokesman Jack Carson of the Oklahoma Department of Agriculture says that they investigate 100 to 150 livestock killings a year that appear to be the work of a large cat. Several mountain lions have been killed in the state through the years, but all are thought to have been transients. If a mountain lion is shot within the state, the law requires that the carcass is brought to the Wildlife Department for analysis. The livestock killing is an important point, because big cat kills have a very specific methodology. Thanks to Micha Singleton, a southern gentleman and excellent big cat researchers, I've been able to analyze photographs of livestock and even a horse that show the typical signs of a big cat kill; claw marks across the side of the animal and puncture of the throat.

It's important to understand the term Black Panther as it used in this field, as it does not point to a specific specie. Rather, it refers to any large non identified large black cat in the United States, and elsewhere in the world for that matter. These animals may turn out to be a variety of things. Some, perhaps are jaguars, whose range extends further north than previously believed. This hypothesis is a serious consideration for many of the Southern States, not so far from the Mexican border; or perhaps even true for Northern California. There's doesn't necessarily need to be an established breeding population for these sightings to take place, just a few specimen's from time to time that venture north.

Another hypothesis, while highly controversial, is the possibility of a melanistic mountain lion. Officially, the black mountain lion is an abomination in the eyes of science, it doesn't exist. It, has never been seen. That said, the gene responsible for melanism is present in mountain lion populations. I cannot overstate the importance of that fact. There is no biological barrier to a black mountain lion. This animal is not an impossibility; and how often I hear from eyewitnesses who are familiar with mountain lions that the animal observed was such an animal.

A last possibility is that we have a breeding population of another type of big cat, that only exhibit a black, or very dark coat. Here in the United States, unlike the situation in the UK, big cat sightings generally fall into two main categories; recognizable specie outside their habitual accepted range, and a large black unidentified big cat.

From the evidence it appears that certain states where mountain lions were extirpated, are making a comeback. South and North Carolina for sure, and possibly small populations in Louisiana, Kansas, Kentucky and New York State. Other states near these six just mentioned may have small populations as well, or the occasional wandering specimen. More data is needed in order to fully determined where breeding populations reside. What I do know, is that there are breeding populations of mountain lions outside their accepted range.

Within this new population, with certainly a smaller number of animals then within their official range, some mutation was inevitable. In order for these animals to remain undetected, they may have had to switch their hunting patterns slightly; perhaps from dawn and dusk to night. This may have reinforced certain mutations that became advantageous, such as melanism. Being black in this case would help the animal stay hidden from men at night, and be camouflaged while hunting prey. The later is the reason African black panthers and black jaguars in South america are mostly found in jungle environments, as it helps them stay hidden.

THE ONZA

There's one last portion of mystery related to the mountain lion that I wanted to briefly mention. The Aztec's called it Cuitlamiztli and today's resident's of Mexico's Sierra Madre Occidental range call it the Onza. They claim that it is a third big cat specie, separate from the mountain lion and the jaguar. This cat is reputed to be somewhat smaller than the average mountain lion, or at least more gracile, but more aggressive. Locals tend to avoid the Onza, fearing an attack.

Several Onza's have been killed and a handful of skulls have been studied. DNA analysis on one specimen came back as mountain lion. Pictures of the animals do show superficial differences such a more slender body and skinnier legs as compared to the mountain lion. The paws are also slightly longer with non retractable claws, like African cheetahs. Mountain lions have retractable claws. The questions remains, why the differences; and also, was the DNA study conducted on an Onza or on a regular mountain lion?

SECTION IV:
PARA-ANTHROPOLOGY

1

GIANTS

Cryptozoology usually concerns itself with undocumented animal species; the focus primarily on potential prehistoric survivors, big cats, new ocean species and large primates. The later, the more press friendly avenue of study as it includes potential hominids such as Bigfoot and the Yeti. Hominids, or the now preferred term hominins, from a strict anthropological standpoint includes man, primitive and otherwise. From a zoological standpoint, man is also part of the animal kingdom; and thus strange species of man, including mysterious pygmies, can fall within the cryptozoological paradigm.

The section on giants ventures closer to the ufological border, especially when discussing giants in ancient times, called the Nephilim. There was a UFO wave in Israel in the 1990's which included sightings of giants, as I recounted in an earlier chapter, that many linked with the Nephilim. Truth be told, the lines separating angels, aliens, gods and even ancient advanced cultures are very thin indeed. Those identities are more often than not created by the observer. Not even history escapes the observer effect.

All that stated, I wanted to keep this chapter separate from the cryptozoological and ufological sections, because as you're about to see it ventures into other arenas. Arenas that are closer in tone with this section of the book. Furthermore, this chapter is very much related to anthropology and archeology, which fit with our theme of para-anthropology and para-archeology. Here I wanted to focus on a much more obscure corner of our world, sightings of undocumented pygmies and the historical existence of giants.

PATAGONIA

The history books are quite detailed when it comes to Portuguese explorer Magellan and his travels into Patagonia. All this is thanks to Franscesco Antonio Pigafetta, Magellan's official chronicler. What the history books tend to omit, or at the very least dilute, are the tales of giants encountered by Magellan and his me. These tales are not featured in apocryphal works, or in rumored lost manuscripts, the giants are talked about and described in Pigafetta official chronicles.

This brings up a rather overlooked point about research into any ostracized phenomenon. The amount of data and facts that are actually in accepted historical works, in well respected newspapers, and in books by reputable writers and journalists is much higher than people realize. The problem is that, those parts are ignored because of the "everybody knows that it doesn't exist" attitude. Yes, it's sometimes that simple. There are sections of historical manuscripts that are taught as fact in universities the world over, while parts of the same manuscript, sometimes on the same page, are ignored because they do not fit with the version of history or reality that we already know. I've known of scientists and laboratories that refused to look at potential evidence, because they already knew that it wasn't real. This attitudes that has become so prevalent today is against everything science is supposed to stand for. Unfortunately, academia has forgotten this, and like the priests of old are more concerned with keeping the status quo than rewriting even a small portion of the history books.

Pigafetta's chronicles tells us that the giants encountered by Magellan's were clearly natives of Patagonia in all appearances, but size. While native Patagonians were small in relation to Europeans, in this case Magellan's party only reached up to the

Patagonian giants waists. In time, tales of the Patagonian giants would fade; but not before encounters with the Spanish, Dutch and English made their way back to Europe. The giants were described as between 9 and 13 feet in height, which dwarfs all known races short of the Bible's Nephilim. According to the Old Testament, and certain apocryphal works, giants were quite common in biblical times. Then, they disagreed, and wether a relationship exists between Goliath and other biblical giants and the Patagonian giants remains to be seen. If a link does exist however, it would imply a migration into the New World in pre Columbian times, even pre Viking.

John Drake, another English explorer who is more known for being Sir Francis Drake's cousin than any of his actual explorations, mentions a violent encounter he and his men had with the Patagonian giants. Unfortunately, not much more is known about that particular encounter. Thankfully, more details on the giants would emerge; thanks to the Commander of the HMS Dolphin, John Byron. Byron debarked in Patagonia in the late 1770's and described encountering giants that he called "monsters in human shape". His quotes weren't because of any deformities on the part of the giants, as they looked quite human, but due to their enormous size. He described the shortest at around 8 feet in height and the tallest at a little more than 9 feet (Whitthall, 2012).

By the mid 1800's, the giants vanished from tales brought back from explorers and settlers alike. Many thought them extinct and native Patagonian told Europeans that the giants retreated deep into the interior of the land. In the next 200 years, unproven tales of the discovery of giant human bones and skeletons, from various locations worldwide, would occasionally surface; but the giants themselves had both disappeared from history and were waiting at the same time to be discovered.

GIANTS IN NORTH AMERICA

Lovelock cave is an archeological site discovered in 1911 by David Pugh and James Hart who where there to mine bat guano. A fairly common occupation in those days, as guano was used as fertilizer. In any case, Pugh and Hart found more than just guano, as several archeological artifacts and bodies were discovered by the two men. There were nothing particularly alarming about any of the ancient artifacts found; but the bodies who were mummified, depending on whom you believe were rather unique. According to some sources, the skeletons were eight feet tall with red hair, and most unusual of all, a double row of teeth.

It's doubtful that the two men were aware that the Paiute people, who were native to the area, had legends of cannibalistic red haired giants, that were said to have once lived in the area. They called them Si-Te-Cah. Oral traditions talk of war between the giants and local Native Americans; and yes these tales were around many years before the Lovelock cave discovery.

Pugh and Hart reported their discovery to the proper authorities, and The University of California took over the find. According to the university's archeologists Mark Harrington and Llewellyn Loud, the cave was occupied around 1 000 BC. Ultimately, over 50 bodies were identified at the cave. How many of those, were said to be of unusual size is unknown.

Today, all that is left from Lovelock Cave are a few bones in a back-room at a local museum, with some of the artifacts scattered at different locations. There were pictures taken of the giants, but they've disappeared. There is one picture of a 7 foot tall mummy of a woman holding an infant still in existence; but is from a different location. That picture is actually from another find in Yosemite. The actual remains of the mummy's from Lovelock were destroyed in a fire years ago.

We know that the Lovelock Cave site was a bona fide archeological find; it's in the textbooks. What the textbooks wont say is wether giants were found among the native bodies and artifacts. It does all sound like fiction based on Native American myths, except for the fact that Lovelock Cave wasn't the only location where giants have been found; and not just in the American Southwest either, but all over the country. Not all of these so called giants, were reported as having that extra row of teeth; but all are described as in the 7 to 9 feet range and having European features. The majority of stories of skeletons found with unusual dentition are mostly from California, Nevada and Arizona. One of the more famous case was a giant with the double row of teeth unearthed in Lompoc California in 1833.

If you do your research, you'll find that there are literary dozens of reports, some from professional archeologists, in newspapers and books, of giants exceeding 8 feet in height. One interesting side note to these stories is that in many of these finds, state archeologists and scientists from the Smithsonian are mentioned has having examined the bodies. In some cases, they take the bones, and are never heard from again; or the remains are re-buried and declared Native American, preventing any one from digging them back up. This includes recent cases as well, and most of these appear to be giants with regular dentition. Is there a cover-up? I don't know, but if there is; is it only in place in order to refrain from re-writing the history books? Or, is there a much bigger story hidden? There is of course a very politically sensitive issue in regards to Native Americans, in terms of who was here doing what first. My guess, is that if there is a cover up, it's most likely a combination of all the factors above.

Bones and mummies of giants have also been discovered in Mexico, and the cover-up rumors extends across the border as well. The literature from the 1920's mentions quite a few finds of unusual large skeletons. Official archeologists from the United States and Mexico were involved in these discoveries, but there is no way to determine today if the bodies really were of bona fide giants. There is no official paper trail. There does appear to be evidence that many of these finds were officially "buried" if you will, and once again I don't think that it was necessarily the subject of giants that are so off limit.

Adding to the issues mentioned above is the problem that, academia refuses to look at any evidence of pre columbian contact in the Americas. The idea of diffusionism in the Americas borders on racism for much of the academic world. It's a ridiculous point of view. Pre-columbian contact doesn't negate any of the achievements attributed to Native Americans in North and South America. All it says, is that people met earlier that we thought. As a former anthropology student, I can tell you, do not ever mention that native American's had contacts with other cultures before Columbus. That never ends well.

As far as the southwestern giants with unusual dentition; from a biological standpoint, having two rows of teeth isn't a physiological impossibility. In fact, scientists have discovered that a particular gene inhibits the formation of additional rows of teeth; and thus two rows of teeth within the human population is extremely rare, but not unheard off. I honestly have no idea if this has any impact of the stories giants. I don't know either if there's a correlation between the turning off of this gene in certain populations, such as let's say individuals with red hair, or individual from a certain geographical location; making certain groups more likely to develop this condition. We're in a highly speculative model here, but this kind of study could certainly be of value.

Furthermore, I'm not aware of any mention of double rows of teeth in any of the Patagonian giant stories, or in any religious text. The Old Testament does mention six toes and fingers on the Nephilim. A feature I've heard mentioned on several found bodies, but nothing that i can confirm as fact. If you look through the Old Testament, giants are mentioned everywhere. The prophet Amos even goes as far as giving a specific point of origin for a race of giants in the land of Canaan (Childress, 2010). There's actually a Book of Giants that was omitted from the Old Testament, that according to various biblical scholars is actually a continuation of the Book of Enoch. The Book of Giants was discovered at Qumran, home of the Dead Sea Scrolls. While the Dead Sea Scrolls are considered canon by scholars and historians, the Book of Giants has been virtually forgotten.

Within certain physiological limits in relation to size, imposed by our planets gravity, were there giants in those days? The answer is, possibly. The evidence from North America is elusive; and the stories from the Bible and from Native American traditions are compelling, but still stories. The Patagonian Giants, on the other hand, appear to point to real events. The question is, where these bona fide giants, or just tall natives?

Is it functional for a bipedal specie to be over 9 feet in height? Were their bones thicker in order to deal with the extra weight; and feet wider and flat in order to compensate for that weight? Perhaps, the six toes, mentioned in the old testament, created more of a platform to increase balance. Without a body, I can't really answer these questions with certainty; and unfortunately, the Giants are extinct both in myth and in reality, for now.

2

STRANGE PYGMIES

ALUX

The Alux holds a semi mythological status in Central America. Tales of the little people in this region of the world originated with the Mayan's and seem most abundant in the Yucatan peninsula of Mexico. I had first heard of the Alux from my anthropological studies that took a mythological approach; and from Loren Coleman's book "Curious Encounter" that took a cryptozoological approach, and spoke of modern sightings. I was at first somewhat skeptical of their objective existence; but once you strip the subject of its mythological subtext you are left with bona fide sightings, in modern times no less. So within this duality where I apparently live most of my life, the possibility of a hidden pygmy group, perhaps extremely primitive, in the Yucatan forest and elsewhere in Central America becomes an intriguing possibility.

One of the more recent sighting of an Alux occurred in 2007 by a man named Dan Gannon. Gannon was driving with his wife and a couple of passengers, in the Yucatan, when at around 9 PM on the right side of the vehicle the headlights illuminated what appeared to be a small man about two feet in height. He estimated the height based on some weeds the man was standing next too. Half the body was initially hidden by the three feet tall weeds. What set the small man apart was that he was extremely muscular and appeared to have dark skin, but lighter than natives that work in the sun. Apparently startled, the small man moved to hide behind the weeds. The driver, a native Mayan refused to stop, fearful of the Alux.

Blurring the line with diminutive hominids similar to Bigfoot reported in various central and south American locals, the Alux is at times reported as hairy. In these cases the Alux is confused with the Duende, which is the Central American version of Bigfoot. While a considerate amount of folklore surrounds the Alux, much of it similar to faeries and elves of Europe; the little people sighted deep in the jungle appear to be free of any supernatural and mythical overtones. This is a case where one term, Alux, is used interchangeably to depict both folkloric entities and a possible anthropological mystery. Sightings of the anthropological Alux usually occur near Mayan sites or deep in the jungles. If the Alux is real, he in all likelihood represents a small pocket of a native pygmy population. The evolutionary reasons for the developments of pygmies isn't clear. What we do now is that traits associated with what constitute a pygmy is a response to certain environmental conditions, such as ones found in central Africa, southeastern Asia and possibly Central and South America.

NEGROES OF THE WATER

Remote areas of northern Argentina has a mystery pygmy that goes by the unfortunate name of Negroes of the Water. Very little has been written about this subject. You can look it up on the internet and you wont find much; a brief mention here and there maybe. As is the case with the Alux, there is some conflicting information, both on the internet and in the literature. Negroes of the Water have at times been described as hairy and resembling little Bigfoots, which complicates the issue somewhat. It seems though, that for most part, native traditions speak of a very small human that is rather fond of tobacco. A trait also associated with the Alux.

The evidence for the existence of pygmies in northern

Argentina, I'll admit, is based on a handful of reports. Anthropologists will explain to you that Negroes of the Water do not really exist, rather it is a racist term uses to denigrate certain individuals considered of lower class. This in part may be true, but still doesn't explain the actual sightings. The more reliable sightings on record describe the Negroes of the Water as non hairy with a dark red complexion, and no taller then 4 feet in height. Very primitive in culture, as they do not seem to possess any form of language.

Sightings of similar red skinned pygmies were also recorded in the American mid-west, around the Detroit area, back in the 1700's. They were called Nain Rouge by locals which is French for red dwarf. There are also stories, associated with some of the American southwestern sites, of smallish primitive people. These stories, admittedly dubious, date from the early 1900's and usually involve sightings in cave systems or tunnels. I once read a story, and I quite honestly cannot remember exactly where, about a group of explorers that were attacked by hairy pygmies while exploring a cave/tunnel system in the region.

Unfortunately, the late 1800's and early 1900's was a time where newspapers made stories up on a regular basis, in order to boost circulation. Determining what is real news, and what are tall tales from that time period, isn't always easy. Come to think of it, it isn't easy today either, as media agendas have evolved beyond the need to just sell newspapers. As far as modern pygmy sightings are concerned, a case can be made for the possibility of surviving stone age level pygmies in central and South America. Encounters, albeit from over a hundred years ago, from places like Arizona are more problematic. Stories of extensive cave and tunnel systems in the region are intriguing, but have yet to be proven as fact. Even if there were caverns and an underground system large enough to conceal a pygmy tribe, there's still the question of obtaining enough resources for survival.

All that said, there are certainly Native American traditions of little people. For example, the Hopi tribe speak of the Ant

People that live underground. But again, this leads us into the crazy world of underground lore and inner earth. As interesting as that may be, and I'll admit that the underground is a part of our planet that is very much unexplored filled with unusual organisms, river systems, and enormous cave systems; the idea of an underground intelligence remains unlikely. Still, if anyone wants to spend the money, go deep underground and check, I'm in. Oh yeah, I almost forgot; and then there's Pedro

PEDRO

In 1932, two gold prospectors were blasting in the San Pedro mountains of Wyoming, when they found a mummy. It was 14 inches tall. It was also extremely well preserved, fingernails included. The flattened head and bulging eyes indicated some kind of head trauma. X-rays confirmed this, as several of his bones were broken. Pedro also had unusually large canines. What the x-ray also revealed was that the skeleton appeared to be of a fully formed adult. There is no arguing that this was a real body; but, was this really a 14 inch adult or a deformed infant?

The initial x-rays were conducted in 1950 by Dr Henry Shapiro of the American Museum of Natural History. The body was also examined at Harvard, where the findings of the American Museum of Natural History were upheld. It was also estimated, by Dr Shapiro, that Pedro was 65 years old when he was killed. Neither institution were able to explain Pedro's size.

Thirty years later, another anthropologist named George Gill declared Pedro a native infant suffering from 9;anencephaly. Anencephaly is a rare condition in fetuses where the majority of brain and skull fail to develop. The infant usually dies shortly after birth. Infants that are born with this condition do resemble Pedro, with a large flat head and bulging eyes. I've seen a number of pictures, and there is no denying the resemblance, and Gill most certainly based his theory of Pedro on that same physical resemblance. A reasonable assumption; unfortunately,

Gill only looked at the x-rays, since the body of Pedro disappeared decades ago. Resemblance doesn't necessarily make Pedro a anencephalic infant. Some of the other traits are still in need of explanation.

The Shoshone people do have stories of little people that once inhabited Wyoming, and more specifically the San Pedro mountains. They were called the Nimerigar, and were known as very aggressive, and skilled with poison arrows. According to the Shoshone, the little people can still be found in these mountains. The Crow Nation also tell of a race on little people in the Pryor Mountains of Montana. All that said, these stories aren't necessarily tied to Pedro, even if he was found in the San Pedro mountains. We just don't know. The enencephalic infant theory versus the little people theory remains an ongoing conflict.

AUSTRALIAN PYGMIES

Back to more regular sized pygmies; there's one more area where smallish primitive people are still said to go about their primitive ways, and that's in Australia. Tales of a lost tribe of pygmies date back to European settlers, and in modern day Australia appear to focus on Queensland, and the Carrai range of New South Wells. Sightings occur deep in the bush, and describe dark skinned primitive people at a little above 4 feet in height. Some of the sightings originate from park rangers, who also occasionally find small fires and sign of occupation from unknown sources in remote areas.

Pygmies in Australia are a sensitive topic. This is a country that has had a number of racial issues in regards to the aborigines, most of it fairly recent. All, those issues aside, the truth is that unbeknownst to many people, Australia did indeed have a population of pygmies in the past, and yes some did live in Queensland.

Pygmies are generally thought of as African people, but

modern pygmy people exist outside of Africa. Genetically distant from Africans, Asian pygmies are more correctly called Negritoes, and can be found all over Southeast Asia. There is also a pygmy population near Australia in New Guinea. There's no real agreed anthropological definition of what constitute a pygmy. Some anthropologist, feel that any tribe or genetically related group whose population falls under 4 feet 11 inches are pygmies. Not everyone agrees, and as you can imagine, there's a good amount of racial and political correctness issues involved with the term pygmy. Some find it offensive, which I find kind of silly. I personally have a strong distaste for political correctness, because I firmly believe it creates more barriers then it breaks-down. All that really matters, is wether you're an asshole or your not, and that goes for pygmies as well.

3

PARACRYPTOZOOLOGY

This is about creatures on the extreme fringe of Cryptozoological studies. Lizardmen, Merfolks, Dogmen, Flying Humanoids; ones that seem unaware of their non existence. The Chupacapra certainly falls within this category; but due to the Chupacabra's association with the UFO phenomenon, I covered it within the UFO section of this book. Plus, the Chupacabra is a star in cryptozoological and paranormal research, he doesn't share his trailer with "mythical creatures".

What all these creatures do share is a new found popularity in the media of late, in the forms of documentaries, internet websites and books. As a response, I can no longer ignore them, and felt that a new designation was required; hence the term Paracryptozoology. Furthermore, popularity is always good; yes research for its own sake does have certain rewards, but I got to eat. All that said, due to certain inescapable realistic biological barriers that these creatures appear to ignore, it can be argued that these paracryptozoological creatures fall within the UFO's grand experiment as well. Possibly, but we've been warned once or twice about explaining one mystery with another. Inference on the other hand, well that's an entire different matter altogether.

While the fossil record can help explain the presence of Bigfoot, Mokele Mbembe and Nessie, here it falls silent. Admittedly, the existence of these creatures is a stretch in credulity. Yet, the eyewitness accounts come from people who in another time or place would be the eyewitnesses we as researchers site so often as validation for a bona fide UFO encounter or Bigfoot sighting. This is a problem on many levels; and I wish I could ignore them, but I can't. What is so disconcerting is that some of these guys, not all mind you, share common human attributes; such as a similar body to head ration to man, arms and legs and the ability to stand or walk on two legs.

MERMEN

During the summer of 2013 Animal Planet began running a documentary film exploring and ultimately proving the existence of Mermaids. They claim several scientists had proof and had obtained footage. The program was called "Mermaids: The Body Found", and it garnered huge ratings. As you can probably guess it was also fiction. Scientists and people of great self importance were outraged; and some people fell for it. The internet briefly exploded, and four months later, no one cared. But, the concept struck a chord for whatever reason. An unconscious vestigial memory of our gilled endowed pre-mammalian ancestors perhaps?

The show was based in part on the aquatic ape theory which states that humans went through a semi aquatic period in our evolution. Proponents of this theory base it on several traits that differentiates us from our fellow primates; less body hair, a descended larynx and subcutaneous fat. In truth, all these traits can be explained in other ways, and the aquatic ape theory is not generally endorsed by mainstream evolutionary scientists. Still, it does hold a few adepts in the hall of academia. Was is true, independently of the aquatic ape theory is that we, as a specie, do possess traits that hark back to aquatic ancestors. Traits such as webbed feet or hands, embryo with gills (non functioning however), and even perhaps the hiccup which may actually be an amphibian and lungfish trait related to the switching between breathing water and air.

As with the other members of this chapter, mermaids sit at

the threshold of Cryptozoology, and mythology. But, what are we talking about here, when we say mermaid and Mermen? As you may imagine, we are not talking about sirens or Ariel, but rather humanoid creatures reported at sea and in lakes that do not fit any known biological organism that we are aware off.

One of the most unlikely sources for reports of mysterious underwater humanoids was the former Soviet Union military. I go into much more detail within the Russian UFO chapter, but here is a quick refresher. The Soviets were training divers at Baikal Lake when at about 164 feet under the lake, they spotted what was called mysterious underwater swimmers. They were described as 10 feet in length, humanoid, and wearing what appeared to be silvery suits, but no scuba equipment. They attempted to capture the creatures, with no success. Major General Demyanko claimed that a force pushed the divers away from the creatures towards the surface. It resulted in decompression sickness with several divers losing their lives. Demyanko stated to Lt Colonel Gennady Zverez who was conducting similar training exercises in Issik Kul Lake that the "swimmers" may be present in this lake as well; and in fact elsewhere in Siberia. Identical creatures were also reported in the 1990's by a handglider D. Povaliyayev over a lake in kavgolov (Stonehill).

Anapa is a coastal town in Russia facing the Black Sea. Borovikoz was a shark fisherman in the area, who retired after a strange encounter. Borovikov claims that at a depth of about 28 feet he saw down below three white humanoid creatures swimming towards him. They were aware of his presence and came closer, with Borovikoz frozen in both astonishment and fright. They looked at him briefly before swimming away. He claims that they had huge bulging eyes and what he can best describe as fish tails.

LIZARDMAN

Sightings of Lizardmen, excluding Hopi stories, which will get to shortly, tend to occur primarily in the Midwest and Southern United States; with a particular high concentration of sightings around the Ohio River valley and South Carolina. This may be of importance, as sightings in a specific geographical area suggest a real animal and not a delusion, or member of the goblin universe. Otherwise, we would expect a random lack of pattern with no finite geographical area. Unless of course, we are staring at a form of social mass delusion tailored to very specific environments. An argument, I suppose, that could be used for any cryptozoological animal, UFO story or ghostly activity. In theory, not an impossible psychological paradigm, but yet to be proven in the real world.

Stories of Lizardmen date back to at least the late 1800's when one was allegedly captured in Tennessee in 1878. It was described as scaly and walking on two legs, which I must confess, is not much to go on. More recently, similar creatures have been spotted in the Evansville, Indiana area near the Ohio river. One of the more publicized account come from two police officers. They describe a creature running on two legs, about four feet in height with the face of a lizard or frog. In this part of the Ohio river valley the creature is called the Loveland Frogman. As a quick note, whether the creature is called Frogman or Lizardman is of little importance, since its true biological identity is yet to be determined. The names are just a visual point of reference used to somewhat categorize an unknown. If these creature are real, they will turn out to have a specific biological identity, and half man and lizard or half man and frog is probably not among them.

In South Carolina the creature is simply called Lizardman or the Lizard Man of Scape Ore Swamp. Scape Or Swamp is located in Lee County and the descriptions are similar to the Ohio river valley creature, perhaps a little taller at about six to seven feet in height with dark scaly skin. Some tracks have been found indicating three clawed toes. Some of the tracks have also proven to be fakes.

The creature gain national prominence in 1988 when 17 year old Christopher Davis came forward with his story. Davis was driving home at two in the morning on June 29 th, when he was forced to pull over due to a blown tire. He heard what he described as a thumping noise and turned around to see this creature, initially about 20 feet away, coming towards him in what he assumed to be a menacing manner. Davis who luckily was finished with his tire change got back in the car in order to flee, and the creature jumped on the roof before he got away. Scratch marks were found on the car's roof. In the next month or so, several more sightings by others led the police to take the matter seriously.

In fact, a couple weeks after Davis's sighting the police department made several plaster casts of these large three toad tracks. Not knowing what to do with them, they turned to the South Carolina Marine Resources Department. The later informed the police that the tracks were unclassifiable and "neither matched or could be mistaken for any known animal". Reports of sightings have increased the last few years, some more believable than others. It must be pointed out that, the area has economically benefited from these stories.

A similar creature has also been seen in Thetis Lake, British Columbia. Described as bipedal, scaly skin, big ears and a pointed projection on top of it's head. The last description pointing to perhaps a sagittal crest, which is an attachment on top of the skull for jaw muscles. Usually a prominent feature on large primates such as gorillas. Speculating upon a common biological identity is a fairly sizable assumption at this stage. But, paranormal and UFO theories aside, and if we assume that these creatures belong to the animal kingdom; logic would than dictate a certain biological relationship between these locations.

If not, we start heading into some very strange places, both figuratively and geographically. As such, the concept of lizard people has taken a new twist within the last 20 years or so. It is now very much associated with the UFO phenomenon, and within this paradigm lizard people are called reptilians. More crap, I'm convinced, has been written on this subject than any other; including claims of people shapeshifting into a reptilian form, and a reptilian presence under Los Angeles and New York. The internet is filled with eyewitness accounts, pictures and videos that claim to prove this. Some of the accounts are puzzling, and I've been called on some of these myself. The pictures and videos, not so much; they show nothing.

Native Americans and especially the Hopi people have many stories of the Lizard people that live underground, in certain desert locations. I've travelled to one or two of those locations personally, and yes I did see something that I truly cannot explain. But, as I've made clear in previous chapters, perception is tricky and at times even cruel.

From Quetzacoatl, to the snake in the Bible, and to the Caduceus; the reptilian archetype is a ubiquitous motif in our cultural evolution. But, it is much more than that, it also has, much like the vestigial traits associated with the Mermen concept, an evolutionary connection. We as a specie possess a reptilian brain; which in reality, speaks more in favor of evolution and a shared ancestry than a link with reptilian aliens. Our reptilian brain is the most ancient part of the brain and controls breathing and heart rate among other critical functions. It includes the cerebellum and the brain stem. This part of our brain is very similar to modern reptilian brain. It's very primitive in the sense that it also deals with basic emotions and needs, such as aggressiveness and feeding, that predates and at times override the more rational aspects of our modern brain. This is a biological fact.

What is interesting here is that both creatures described above, Mermen and Lizardmen, represent certain primitive and vestigial traits taken to a evolutionary conclusion. If I was a smarter man, I would say something grandiose such as; it's a hypothetical quantum what if.

Quetzalcoatl for the Aztecs, Kukulman for the Mayan is called the feathered serpent. The caduceus, the symbol for modern medicine, is two snakes intertwine under a pair of wings. The later may also be a representation of DNA which then represents evolution and genetics. Taking this a step further; which some may feel a little too far (the middle ground is not my friend); it also represents knowledge. And who gave knowledge to mankind and Adam? We are also introduced to a new theme her, wings and flight, which brings us to the our next topic, Flying Humanoids.

FLYING HUMANOIDS

Flying humanoids are the least localized of all the creatures in this chapter. This reflects the fact that the flying humanoid phenomenon is a sort of catch all category. It includes creatures such as Mothman, and its British counterpart Owlman, which are intrinsically tied to the UFO phenomenon. It also includes creatures that perhaps are more of a standard cryptozoology matter, where the humanoid form is more subjective. Some of these, I've already discussed briefly in the cryptozoology section, but I'll get into a little more detail here.

Out of Seram, Indonesia, comes reports of a creature called the Orang Bati. They are described as human in form, from four to five feet in height, with black wings, red skin and a long thin tail. A similar description came In 1969 from Vietnam. Three US marines witnessed a flying humanoid, apparently female at close range. The creature flew over their heads, so close that the soldiers could hear the sound of the wings flapping. They said the creature resembled a five foot naked woman with black furry skin and wings. Attached to the wings were what seemed like normal looking human hands. The three marines were adamant about what they saw, and at close range it's hard to imagine that this was a case of misidentification.

Still, the possibility exist of a contaminant in the air, leading to perhaps a hallucinatory episode. That itself is a controversial subject. There were stories, denied by the United States military, of the testing of a hallucinogen known as BZ during the Vietnam war. We know, that there was an interest in BZ and other drugs for chemical warfare usage during the Vietnam war. Agent Orange being an example of the usage of chemicals in Vietnam. Wether BZ or a derivative was ever used on U. S soldiers is another story however.

About three years before that sighting in Vietnam, the creature known as Mothman made its first appearance in Point Pleasant, West Virginia. Described as a little more animalistic and taller at around six feet in height, humanoid, with gray fur and large wings. From 1966 to 1967, Point Pleasant became the epicenter of Mothman sightings (many at close range). Numerous UFO sightings and Men in Black visitations during that time in Point Pleasant suggests, even necessitates, a direct link between these phenomena. Figuring out how that link operates, would go a long way in solving these mysteries.

Not to be outdone, in 1976 Cornwall, England introduced the Owlman, which is almost identical in description to the Mothman. Again, an area with a severe paranormal reputation and numerous UFO sightings. It is as if, during those years between 1966 and 1976, we witnessed the birth of a new archetype, the Flying Humanoid. The question is, what does it represent?

Perhaps, for the intelligence behind these event, the representation of these creatures serve as a form of non verbal communication. A message obviously we have yet to decipher. Or, maybe by observing our collective response to these event, they are learning about us as a specie. So, what is the message? Or what are they learning about us, and more importantly, why?

What it all means, remains to be seen, but flying humanoids are not exclusive to Seram, Vietnam, West Virginia and Cornwall. Washington state, for example has had sightings of a creature with the unfortunate name of Batsquatch. The name sounds ridiculous, which has resulted in very little research on the subject. Last thing most UFO researchers, cryptozoologists or

paranormal investigators want, is to be associated with something called the Batsquatch. A sentiment I fully understand, and
one I use to share on a full time basis. Quite honestly, a few
years ago I would have never released this chapter publicly. Yes,
I'm now out of the Paracryptozoology closet, and talking about
Batsquatch is the result.

On to a more realistic side of the Flying Humanoid phenomenon, where the Orang Bati from Seram is relatively free of any
paranormal or UFO related association. So is the similar Chick
Charney from Andros island in the Bahamas. It is described as
having a human like body, big eyes, three toed feet and birdlike
face minus the feathers. The evidence for these two isn't overwhelming I must say, and we are dealing with a limited amount
of data. Placing these two within a biological framework is
thus problematic. But, let's explore the possibility that they are
undiscovered species, nonetheless.

These Flying Humanoids are undoubtedly very impressive
creatures to observe. They are big and mysterious and it isn't
a stretch to see why human attributes are given to them. On
the other hand, the possibility that these creatures are related
to man may not be utterly preposterous either. In 1986 a neuro-
biologist by the name of Dr John D Pettigrew came up with
an interesting theory. He proposed that certain bats are very
closely related to primates.

As Batman likes to point out, bats aren't rodents, they belong
to the mammalian order called Chiroptera which includes the
Megachiroptera and the Microchiroptera. The Microchiropteras
are the weird looking ones with big ears, pudged noses and so
forth. The Megachiropteras are the ones we are more concerned
with here. They are more furry and their faces resemble more
traditional mammals. Pettigrew was interested in the connections of the retina to the brain of bats, and in comparing these
connections in Microchiropteras and Megachiroptera. He used
the Australian ghost bat for the former and a specie of fruit
bat for the later. What he found was that the pattern of neural
connections in the Megachiropteras differed from the Microchi-

ropteras and was very similar to primates; which prior to this was thought to be a pattern unique to primates.

Such similarities point to either a link ancestry or a case of parallel evolution where two distinct species developed over time identical traits. Both types of bats are classified as belonging to the same order, Chiroptera, because it seemed very unlikely that two different mammalian species could have evolved powered flight. It is also true that there are definite skeletal differences between Megachiroptera and Microchiroptera. Subsequent studies have also shown similarities between proteins in the blood of both Megachiropteras and primates. Not everyone agrees however, as other DNA studies show that primates and Megachiropteras aren't as closely related as Megachiropteras and Microchlropteras.

So, perhaps this can lend support to the possibility of other flying mammals existing today, and having developed the ability to fly as well. Taking this speculative model to its logical conclusion, and I'm using logical conclusion loosely here, brings up the possibility of some Flying Humanoids being undiscovered flying primates. Flying Humanoids and even Lizardmen may suggest a kind of evolutionary pattern encoded in DNA organisms. A kind of directed evolution towards the humanoid form. Perhaps it is time to realize that man's morphology isn't so special after all. A number of scientist have hypothesized that if a mass extinction hadn't occurred 65 million years ago, the dinosaurs may have evolved to be very much like us. Perhaps the human look is in, evolutionary speaking. It might just be the rule and not the exception. A side effect of higher cognitive development in the brain, both on this planet and elsewhere?

DOGMAN

A three hour car ride from Los Angeles, finds you in a completely different environment from the traditional Southern California. You'll find yourself in a small mountain town called

Big Bear with snow and skiing in the winter. This is the real reason to live in Southern California; you can ski all morning and early afternoon, make it back to surf or bodyboard in the late afternoon and still have time to go to Tito's Tacos for dinner. Big Bear was a place I would occasionally go on weekends as a child. We would often arrive after dark, take a right on a small road until we arrived at a cabin at the very end of the road; last cabin on the right.

The time between the ages of 9 and 12 is a strange one. it's when reality begins to encroach on imagination. Yes, I'm well aware that in my case reality may not have completely encroached, hence this chapter. In any case, one night at age 10 or 11 I heard howling and growling outside in the woods. I walked out to investigate and as I walked into the woods, it became louder. It was clear something was attacking something else, and I had to see it. My first thought was of Bigfoot, which in retrospect was very unlikely in that part of the country. A little voice saying Werewolf begin to creep in the back of my head, which is even more unlikely because, you know, they don't exist. Eventually the growling and howling stopped and I never found the source, which quite honestly were most likely coyotes, dogs or perhaps a mountain lion.

Years later, the Beast of Bray Road, the so called Wisconsin werewolf, made it's appearance in the cryptozoological world. Initially, I assumed a localized phenomenon from rural Wisconsin. I ignored it at first, overshadowed by other denizen's of the strange, until I started hearing stories of the Dogman in Michigan and Kentucky, among others, and the little voice was back.

I briefly discussed the Beast of Bray Road in a prior chapter from a strictly cryptozoological standpoint; and initially it appeared to be just that. Yet, something about it bothered me. For one, could an animal as big and aggressive as the Beast of Bray road truly remained hidden in a state like Wisconsin, even in remote rural areas. As I researched the subject a little further and kept tracked of seemingly the only investigator on the case, Linda Godfrey, I realized that things were escalating into another arena. Sightings were coming in of this creature taking a bipedal stance and running on two legs. Not just a handful of sightings either, but dozens from multiple states, many in broad daylight and at close range.

All the descriptions match, 6 to 7 feet tall, very muscular, covered with hair with an elongated muzzle, long ears and claws. Tracks are similar to canines, only much larger and some tracks include a heel. The later, a very important point. Dogs, wolves, coyotes are digitigrade where the heel is raised away from the ground, and thus does not show up in tracks. These type of animals walk on their toes, whereas humans and bears for example are plantigrade. We walk with the entire foot, from heel to toe flat on the ground. Plantigrade locomotion actually precedes digitigrade locomotion in mammal evolution. Digitigrade locomotion is a more modern adaptation. So, if these tracks have a heel, they weren't made by a wolf or dog. There is no getting around that. Sightings indicate that these creatures are very adept at walking bipedally, but have a tendency to get down on all fours when running. Even, in that position though, the back legs appear to be longer than the front given the creature a awkward type of quadrupedal run.

The concept of dog people, or more precisely dog headed people isn't a new one, it is called cynocephaly. Many ancient cultures had tales about such a specie; Marco Polo himself claimed to have seen dog headed people in Asia. Although, according to Greek historian George Alexandrou, this may have been a tribe in Pakistan that were known to slash their cheeks up to the ears in order to display their teeth (Alexandrou, 2010). The Greek Megasthenes claimed that dog headed people lived in India, and various Europeans writers and scholars through out the ages have mentioned tribes of dog people. Am I implying that there are a specie of dog like people hidden among us? Not necessarily, but I am following that line of questioning to see where it leads; no matter how improbable. It is after all, what Holmes would have done.

Sightings of these creatures have often been grouped with Bigfoot sightings which in some cases may just be that, Bigfoot. But, this cannot account for sightings where the creature is described as having a snout and elongated ears, neither are traits associated with Bigfoot. Bigfoot also has a very specific geographical distribution, which doesn't always coincide with Dogman sightings. So, what the hell?

A case in Texas dating back to the 1960's includes one of these creatures actually killing a thirteen year old boy, with witnesses. Sightings across North America is now in the hundreds, including one dead body from Alabama in the mid 1940's. In a little school in Crenshaw County, several students, around the age of 11, found the upper torso a strange creature in the schoolyard one morning. The legs were missing, but the torso, head, arms and hands were in good shape. According to eyewitnesses, the creature looked half human and half dog, with claws on the hands; and quite a few people saw the creature, as the body was left there for all to see for over 24 hours. The description above seem to match the description for the Dogman, and if true it does speak to the biological and not paranormal aspect of the Dogman phenomena. Even though, both concepts may not be mutually exclusive; at least in this case.

These creatures have been seen hunting, eating fish and deer, and there is even a report of one with pups crossing the road. One account that always makes it on television on various documentaries occurred to a Department of Natural Resources employee by the name of Steven Krueger in Wisconsin. krueger was picking up a deer carcass in the middle of the night, that was laid out in the middle of the road. He loaded the carcass in the back of the truck and went inside to fill out some paper work. Suddenly, the truck begin to rock violently. He looked in the back mirror and he saw a 6 to 7 foot dog or wolf like creature standing on two feet and stealing the deer carcass. Krueger who as part of his job was very familiar with all local wildlife could not identify the creature. Krueger, frighten, sped away as fast as he could, only stopping a few miles down the road.

PARA-ANTHROPOLOGY

Native Americans, such as Cherokees have traditional stories of such creatures, called Hattack Ofi. There are also sightings on record from settlers and early inhabitants of the New World. Louisiana for example has a long history of the Loup Garoux, french for werewolf. Still, I find it difficult to fully commit to the possibility of a breeding population of these creatures in the United States.

A recent sighting in Maine by a family was recently documented on television by the show Paranormal Witness. Preceding their sighting of multiple creatures outside their house, the wife and husband witnessed some strange lights in the forest. When they went to investigate the lights ceased and the source never identified. This is not isolated event, where strange lights and even UFOs preceded or follow a Dogman sighting. Any type of correlation hints at a paranormal connection.

The nature of this chapter makes it somewhat impossible to ignore the concept of werewolves; which in reality is many things grouped together, with the result being the hollywood movie version of a werewolf. That guy doesn't really exist, but makes for some great horror films. I adore werewolf movies, and none is better than "An American Werewolf in London", which ironically is portrayed more like traditional werewolves in European lore. When belief in werewolves were common in Europe, the beast was not described as bipedal and looking human at all. It was actually described as a very large wolf, often lacking a tail. The one aspect that is similar to the movie werewolf is that the werewolf was a real person during the day time.

Lycanthropy which is another term was being a werewolf is actually a psychiatric condition. Referred to as clinical lycanthropy, symptoms include the delusion of transformation into an animal, and acting out upon that delusion. Hypertrichosis, know as the werewolf syndrome is a genetic condition where the entire body, or parts of the body, is completely covered with hair; resulting in the afflicted looking very much like the hollywood werewolf. And the, there's the British Werewolf.

Remember Cannock Chase from the Spectral chapter? This is the area of Britain where sightings of Black Dogs and the British Bigfoot are so common. In that chapter I speculated that these two phenomena were related and maybe a representation of the same source through two different archetypes. Remember, you cannot always separate the observed from the observer. In any case in Cannock Chase, you can also add werewolf sightings. Similar to the Dogman sightings in America, this creature has been seen on all fours, with the ability to stand and run on two legs. Sightings go back for generations, and this version of Dogman appears to have inherited the ability to disappear quickly like the other creatures of Cannock Chase.

Outside, of the United states where the Dogman phenomenon resembles a Hollywood movie and England where the phenomenon takes a paranormal ghostly turn, there is one more location of stories of these creatures. I've personally heard some very strange stories from soldiers coming back from the middle east. None of these, that I could verify; but these stories involve disappearances and UFOs in the desert. As a result any mention of that part of the world as it relates to any subject in this book tends to catch my attention. As we have seen, the middle east is of particular interest when it comes to UFO history, but werewolves, not so much. That has now changed.

I started hearing rumors, but in this line of work you hear a lot rumors. I honestly didn't give the subject much thought, until I started to see the subject mentioned online and more importantly in books by excellent well respected authors in this field. The stories were of soldiers coming back from Iraq and Pakistan with stories of dog or wolf like people that lived in remote areas. They were instructed not to engage these creatures, as presumably the military was, one unsure of how to proceed in this regard, and two, were more preoccupied with the war. Stories that pertains to various strange phenomena and a chance encounters with various branches of the United State military or foreign military are usually impossible to verify. Wars tend to breed a very specific type of paranoia, where stories of top secret encounter with aliens and monsters serve a very real sociological function. A type of urban legend syndrome if you will. All that being said, top secret operations in exotic and remote parts of the world may indeed lead to chance encounters with unusual things, since unusual things are still more likely to be found in remote places.

4

ZOMBI

The wind tunnel is what we called it. It wasn't a long walk, but in Chicago in the middle of winter, anywhere is a long walk. As I left the dorms and turned the corner, there was no avoiding it; and it was windy that day. I was on my way to meet my Anthropology professor. I was just approved for an independent study of a subject of my own choosing, as long as it fell under the Anthropology paradigm. I knew precisely what I wanted to study; hoping that It would turn into field work. In retrospect, that may have been slightly over optimistic since it would involve going to Haiti. Twenty years later, and I'm still trying to go to Haiti. It's one of those places that calls, unquantifiable, but there.

I liked the Anthropology department; they were always more accommodating than the Psychology department, my other avenue of study. To be fair though, I did test the limit of the Psychology department with some of my paper topics. If you're reading this book, you can probably imagine; or check the Parapsychology section and understand the source of their discontent.

Back on that cold winter day, I arrived at the Anthropology building and navigated the narrow corridors until I reached my professors office. The door was open and I went right in. We had always gotten along very well. He was also from California, but from Northern California, which quite honestly is like another state. He was from the University of California at Berkeley, and played the part well. Still, we had a state in common and an interest in hominids and human evolution. The later is what he expected me to choose, a project based on primate or human evolution or anything along those lines. So what do you want to study? Zombis I said. He looked at me briefly and said Ok.

As it turned out he was familiar with the subject. By the subject, I don't mean the walking dead as portrayed in movies. Rather, medically verifiable individuals in Haiti whom had been pronounced dead and buried; and subsequently turned up alive some years later. A rare phenomena, even by voodoo standards, but it is real. There was nothing supernatural about it, a drug was the culprit; the quixotic Zombi powder.

CLAIRVIUS NARCISSE

The Albert Schweitzer Hospital In Deschapelles is an American institution in the Artibonite Valley of West Central Haiti. Founded in 1956 its doors are still opened today. On the 30 th of April 1962 at precisely 9:45 PM a man walked in spitting blood. For the next two days he would suffer hypothermia, paresthesis, cyanosis, hypertension, loss of weight and a difficulty in breathing; all from an unknown source. At 1:15 PM on May 2, Clairvius Narcisse would be declared dead, and in the morning of May 3 Narcisse was buried in his native village of L'Estere. Angelina Narcisse was the last person to see her brother alive, as she was present at the hospital when he died. Angelina Narcisse would also be the first person to see Clairvius alive eighteen years later.

A regular at the L'ester marketplace Angelina was shopping when a man approached her and introducing himself by a nickname they had used as children. The man was Clairvius Narcisse. He would later tell his full story, claiming that he had been made a Zombi because of a land dispute with his brother, when Clairvius had refused to share inherited land.

It is said in Haiti that the country is one hundred percent catholic and one hundred and ten percent voodoo. Haiti is land of dichotomy and contradictions. That one hundred and ten percent follows certain protocols set by the Bizango society, the real power in rural Haiti. A secret society that isn't particularly that secret.

Voodoo and the society are not inherently evil, that's a misconception. Voodoo is a powerful force; but a force in itself is directionless. It is only when applied to a goal that it may become good or evil. To some extent, this philosophy is offered as well by Carlos Casteneda in his books about sorcery among the Yaqui Indians. Another interesting parallel between both cultures is that both the Yaqui and Haitians were victorious against foreign invaders; the Yaqui in 1608 versus the Spanish, and the Haitian in 1804 against the French.

Narcisse's brother sold to a Bokor who made him into a Zombi. A Bokor is a sorcerer in Haiti, and the only one who knows the secret of Zombification. At this point it would be wise to forget all that you know about Zombis from television and the movies. The reality is that the fear is not of Zombis, but the fear is of becoming one. In rural Haiti, Zombification serves as a punishment, a death penalty if you will, courtesy of the Bizango Society.

Obviously, not all transgressions lead to Zombification. There are various punishments set by the Bizango society, but the more serious offenses can lead to Zombification. These are, material advancement at the expense of others and lack of respect towards fellow Haitians. Taking another man's woman, causing harm to one's family, defaming the Bizango society and cheating in regard to land issues are all considered serious offenses (Davis, 1985). Clairvius Narcisse had at one time or another committed many of these crimes; he had a reputation for being greedy, had refused to share his land with his brother, and had refused to help his family out financially on several occasion. To add to his growing shaky reputation, he had fathered children with a number of women and had refused to take responsibility, financial or otherwise. On the Bizango's ten most wanted for Zombification list, Clairvius Narcisse was at the top of the list.

As I alluded briefly, the official religion of Haiti is Catholicism. This is what the outside world sees of Haiti. On the inside, it is a country run by much older traditions. Voodoo is a religion, and like all religions it serves a dual purpose; a religious one and a political purpose. Zombification and thus the Bizango society expresses this model quite well. The act of becoming a Zombi is equivalent to the death penalty, and the fear of such a fate is a form of social control.

Narcisse, was aware of being declared dead; completely paralyzed and unable to do anything about it. He was also aware of being buried and the nail that pierced his skin as it went through the cheap wood of the coffin. The scar still visible 18 years later. He remained in that coffin, buried for 72 hours; and then he was taken out, taken away to work at a plantation. This is standard protocol apparently. Zombis are used as slave labor as a way to repay society with the production of goods. In Narcisse's case he escaped when the plantation's owner died.

The case was investigated by the family, the BBC and head of the Centre de Psychiatrie et Neurologie in Port-au-Prince, lamarque Douyon. It was declared a legitimate case of Zombification by all involved. Narcisse wasn't the first or last individual case of Zombification; but before Narcisse, it wasn't taken seriously outside of Haiti. I was told personally of a case that took place in the 1960's where an american while in the military found himself in Haiti visiting a plantation. The plantation owner had a number of individuals working for him that seemed to be in a strange stupor like state. He called them Zombis.

In fact it wasn't until Harvard ethnobiologist Wade Davis came back from Haiti with samples of the Zombi powder, that scientists were even aware of the concept of Zombification. Davis wrote a book entitled "The Serpent and the Rainbow" and in detail explained that Zombis were not the living dead, but rather under the influence of a drug. What remains a mystery is how the inflected remain in that Zombi state for years, and what occurs from a physiological standpoint when they "snap out" of it. What triggers the later?

ZOMBI POWDER

Paresthesia (tingling sensation of the skin), cyanosis (oxygen deficiency in the blood leading to a bluish tint to the skin), respiratory failure, uremia (toxins in the blood), vomiting, general weakness, complete paralysis while remaining conscious are all symptoms associated with Zombification. All these symptoms were experienced by Clairvius Narcisse and others before their "deaths". Narcisse also complained that his skin felt like it was on fire.

Studies on the Zombi powder indicated that the ingredient responsible for the majority of the conditions listed above is tetrodotoxin, or TTX for short.

The drug tetrodotoxin comes from the following marine species; Crapaud du mer (Sphoeroides testudineus), the poisson fufu (Diodon hystrix), and the bilan (Diodon holacanthus). All three of these are species are pufferfish. Tetrodotoxin is found in the intestines, ovaries, testicles, liver and in the skin of these animals. Pure tetrodotoxin is 160,000 times more effective in axonal blockage than cocaine. It is also 1 000 times more potent than sodium cyanide. Half a milligram is all that is needed to kill a grown man. Used in proper dosage the drug causes complete neuro-muscular paralysis.

Axons relay nerve impulses between the central nervous system and neuromuscular junctions. The relay or inhibition of these impulses depend on the concentration of sodium and potassium ions inside and outside the axon. Most drugs make an axon equally permeable to both, resulting in the inhibition of nerve impulses. Tetrodotoxin doesn't affect the flow of both sodium and potassium, instead it inhibits the flow of sodium alone. The result is complete neuromuscular paralysis.

Case studies of Tetrodotoxin poisoning reveal identical symptoms to the effect of the Zombi powder. These symptoms include nausea, vomiting, paresthesia, hypersalivation, extreme sweating, weakness, headache, pulmonary edema, cyanosis, dilation of the pupils and hypothermia. Individuals affected by the Zombi powder claim that they remain conscious through out the entire episode. Again, case studies in tetrodotoxin poisoning confirms this fact. The victims retain complete awareness but otherwise show no signs of life. Tetrodotoxin is topically active meaning that just handling the toxin can induce some of these symptoms.

VOODOO DEATH

It was assumed by Davis that a another drug was administered to the Zombi upon "resurrection". I've thought about this at length and discussed it with my professor back in school; and I have to agree. Yet the drug has never been identified. There are several reason for this. For one, there has been a serious lack of interest, and thus funding in regards to the Zombi phenomena. Even with the successful acquisition of the Zombi powder by Davis; academia still retains a very skeptical view of the phenomena. It's association with Voodoo, certainly does not help matters. The only on location investigations that I'm aware off within the last twenty years have been from free lance writers and various film crews. Those were much more interested in Voodoo and the sensational then the pharmacological aspect of Zombification. Furthermore, none of these later investigations have produced a Zombi.

One thing that is immeasurably important here is the close relationship between the science in regard to the powder and the Voodoo phenomena. This is the main reason I wanted to include this subject in this book; and why this subject is an important model for research in other borderline areas. Both aspects are not mutually exclusive, here and elsewhere. To Haitians, the source of a Bokors power is both a knowledge of the ingredients necessary for the preparation of the powder, but also the supernatural. They are two sides of the same coin. You may split the coin in half, but then you don't have a real coin anymore; it becomes worthless.

Tetradotoxin is without doubt responsible for the onset of zombification; but in theory the afflicted should come out of its spell once he or she is unburied, or shortly thereafter. Yet Zombis remain in their state for an undetermined amount of time, which can be years or decades. Lore has it that the death of a Zombis master, usually the plantation owner, results in the Zombi regaining its "human" faculties More than superstition, this may point to the existence of another drug, a maintenance drug. Once a Zombi's owner dies, and no one continues to administer the maintenance drug, the afflicted simply snaps out of it.

Last but not least is the phenomenon of voodoo death. Voodoo death is a term common in Anthropology and points to the power of cultural expectations. Contrary to popular belief the origin of the term has no relationship to actual Voodoo.

It originated in cultures where a witch doctor, or sorcerer, plays a very important social role. In these cultures it has been observed that in certain cases where the witch doctor points to an individual and declares him dead in an hour, that individual dies. This is of course is an extreme rare example, and the concept can be applied to less severe declarations by the witch doctor. The point is not the witch doctor's supernatural power, but the social expectations and "knowledge" of what is about to occur. Its self fulfilling prophecy in its purest form.

This may seem strange to us, but to cultures who believe in the powers of their witch doctor or sorcerer, the results are inevitable. Haitians believe in the power of the Zombi powder, they know what it's like to become a Zombi; so perhaps what we have here, at least in part, is a sociological placebo effect. Still, for the most part, personally I'm going to go with the drug thing.

5

LOST

PART I

LOST RACES

MYSTERIES IN THE DESERT

On April 5 1909 the Phoenix Gazette ran a front page story involving the discovery of what they called an Egyptian cavern city in the Grand Canyon. The man who made the discovery was a G.E. Kinkaid, an explorer for the Smithsonian. As a result, the investigation and exploration of the site was conducted by the Smithsonian Institute and led by S. A Jordan.

Kinkaid found the site while traveling on the Colorado river, about 42 miles downstream from the El Tovar crystal canyon.

The "cave" as he called it was built in the side of the rocks, and extends at least one mile downwards. Kinkaid's solo exploration and Jordan's team of archeologists gave this account of the interior. "There are numerous passageways leading to hundreds of rooms. Rooms were ventilated by holes on the side that led to corridors. Numerous artifacts such as weapons have been found. Certain idols have been found that do not appear to resemble known Egyptian deities". What was described as a large hall was located about 100 feet from the entrance, where an idol was found seated cross legged holding flowers in each hand. Kinkaid felt that it looked Asian. Pottery, various metal instruments, seeds and tablets with hieroglyphics were also found.

Hieroglyphics regularly appeared on urns, tablets and doorways. There is no mention of a translation for the hieroglyphics in the original article or in subsequent sources. This leaves the Egyptian hypothesis uncertain, but Kinkaid did mention that he felt that they looked Egyptian. Pictorial writings were also found. There were two animals depicted in the writing; one is mentioned as a prehistoric animal and the other is not identified. This is unfortunate, because if a non local animal was depicted, it may have given us a clue as the origin of the culture that once lived here and thus settle the Egyptian or not argument.

What came next borders on the extraordinary; mummies were found. All male, and found on shelves, each it's own. Copper cups and pieces of broken swords were found next to each mummy, suggesting that these were once soldiers. One of the rooms was avoided and not explored due to a strong smell and extreme darkness. Kinkaid noticed that there was no ventilation in this room and thus feared some kind of gas. Nothing further was said of this room. The team estimated that 50,000 people could have lived in this "city". This to me seems excessive, but nonetheless, this was the figure given in the article.

True story, hoax, or a little bit of both? The Smithsonian denies such a find, claiming that it is common knowledge that no Egyptian ever set foot in North America prior to Columbus. Tantalizingly, certain formations on the North Side of the Grand Canyon have names such as Isis temple, the Cheops Pyramid, the Tower of Ra and Horus Temple. There is a tradition among the Hopi people, it tells of their ancestors who lived in the underworld in the Grand Canyon. A dispute evolved between two factions which resulted in one group staying in the underworld and another reaching the outside world, eventually becoming the Hopi tribe. But, this isn't the only mystery involving lost races in the Americas.

MYSTERIOUS RACE IN GREEN HELL

Manuscript 512 in the National Library of Rio de Janeiro tells us that in 1753 a group of Portuguese treasure hunters came upon a lost city deep in the jungles of Brazil. The treasure hunters were exploring the Central Plateau in Minas Gerais when in the mountain passes they came upon a forgotten city made of stones. A man made road led into the city through three large archways, one of them inscribed with unknown letters. The broken pillars, the vegetation and the state of the buildings led to the conclusion that the city, like many in this part of the world, was abandoned long ago.

In the center of the city lay a statue upon a black column, a man pointing north. The majority of the city was in such ruin that they concluded that it had been devastated by an earthquake. The city itself is next to a river and several small lakes; and the explorers followed the river downstream for three days, until they reached a waterfall. Past the waterfall the river became very large. To the east, mines were found with a flagstone carved with unknown symbols. Bars of silver were also discovered, and nearby, a temple lay in ruins with more unknown symbols.

They decided to keep following the river downstream for another nine days when they came upon an area where the river spread out once again. There, to their surprise, they encountered two white skinned individuals with long black hair in a canoe. The explorers fired their guns to get their attention. Predictively the two men paddled away. The manuscript also mentions a gold coin was found in the area, with the image of a kneeling boy on one side. At this point Manuscript 512 ends; but less than 200 hundred years later the story would continue.

British Lieutenant Colonel Percy Fawcett had also read the manuscript, and having spent a considerable time in Brazil had heard the tales of the white skinned indians said to live in the deep interior of Brazil. Determined he would find this lost white race, he set out into the jungle to do just that.

Fawcett had a theory that Atlantean survivors had found their way into South America and more specifically the Matto Grosso. He spoke of three cities; the one from Manuscript 512, a second abandoned city he himself had seen, and a city deep in the jungle where native say "European" looking people live. In 1924, accompanied by his son Jack and Raleigh Rinell, Fawcett left civilization in search of the third city. They headed for what is today Cuiba, the capital of the Matto Grosso; and then headed north somewhere between the Xingu and Araguaya rivers. In May of 1925 they reached the village of Bacairy, and then Kalapalo on the river Kuluene. What happened next is a mystery. Kalapalo is the last place the three men were seen alive. Poetically, like Atlantis, Percy Fawcett has never found, alive or dead. Many have gone looking. Some, have come back with tales of lost decrepit cities deep in the jungle, tales of gold, undiscovered pyramids and white Indians; hints of all the things Fawcett was looking for, but never a hint of Fawcett himself.

THE WHITE PYRAMID

On march 28, 1947 the New York Times reported that Colonel Maurice Sheahan, while flying over the Shaanxi province in China, spotted a huge pyramid 1 000 feet in height. An event largely forgotten in a post World War world that was more concerned with the future and the emergence of communism, then pyramids that belonged in the past. It wasn't until 1961 that the story was revisited. It was determined that an error in calculating the height of the pyramid had occurred, and that the pyramid was actually between 500 and 600 feet in height. The location was calculated to be about 40 miles southwest of Xian at the foot of the Tsinling mountains. Another smaller pyramid is reported nearby along with hundreds of yet smaller pyramid structures that may be burial tombs.

Two years prior to Colonel Sheahan fly by, US pilot James Gaussman claims to also have seen a huge white pyramid while flying over China. Whether this was the same pyramid is unconfirmed, but most likely it was. While Sheahan never actually mentioned that the pyramid was white, one of the photographs of the pyramid attributed to Gaussman shows a village in the background as depicted by Sheahan. In an interview in 1999, Sheahan's son confirmed the story and added that his father had seen the pyramid on two separate occasions.

There is no denying that China has a number of pyramids, recent satellite pictures have confirmed this. Furthermore, Hartwig Hausdorf, author of Die Weisse Pyramide, which was given the title "The Chinese Roswell" for the English speaking market, also managed to photograph several smaller pyramids from the ground in his travel though China. I concur with the more conservative mainstream academia that several of the smaller or medium sized structures are most likely burial mounds, but the function and provenance of the larger structures remain a mystery. Unfortunately, it appears that the Chinese government has no intention in sharing information about these structures.

Ethnocentrism, certainly plays a part, as it does in Egypt and in the Americas. Regional academics and officials have always been against the idea that other cultures, especially very ancient ones, may have had a hand in creating some of the historical monuments in their sandbox. These ideas must never be entertained they say, even when there's considerable evidence to the contrary. But I ask you this, is it more likely that cultures the world over came up with the concept of pyramids independently of one another, or is it more likely that there's a lost connection hidden among the pyramids. Oh, and for what it's worth, satellite photographs of what appears to be pyramids also exist from a very different location, Mars.

ATLANTIS, THE ANTEDILUVIAN PARADIGM

Location, location, location, has been the focus of Atlantean research since Plato, beyond the pillars of Hercules and all that. But, what if looking for the exact location of Atlantis in order to find Atlantis is the wrong approach? Perhaps, we should start looking at the concept of Atlantis as a culture, and not a specific location. What if, there are clues all over the world that we have failed to identify, Percy Fawcett's South America, China's White Pyramid, the Sphinx, underwater structures off the coast of Cuba and off the coast of Japan, and of course the Bimini road?

The Sphinx is a particularly interesting structure for many reasons. One of which is the amount of weathering/erosion upon the Sphinx. There is no real way to date the monument, and contrary to popular belief, there are no records anywhere of the Sphinx actually being built. The construction of the Sphinx is attributed to the Pharaoh khafre in the Old Kingdom, for no other reason that the Sphinx lies close to the pyramid of khafre, which may or may not have been built by the Pharaoh. I'm not making this up. The problem is that the amount of weathering on the Sphinx itself indicates severe rainfall, which hasn't occurred in Egypt since a few thousand years before anyone was capable to build such a structure.

So, what is Atlantis really about? It's about an undiscovered pre-Sumerian civilization, that started at a central point and spread out in all directions. The key is of course identifying remains of that civilization, and then, and only then, triangulating a specific area on the map that may have originated these markers. In essence, we are working backwards. We are looking at how Atlantis may have affected the world and working our way back to that ancient civilization.

In this model, Atlantis may turn out to be more of a concept, a much advanced ancient past, than an actual island or continent. That said, there has to be a point of origin. But, by focusing on that area specifically, we are missing all the signs of what Atlantis really was, or represents. Bruce Lee said it best, "Its like a finger pointed to the moon, don't concentrate on the finger or you'll miss all that heavenly glory". Whatever the case may be, there is something wrong with the historical and archeological paradigm as it stands today. The past is not what it used to be.

One avenue of research that I believe show great promise in the search for Atlantis, or any undiscovered ancient culture, antediluvian or otherwise, is language. Or more precisely, the presence of common root words across ancient cultures that should have had no contact with one another. Language does not lie. The brain is pre-disposed to interpret events in a certain way and even to formulate a set of belief systems. But, is it pre-disposed to the formation of similar language across cultures?

Is the Aztec long lost land of Aztland related to Atlantis? Why is the pyramid a world wide archetype? Who are the bearded men depicted in Aztec art? Underwater ruins, crystal skulls, ruins at Baalbek, Sphinx, Bimini road, even possibly the enigmatic structure on top mount Ararat; all point to an extended view of the past not seen since the days of the great libraries.

PART II

DEUS ABSCONDITUS

RENNES LE CHATEAU

It's a long ride up the road that Sauniere built. There are many mountain turns before reaching the village; and in March with no tourists in site, Rennes Le Chateau is quite unassuming with no hint of mystery or particular importance. Very few people live here, and one can imagine the isolation of this village during the time of the mystery. I remember walking towards the church when an older gentleman said hello in perfect british English. We chatted briefly, but warmly. He came here to write a book some years ago and I suppose at some point never left. The church itself is small and at first glance unremarkable, but there is a mystery here. Just above the door is an inscription "Terribillis Es Locus Iste"; terrible is this place.

1885 was the year Berenger Sauniere arrived at the church in Rennes Le Chateau. His first six years as a priest were rather tranquil. And then, in 1891 inside one of the hollow columns supporting the altar, Sauniere found four parchments. Two of them, dating from 1244 and 1644, contained genealogies. The other two were much more recent and in fact dated from the 1780's and are thought to have been written by Antoine Bijou, whom at that time had held the same position as Sauniere. They, contained Latin exerts from the New Testament, but with certain irregularities such as letters raised above others, words and sentences run together with no space in between, and out of place letters. If it was a hidden code, it was meant to be revealed.

One of the messages, which is assumed Sauniere deciphered himself since all one had to do was to take the raised letters, spelled: «A Dagobert roi et a scion est ce tresor et ilia mort.» In English it gives: «To Dagobert king and to sion belongs this treasure and he is there dead» (Baigent, Leigh, Lincoln, 1982). The other gives: « Bergere pas de tentation que Poussin Teniers gardent la clef; pac DCLXXXI par la croix et ce cheval de dieu j' achieve ce daemon de gardien a midi pommes bleues.» In English it gives: «Shepherdess no temptation that Poussin Teniers hold the key, peace 681 by the cross and this horse of God I complete (or destroy) this daemon of the gardien at noon blue apples» (Baigent, Leigh, Lincoln, 1982). Deciphering the parchments is one thing, but making sense of it quite another. Sauniere approached his superior with this and was subsequently sent to Paris.

Before he left, he bought three paintings; a David Teniers painting, the portrait of Pope Celestine V by an unknown artist, and «Les Bergers D'arcadie» by Nicolas Poussin. Once in Paris he met with Abbe Bieil and Emile Hoffet. Hoffet was well versed in linguistics and cryptography as well as a «friend» of esoteric circles and societies that flourished abundantly in Europe at this time. What ultimately when on in Paris for those three weeks isn't very well known, except that Sauniere did present the parchments to these two men and that he also met a friend of Hoffet named Emma Calve, whom was quite a renown Opera singer and a high priestess in esoteric circles. Rumors have it that Sauniere did very un-priestly things in Paris.

Upon his return he preceded to completely remodel the church. He also built the town's water tower and paved the road leading up to the village, perhaps anticipating the twentieth century. He was now a very rich man, and from this point on the story of Sauniere and this little village becomes an amalgam of historical facts, rumors, philosophical agenda, speculation and legend.

It is said that Sauniere found a crypt under a flagstone dating from the seventh or eighth century which contained human remains. He also removed inscriptions on the grave of Marie, Marquise D' Hautpoul de Blanchefort. Her grave and inscriptions had been installed by Antoine Bijou, the same man who had written the parchments. The inscription on her grave gave the same message as the parchments attributed to Bijou. At this point, Sauniere became quite extravagant. He started spending a large amount of money whose source is a mystery. This fact led to the theory that Sauniere had found a treasure at Rennes Le Chateau. This in my opinion is an over simplistic deduction, and fails to take into accounts all the symbolism associated with this story.

Sauniere built a tower called Magdala and a house called Villa Bethania. The church itself had been consecrated to the Magdelen in 1059.   Obviously, Sauniere thought that both Maries were important; Mary Magdelene and Mary of Bethany. The Magdelen was a former prostitute who according to the gospels reforms and decides to follow Jesus. Yet it seems that she holds some special place in the life of Jesus as she is the first to see Jesus after the resurrection. She also figures in some medieval legends were she is the one who brings the Grail to Britain and France instead of Joseph of Arimathea. Mary of Bethany is the sister of Lazarus who is said to have risen from the grave. She was the one who anointed the feet of Jesus in the Gospel of John. Maybe, what is important aren't the two Mary's, but what they are associated with, the Grail and resurrection; two themes explicitly represented in much of the artwork within the church.

Back at Rennes Le Chateau our debonair priest had grown found of taking long walks in the country side with his housekeeper Marie Denardaud. Where he went and what he did, he kept secret. Some reports have him collecting rocks. He also began corresponding with unknown individuals across western Europe. He had also opened some rather large bank accounts with various banks. He had a road built leading up to the church and was involved in other public enterprises. But it was at the church itself that he made the most enigmatic changes. Above the entrance he had inscribed «Terribilis est locus iste» meaning, this place is terrible. Just inside, he had a statue placed of the demon Asmodeus. Legends have it that Asmodeus is a guardian of secrets and the builder of Solomon's temple. There are also painted plaques that depict various scenes surrounding the life and death of Jesus, but with some differences to accepted theology, such as a painting of Jesus being carried to or from his tomb at night under a full moon.

By now Sauniere was throwing banquets and parties the like Rennes Le Chateau had never seen. Emma Calve was a regular visitor as well as Archduke Johann Von Hapsburg, cousin of Austria's emperor. Bank records show that the Archduke had versed a considerable amount of money into Sauniere's account. By this time, a new bishop in the area, at Carcassonne to be exact, was suspicious to say the least of Sauniere's fortune. Sauniere refused to tell the new bishop anything about anything and a local tribunal suspended him. However, that suspension would be short lived as the Vatican intervened and reinstated Sauniere immediately.

On January 17, 1917 Sauniere suffered a stroke and died five days later, even though just a few days earlier he was reported as being in perfect health. Yet, that did not stop Marie Denarnaud from ordering a coffin on January 12. This was obviously a good deal for Denarnaud since he had transferred all of his money to her. Poetically enough, he died a broke man.

As all good stories go, there is one final component to the story. A priest came to Sauniere to administer the last rites. He never finished because after talking with the dying Sauniere he refused to administer Extreme Unction and left only to fall into a severe depression. Legend has it that he never smiled again. As for Marie Denarnaud, she settled into Villa Bethania until after the second world war. As the French government was establishing a new currency, «old money» had to be accounted for. Instead of explaining how she came to posses such a fortune, she decided to burn all of her old francs. Now poor, Marie sold Villa Bethania to a Noel Corbu who she promised to tell of secrets that would make him rich and powerful. That never came to pass as in 1953 she suffered a stroke and until her death was unable to speak, leaving Corbu a most frustrated man.

The church is only open to the public for a half hour at a time, at one hour intervals. With a small fee Sauniere's house and "the tower Magdala" can also be visited. The church itself and the house is now a museum, containing various artifacts belonging to Sauniere, including his financial records. They don't shy away from the mystery here either as a somewhat conservative summary is given, but one can sense that this is accompanied by a certain nondescript uneasiness.

Once passed the entrance to this terrible place, you are indeed greeted by Asmodeus. A statue of course, but quite intimidating nonetheless. Some researchers and historians believe that the statue is not Asmodeus but Rex Mundi instead. Asmodeus is the guardian of Solomon's temple and Rex Mundi is the Cathar's creator of the earth and materialism. He is often equated with the devil by Christianity. Whichever the case may be, it does set us upon an unexpected course in our search for answers.

After looking at this figure, I remember turning around and looking at the other end of the church where the altar lies. At this point you cannot help but be smitten with all its symbolism. On the front bottom of the altar is Mary Magdelene represented kneeling next to a skull. On one side of the altar is a statue of Joseph holding an infant and on the other side Mary doing the same. On the walls lining the church are paintings and smaller statues representing the story of the Christ; all with various degree of deviation from the accepted gospels.

The paintings and statues are numbered by stations. Between station thirteen and twelve is a statue of the Magdalene standing next to a skull, just at her feet. With her right arm she holds a cross, with her left a cup or urn, some think the Holy Grail or a symbol for the grail. Every station is loaded with symbolism and meaning, with no agreed upon final message. Answers, are beyond the scope of this book; and to go any further would be an oeuvre in itself. So for now, I'll leave this mystery as it is.

TEARS OF THE VIRGIN

"I saw clearly a luminous globe, which moved from the east to the west, gliding slowly and majestically through space"; said Monsignor John Quaresma. Another witness described the object this way: "It was not the sun (...) it was a huge disc that moved in front of the sun". A seemingly routine UFO sighting, the kind I receive on a fairly expected schedule. But, this wasn't a routine UFO sighting: the year was 1917, and in Fatima, Portugal, 70 thousand people were on location awaiting a Marian apparition and watching the sun dance in the sky.

The miracle of the sun, as the event described above would eventually be known, occurred on October 13, 1917. The last day that the Lady appeared in Fatima, and had promised a miracle on that very date. The apparitions began six months earlier on the 13 th of May to three local children, Lucia dos Santos, age 10, and her two cousins Francisco Marto and his sister Jacinta, the youngest by two years. They were tending to their sheep in an area near Fatima called Cova da Iria, when Lucia noticed a couple of flashes in the sky. The weather was promising and there was not a single cloud in the sky, but Lucia cautiously thought that perhaps the weather was turning and that they should head back home. To add to her uneasiness, she recalled of a day a couple years earlier when she noticed a lone little cloud in the sky, that seemed to take the form of a person.

Back to the present day, Francisco and Jacinta also noticed the flashes in the sky and were ready to head back to Fatima when by an oak tree a lady appeared. Four feet in height, dressed in white with dark black eyes she was illuminated by a very bright light. When she spoke, she told them not to be afraid and that she was from heaven.

Lucia, the leader of the three asked the lady why was she there. She simply told them that she would appear every 13 th of every month for the next six months. She told them to pray the rosary daily and that, sadly, they would have to suffer greatly for the sins of the world. A month later, on June 13 th, she appeared as promised and informed Lucia that she would be taking Jacinta and Francisco to heaven very soon. A prophecy fulfilled two years later when Jacinta and Francisco both died of the Spanish flu, an epidemic that was sweeping Europe at the time.

Having heard about the May apparition, a small number of villagers came to see the lady. They initially saw nothing, but heard a murmur, voices from far away. When the lady disappeared, a cloud rose up above the oak tree, seen by all heading east. By July 13 th, over a thousand people were now at Cova Da Iria, expecting a vision. Again, the lady could only be seen by the children, but a strange humming could be heard by all, and a large clap like thunder shook the ground. This was the day the lady gave the children what she called the three secrets.

THE SECRETS

The first was a rather stereotypical vision of hell, with demons, fire and burning souls. A warning of what may befell the world. The second was a plea for Russia to be consecrated to "My Immaculate Heart". Otherwise, another great war will erupt. She also went on to say that before this happens a great unknown light will be seen in the sky. It will be a sign of upcoming war and that God is about to punish the world for for its sins. A message that she repeated on following visits.

The third secret, Lucia insisted was not to be revealed right away. She also insisted that perhaps it would be best to wait until 1960, for the secret to be better understood across the world. The third secret written down by Lucia in the 1940's became the most heavily guarded document at the Vatican. Hints were given through out the years, and then subsequently denied. The hints were usually of an apocalyptic nature, and mentioned a great danger to the faith of the world. In any case, the third secret was "revealed" by the Vatican in 2000. The official statement stated that the third Secret was a warning against persecution of the Church, and quite honestly not much else was revealed. A discussion on the veracity of the Vatican's revelation and the behind the scene intrigue associated with it, leads to a very dark and forbidden enclave of the Vatican. Which brings us to October 13, 1917; the day the Lady promised a miracle.

MIRACLE OF THE SUN

A scientist from nearby Coimbra University named Almeida Garret was among the 70,000 people present that day. He himself never saw the actual apparition, instead witnessed a bluish column of smoke. This is how he described what happened next: "It was raining hard, and the rain trickled down everyone's clothes. Suddenly, the sun shone through the dense cloud which covered it; everybody looked in its direction. It looked like a disc, of a very definite contour. it was dazzling. i don't think that it could be compared to a dull silver disk, as someone later said in Fatima. No. It rather possessed a clear, changing brightness, which one could compare to a pearl. It looked like a polished wheel. This is not poetry. My eyes have seen it. This clear shaped disk suddenly began turning. It rotated with increasing speed. Suddenly, the crowd began to cry with anguish. The sun, revolving all the time, began falling towards the earth, reddish and bloody, threatening to crush everyone under its fiery weight.".

The correlation between Marian apparitions and "miracles of the sun" is not solely relegated to Fatima, and thus a pattern does emerge. "It seemed like a shiny wheel separated from the sun and headed towards earth (...) and some sort of shinning balloons began to emerge from the sun..." This last statement is not from Fatima, but from Medjugorje, Croatia in 1981, and was another miracle promised by a lady claiming to be the mother of God.

Since 1917, there has been hundreds of Marian apparitions worldwide, with various degrees of eyewitness reliability. Many, involving unusual cloud movement, unusual movement

of the sun with strange disks seen before and after an apparition. The messages usually involve warnings of doom, war and
destruction. The same type of messages reported by individuals
that claim Alien contact via abduction.

One modern case of Marian apparition reminiscent of Fatima
occurred in north eastern Brazil in April of 1994. A luminous
figure appears to Jose Ernani dos Santos, who was at the time
praying. The figure announced that she would appear again in
the first days of September and October. Word spread quickly,
and an estimated three thousand arrived on September 1 st
to witness the apparition and a unnatural darkening of the
sun. One witness, who was also a UFO investigator, described
seeing a cloud in the sky that was emitting multicolored lights
in all direction, and how the top of the trees were illuminated
by the lights. The illumination of the trees is an important
point, because it points to the physicality of the event and the
lights; hallucinations do not emit photons. Another sign was
promised for the following month. This time, a crowd of over
five thousand believers and a handful of scientists, members of
the Brazilian UFO Research Center, came together on October
1st. At around two in the afternoon while Jose Ernani was
praying, two large clouds moved rapidly towards the sun, in
effect darkening the sun. One of the scientist, Reginaldo de
Atayde, mentioned that there seem to be a large amount of static
electricity in the air.

As people were crying, praying and falling to their knees, a
silver disk appeared briefly before the cloud. By this time, Jose
Ernani was in a trance, apparently receiving a message from the
"holy virgin". The disk disappeared for a few seconds only to
reappear next to the sun. It was described at about the size
of the full moon. It disappeared briefly once again and all was
silent. Until someone shouted "look at the beads of the Virgin's
rosary". In the sky was four metallic looking discs. Three were
lined up in a row, and a fourth was off to the side slightly
obscured by a cloud.

Tears of the Virgin someone called the discs. Others, found

hard to differentiate these objects from standard UFOs. A religious event versus a UFO event is largely dependent on who does the observing, and who writes the books that the world will read. This dichotomous view goes way beyond Fatima and Brazil. Arguing over what constitutes a religious event and what constitutes a paranormal/UFO event is missing the point in my opinion. What may be of more importance is that regardless of the event, we are dealing with the same source. Whatever this source may be, it appears to have a very unique way of communicating. The problem, and looking at the world today I challenge you to disagree, is that in thousands of years of interaction, we have yet to understand the meaning.

THE CAVE

Site N-4 was the official Saudi name for a missile site that was built in the middle of the Arabian desert (Blum, 1988). At around noon, on a day like any other, a Filipino worker took his lunch break from working on clearing the summit for the installment of radar arrays. On this day, he never returned from his break.

The Saudi security team was concerned. This is the Kingdom and this is a top secret installation, he could have been an Israeli spy. Or simply, he may have just fallen over the side of the mountain. Either way, they were unable to locate him. Assuming he was either dead or gone, they left it up to Allah.

The next say, in the middle of the afternoon, he returned. Physically unharmed with not even a scratch, but he appears in shock and initially refuses to reveal where he's been the past 24 hours. One of the site supervisor was a former American Air Force officer, who managed to eventually have the worker tell his story.

At lunch he decided to walk around the mountain until he found a cave, the worker explained. He walked in, and told the American that he was held prisoner for the next 24 hours.

Confused, the American asked who could have kept you prisoner here in such a remote location on a Saudi military base. A ghost replied the worker. This ghost talked and sang, but would not let him go.

This would not be the last time that a presence would be felt in this cave. At first this may seem like a most unlikely scenario, a haunted cave on a military base; but this was not just any mountain, this was Jabal Al Lawz. This was the mountain that many believe is the real Mount Sinai, the place where Moses met with God.

To be fair, not everyone is in agreement over the location of the real Mount Sinai, its a big desert. If Jabal Al lawz is indeed the place where Moses received the ten commandments, then this was the mountain where the Ark was built; and whatever power lies in that place today, is nothing compared to the power contained within the Ark. The Ark was held above the ground and touching it could mean death. It was always carried into battle, for to have the Ark, secured victory. It killed by the thousands, it burned, created lesions on the skin, caused tumors and loss of hair, and it brought down the walls of Jericho. The Jews may have had a terrible sense of direction, lost in the desert for 40 years and all that (its a big desert), but they had one the first weapon of mass destruction.

In light of radiation found at ancient sites, such as at Mohenjo-Daro in Pakistan, warfare may be an ancient art in this part of the world. As such, the power of the Ark extends far beyond the words of the Bible and the Qur'an. There is no denying the fact that the Ark's effect resemble radiation poisoning, and that as a gift from God or from some other source, the Ark was certainly a very dangerous artifact. I find it peculiar that a site that may have once been the source of a great weapon was chosen to be a modern equivalent. Which makes you wonder what else is hidden in places masked by modern wars. Maybe, and just maybe, the weapons of mass destruction are there after all.

www.ingramcontent.com/pod-product-compliance
Lightning Source LLC
Chambersburg PA
CBHW062157270326
41930CB00009B/1565